VOYAGEUR CLASSICS

BOOKS THAT EXPLORE CANADA

Michael Gnarowski — Series Editor

The Dundurn Group presents the Voyageur Classics series, building on the tradition of exploration and rediscovery and bringing forward time-tested writing about the Canadian experience in all its varieties.

This series of original or translated works in the fields of literature, history, politics, and biography has been gathered to enrich and illuminate our understanding of a multi-faceted Canada. Through straightforward, knowledgeable, and reader-friendly introductions the Voyageur Classics series provides context and accessibility while breathing new life into these timeless Canadian masterpieces.

The Voyageur Classics series was designed with the widest possible readership in mind and sees a place for itself with the interested reader as well as in the classroom. Physically attractive and reset in a contemporary format, these books aim at an enlivened and updated sense of Canada's written heritage.

OTHER VOYAGEUR CLASSICS TITLES

The Blue Castle
by Lucy Maud Montgomery, introduced by Dr. Collett Tracey
978-1-55002-666-5

Canadian Exploration Literature: An Anthology,
edited and introduced by Germaine Warkentin
978-1-55002-661-0

Empire and Communications
by Harold A. Innis, introduced by Alexander John Watson
978-1-55002-662-7

In This Poem I Am: Selected Poetry of Robin Skelton,
edited and introduced by Harold Rhenisch
978-1-55002-769-3

The Letters and Journals of Simon Fraser 1806–1808,
edited and introduced by W. Kaye Lamb,
foreword by Michael Gnarowski
978-1-55002-713-6

Maria Chapdelaine: A Tale of French Canada
by Louis Hémon, translated by W.H. Blake,
introduction and notes by Michael Gnarowski
978-1-55002-712-9

Selected Writings
by A.J.M. Smith, edited and introduced by Michael Gnarowski
978-1-55002-665-8

VOYAGEUR CLASSICS

BOOKS THAT EXPLORE CANADA

MRS. SIMCOE'S DIARY

ELIZABETH POSTHUMA SIMCOE

EDITED AND WITH AN INTRODUCTION BY
MARY QUAYLE INNIS

FOREWORD BY MICHAEL GNAROWSKI

DUNDURN PRESS
TORONTO

Editor: Michael Carroll
Copy-editors: Marja Appleford and Allison Hirst
Design: Jennifer Scott
Printer: Marquis

Library and Archives Canada Cataloguing in Publication

Simcoe, Elizabeth, 1766-1850
    Mrs. Simcoe's diary / edited by Mary Quayle Innis.

Includes index.
ISBN 978-1-55002-768-6

    1. Simcoe, Elizabeth, 1766-1850--Diaries. 2. Simcoe, John Graves, 1752-1806. 3. Ontario--Social life and customs--18th century. 4. Ontario--Politics and government--1791-1841. 5. Lieutenant governors--Ontario--Biography. 6. Lieutenant governors' spouses--Ontario--Biography. I. Innis, Mary Quayle, 1899-1972. II. Title.

FC3071.1.S54A3 2007   971.3'02092   C2007-904678-9

1   2   3   4   5   11   10   09   08   07

Conseil des Arts   Canada Council   ONTARIO ARTS COUNCIL
du Canada   for the Arts   CONSEIL DES ARTS DE L'ONTARIO

We acknowledge the support of the Canada Council for the Arts and the Ontario Arts Council for our publishing program. We also acknowledge the financial support of the Government of Canada through the Book Publishing Industry Development Program and The Association for the Export of Canadian Books, and the Government of Ontario through the Ontario Book Publishers Tax Credit program, and the Ontario Media Development Corporation.

Care has been taken to trace the ownership of copyright material used in this book. The author and the publisher welcome any information enabling them to rectify any references or credits in subsequent editions.

                                                            J. Kirk Howard, President

Printed and bound in Canada.
Printed on recycled paper.

www.dundurn.com

Dundurn Press   Gazelle Book Services Limited   Dundurn Press
3 Church Street, Suite 500   White Cross Mills   2250 Military Road
Toronto, Ontario, Canada   High Town, Lancaster, England   Tonawanda, NY
M5E 1M2   LA1 4XS   U.S.A. 14150

CONTENTS

FOREWORD

The present text of the diary/journal of Elizabeth Simcoe (1766–1850) documents her travel to and stay in Canada between 1791 and 1796[1] and varies only slightly from the modern edition prepared by Mary Quayle Innis (1899–1972) that was published by the Macmillan Company of Canada in 1965. That text departed considerably from the 1911 edition prepared with elaborate notes and a biography by John Ross Robertson (1841–1918) and published by William Briggs of Toronto. Robertson, an enthusiastic and energetic individual with an antiquarian collector's instincts (his entry in Henry James Morgan's *The Canadian Men and Women of the Time* [1912] identifies him simply as a journalist and then goes on to list two and a half impressive columns of activities and achievements), crafted a volume of biographical information, extensive notes, and sundry historical addenda that all but obscured the actual diary or journal notes of Elizabeth Simcoe that he had secured from the family's keeping at the Gwillim-Simcoe estate of Wolford in Devon.

What would be, at its best, something just short of two hundred printed pages of Elizabeth Simcoe's jottings were enriched and enlarged by Robertson's historically fascinating textual impedimenta. However, describing Robertson's apparatus as impedimenta is perhaps unfair, since it is really a remarkable collection of historical and biographical detail, some quite trivial, other materially useful and contributing significantly to the context of the Simcoe diary. This material included two hundred and thirty-seven illustrations of which ninety were reproductions of sketches and finished drawings and paintings by Elizabeth Simcoe herself of which fifteen would be reproduced in the edition prepared by Mary Quayle Innis that, in turn, suggests the scope of the reduction imposed by Innis on the number of illustrations that she chose for her edition of the diary. In 1934 Robertson's edition of 1911 was re-issued by his estate.[2] The 1911 edition became, in turn, a facsimile reprint in 1973 as a title in the Coles Canadiana Collection.

While our primary interest in the diary of Mrs. John Graves Simcoe is its relevance to the very earliest days of Upper Canada and its connection to the activities of the first lieutenant-governor of Upper Canada, we are rewarded by insights and observations collateral to the opening of new territory in Canada and the founding of what was to become the Province of Ontario, as well as the laying out of the first sketchy plans of Toronto, destined to become the largest city in the country. What is particularly striking about the diary is that it is not a studied or profound historical record of those days when the site of what is now Toronto was a few modest huts and the forest reached down to the shores of Lake Ontario and Native encampments registered more of a presence than the newly arrived Europeans.

To be sure there was a lot of activity as the recently sworn-in lieutenant-governor drove his garrison to erect housing for him and his family (John Graves had had the foresight to bring what were described as marquee-like tents in which the Simcoes lived bravely at the beginning) and to put up huts as barracks for the soldiers. Although not in the strongest of health, the lieutenant-governor travelled and walked to get a sense of the territory that had become his responsibility and urged his Council to grapple with measures that included everything from the construction of primitive roads (famed Yonge Street had its origins here) to accommodating an influx of new settlers as well as dealing with the shifting alliances of Native peoples. What is forgotten now and is little understood is the difficulty and magnitude of the task that lay before Simcoe whose life was not made easy by a tense relationship with the overall governor, Lord Dorchester. In this enterprise, it is safe to say, Simcoe had the staunch and loving support of his spouse.

Elizabeth Simcoe's watercolour of Joel Stone's mill at Gananoque, Ontario.

Born a Gwillim,[3] Elizabeth Posthuma (she was saddled with the pious Posthuma because her father had died before she was born and her mother died in childbirth) came from a well-to-do upper-class English family that made her an heiress and a desirable matrimonial prospect. Married at sixteen to a man twice her age and recently returned from the wars in America, she became all that a dutiful wife of those times was expected to be. She used some of her wealth to buy an estate, Wolford, of some five thousand acres that became the Simcoe family seat; bore her husband many children; sacrificed a son to Britain's wars on the Continent; and aided and supported her husband in his career, nursing him through frequent bouts of ill health, living out a long widowhood, always prim, proper, and dowager-like almost as if to live up to the tight-lipped severity of her portrait.

But what fascinates us beside the obvious virtues of late-eighteenth-century womanhood is that, at the same time, Elizabeth Posthuma Gwillim-Simcoe can also be seen as a product of that climate of the Enlightenment that marked so many seemingly ordinary people of that time, so much so that they were moved to exercise their imaginations and to develop their talents for languages, music, art, and letters. Thus one places Elizabeth Gwillim readily on a roster of remarkable Englishwomen who accompanied their menfolk (husbands, brothers, et cetera) to the New World and left, certainly in the case of Lower and Upper Canada, a cultural legacy upon which the arts of a new country would be founded.

One thinks here of Frances Brooke, a slightly earlier but near contemporary of Elizabeth Simcoe, and her groundbreaking epistolary novel, *The History of Emily Montague* (1769), which Elizabeth is supposed to have read. Albeit somewhat later, but still very much in the same tradition, there is also Susanna Moodie's *Roughing It in the Bush* (1852); *The Backwoods of Canada* (1836) and *Canadian Wild Flowers* (1868) by Moodie's older sister, Catharine Parr Traill, who had a discerning eye for the flora of Canada; and Anna Brownell Jameson's *Winter Studies and Summer Rambles in Canada* (1838), which reveals uncommon sensitivity, intelligence, and culture. *Observe* and *record* were the watchwords of these travellers and/or settlers in what is now Ontario, thereby creating a wide-ranging context for life in early colonial Canada. What is also especially admirable about these women is that they ventured, seemingly without flinching or hesitation, into the unknown and made lives for themselves and their families in situations of enduring hardship.

The record left us in Mrs. Simcoe's diary spans a period of what are probably the most important five formative years of Upper Canada. The diary is a mixed offering of the briefest of jottings about wind and weather coupled with more discursive and extended journal entries. It is these entries that are the meat and substance that, in particular, draw our attention. There is here a record of travel and the conditions of life in the early colony that informs and fascinates the reader today. What is strikingly impressive in the overall picture is how generally interested and knowledgeable Mrs. Simcoe proved to be. In her "enlightened" makeup she had French and German, was well read, enjoyed music, and drew and sketched with considerable competence. She made it her business to notice everything, and to try to understand and make sense of all that came her way.

Mrs. Simcoe always had a keen eye for whatever customs and natural wonders she encountered in the New World. Here she drew carioles at Quebec City.

Thus, lodged in what must have been unpleasantly spartan conditions — the Royal Navy's HMS *Triton* at twenty-eight guns was not the largest or most sumptuous frigate afloat — Mrs. Simcoe crossed the Atlantic to Canada in what was far from the best season. To relieve the boredom of many weeks of trying travel, she kept busy noting the weather, the wind, the condition of the sea, the longitude, and whatever she sighted. One wonders how she knew enough of seafaring conditions to make such perceptive entries in her journal. Geography was of much interest to her, as well, because she liked to draw maps. When the *Triton* entered North Americans waters, she made detailed observations and displayed admirable knowledge of the islands the vessel passed, citing their names and topography and if they were inhabited.

Arriving in Quebec, and caught in the onset of winter, the Simcoes settled down to the busy round of social life in that old French capital, a habit of long standing designed to enliven the cold months of the winter season now agreeably graced by the presence of the king's son, the Duke of Kent, who was in command of the garrison, and whose band played at the frequent balls as well as at regular church services. Moreover, Quebec was no backwoods village. With a population of some twelve thousand, it had lots of interesting sights to offer the inquisitive and inquiring eye. Had the camera existed then Mrs. Simcoe would have been an inveterate photographer. Instead, she went out to see the sights and drew and sketched with keenness, this enthusiasm for the visual record going on with her when the Simcoes left Quebec in 1792 to travel by bateau[4] up the St. Lawrence River to Montreal, Kingston, and onwards, their destination being Niagara, then also known as Newark, where John Graves Simcoe was to assume the office of lieutenant-governor. There, Simcoe threw himself into the task of laying the foundations of a European model society that was slowly being carved out of what must have seemed to the Simcoes an impenetrable forest wilderness.

Very quickly, the lieutenant-governor became immersed and embroiled in the politics and machinations of a frontier community. Not only did he have to tread carefully in his dealings with a covetous American presence on his doorstep, but there were the tensions arising out of the movement of Native peoples drifting back and forth across what was to them an invisible frontier, as well as the not always accepting attitude of the rough-hewn local

A lovely watercolour by Mrs. Simcoe of a bend in the St. Lawrence River. The hills on the horizon suggest that this spot was not far west of Quebec City.

gentry who liked to see themselves as having precedence and being a law unto themselves. An example of this kind of ultimate authority was the well-connected Thomas Talbot, who served as an aide to Simcoe, and whose perhaps apocryphal method of solving disputes with recalcitrant settlers was to turn to his man servant and say, "Set on the dogs."

Curiously enough, in spite of her interest in all things sundry, and her loyal and supportive role as the spouse of the lieutenant-governor, Mrs. Simcoe does not give us a particularly elaborate or insightful account of her husband's administrative or political activities. An event as significant to him as the taking of the Oaths of Office on July 8, 1792, is recorded in one laconic line in the diary. Nor are the activities of his Council or the Assembly given more generous treatment. They are usually dealt with in a cryptic line or two, meriting almost the same coverage Mrs. Simcoe gives to taking tea with the garrison surgeon's wife.

All of this notwithstanding, one recognizes Mrs. Simcoe's keen, observant, and all-absorbing sensibility, from Montmorency Falls and the Ursuline convent in Quebec, to the abundance of oak, ash,

A rendering by Mrs. Simcoe of Castle Frank in 1796, the rustic summer home of the Simcoes in York (now Toronto). Named for the Simcoes' son, Frank, the house overlooked the Don River. Its Greek columns were white pine logs.

and basswood trees on the lands destined to become the city of Toronto, to the quality and delicious taste of the whitefish brought to her table. John Ross Robertson sums up the great value of the diary well in his biographical chapter on the Simcoes:

> The story of Mrs. Simcoe's life from the day she with her husband left Wolford and sailed in HMS *Triton* from Weymouth, cannot be told better than it is written in her diary....When in 1759, her father, Captain Gwillim, ascended with General Wolfe the rugged path that led to the heights of Abraham, little did he think that thirty-two years later his daughter would give to future generations of Canadians pictures of places in the new land that he and his companions

were winning for the Empire. But the daring
and resolute soldier of Wolfe transmitted to his
daughter not only the courageous qualities that
had been necessary to win this new land for
Britain, but also the foresight and the genius by
which she has preserved by pen and pencil the
spirit of the natural scenery and the social life of
the New Britain that was being planted.

Michael Gnarowski
Voyageur Classics Series Editor

INTRODUCTION

BY MARY QUAYLE INNIS

In 1791, Canada was divided into two provinces, Lower Canada and Upper Canada. An English country gentleman and Member of Parliament, Colonel John Graves Simcoe was appointed lieutenant-governor of Upper Canada. He had fought during the American Revolution and was eager to bring to the wilds of Upper Canada the beneficent British institutions that the Americans had rejected. His wife, Elizabeth, who loved change and excitement, was delighted to find herself a governor's lady.

The Simcoes left an England of growing population, expanding cities, and industrial change. The country was in a chronic state of hot and cold war, but it was prosperous and stable, with a rich inheritance of learning and culture. In the year of the Simcoes' departure, Haydn arrived to receive his degree at Oxford and Boswell's *Life of Johnson* was published.

A part of the Simcoes' young family had to be left behind at the family home, Wolford Lodge, in charge of a friend, Mrs. Hunt. From the day Mrs. Simcoe left home she kept a diary, and in addition to writing letters she sent sections of her diary to Mrs. Hunt.

The voyage, which lasted more than six weeks, brought the Simcoes into a fresh and absorbing world. Lower Canada had a well-established population of about 150,000, while Upper Canada in 1791 had some 10,000 settlers. By the time the Simcoes left Upper Canada in 1796 it had a population of about 25,000.

After spending seven months at Québec, the Simcoes travelled by bateau to Kingston and on to Niagara, the temporary capital of the new province. The next year they founded a new settlement at Toronto, renamed York. They journeyed back and forth between Niagara and York, and Mrs. Simcoe made one visit to Quebec before their final departure in 1796. Throughout the five years, Mrs. Simcoe kept her diary with unresting enthusiasm.

To fill in our picture of the journey up the St. Lawrence, of the lively towns of Lower Canada in the 1790s, and of the scarcely penetrated wilderness of Upper Canada, we could have asked for nothing better than a contemporary diary. We might have hoped for the diary of a woman, with her sharp interest in detail, her leisure and patience to record and keep the record. But in a flight of hopefulness, we could hardly have expected her to be also a botanist, a gifted observer, and an artist with pen, pencil, and watercolour. We could scarcely have hoped, in a word, for Elizabeth Simcoe.

Montmorency Falls, as painted by Mrs. Simcoe, is a short distance east of Quebec City. It was a favoured spot for tourists even before Mrs. Simcoe's time in Canada.

Elizabeth Posthuma Gwillim was born at Whitchurch, Herefordshire, in 1766. Her mother died at her birth and her father, Colonel Thomas Gwillim, who had been an aide-de-camp to General Wolfe in Canada, had died seven months earlier. The child was brought up by her mother's sister, Mrs. Graves.

The girl when she grew up was small and slight, not more than five feet tall. A miniature made when she was a good deal older shows sharp dark eyes in a small face with a strong pointed chin. She spoke French and German, loved dancing and the out-of-doors. Like most young ladies of the day, she learned to draw and paint and showed an unusual degree of talent in these directions.

Admiral Graves, her guardian, was the godfather of John Graves Simcoe, and in 1782 that young soldier, returned from the American campaign, came to visit. He met the lively young Elizabeth, fell in love with her, and in December they were married. The bride was sixteen, her husband thirty years old.

John Graves Simcoe was the son of Captain John Simcoe, commander of the HMS *Pembroke*, who had been at Louisbourg and Halifax, and under whom James Cook, later the famous explorer, had served as master. In 1759, when his son was only seven years old, Captain Simcoe had died of pneumonia on board the *Pembroke* near the island of Anticosti and had been buried at sea.

The widow and her son lived at Exeter, and John Graves went at fourteen to Eton and two years later to Merton College, Oxford. He remained there for only a year; at nineteen he joined the 35th Regiment of Foot as an ensign, and he was sent to New England at the outbreak of the American Revolution. In 1777, he was made captain of the Queen's Rangers; he was wounded at the battle of the Brandywine and later taken prisoner. He was made a lieutenant-colonel in 1781 and returned to England.

The couple lived first at Exeter where three daughters, Eliza, Charlotte, and Henrietta, were born. Mrs. Simcoe was an heiress, and her fortune bought Wolford, an estate of about five thousand acres near Honiton in Devonshire, where they settled in 1788. Three more children were born — Caroline, Sophia, and in 1791 the longed-for son Francis Gwillim.

During these domestic years, Colonel Simcoe occupied himself in building a new house and laying out roads on the estate. He was also fond of reading and of writing, both poetry and prose: his *Journal of the Operations of the Queen's Rangers* was published privately in Exeter in 1787.

In 1790, he was elected to Parliament for St. Mawes in Cornwall and very soon afterward he was appointed lieutenant-governor of the new province of Upper Canada under the governorship of Lord Dorchester.

What to do with the children was suddenly a serious problem for Mrs. Simcoe; even with nursemaids available it seemed impossible to take with them six children, the oldest only seven. In the end, the four older girls were left at home under the care of Mrs. Hunt. Sophia, aged two, and Francis, three months, went with their parents to Canada.

While they waited at Weymouth for a favourable wind, the Simcoes met George III, recovered from his first bout of insanity, who talked to them cordially. On September 26, 1791, they sailed for the St. Lawrence.

Few woman would seem to be less suited to five years of canoes and canvas tents than Elizabeth Simcoe going on board the *Triton* with her ball dresses, her servants, her children and their nurses, her drawing paper and books and watercolours. She was twenty-five years old, she had always lived in luxury, and she was the wife of a colonel and a governor and very proud of the distinction.

Yet she had qualities that prepared her for the hardships of her new life and the unique contribution she was to make to the history of Upper Canada. Like many ladies of her day, she was an assiduous letter writer and her diary writing and sketching were obsessive. In a small notebook found among her papers, she had written:

> I have us'd myself from my Infancy to Read after I am in Bed, it is grown so habitual to me that I cannot sleep without a Dose of Literature. I have in vain tried those pamphlets, plays & which are so universally look'd upon as invaluable Soporifiks to lull me to sleep almost instantaneously. I am obliged therefore to have recourse to my own Writings — & generally catching every thought which accidentally floats on my Brain, I commit it to paper. It serves to waken & amend my breast. My purpose is secured by myself & I am happy that the train of Ideas Lulls me to Slumber & forgetfulness.

In the hurry of shopping in London and preparing her wardrobe, Mrs. Simcoe had time to draw maps of the St. Lawrence River and northern New York — she was always fond of drawing maps — and probably to read those popular travel books, Father Hennepin's highly-coloured account of his North American journeys and Baron Lahontan's lively *Voyages*. That earliest of Canadian novels, *Emily Montague*, Mrs. Simcoe said later gave an excellent picture of Quebec as she found it.

After a voyage that the reader feels in his own nerves — "tacked all day and lost much ground" — the Simcoes reached Quebec on November 11.

Arrived at Quebec, Mrs. Simcoe, depressed at first by the steep, rainy streets, quickly found herself enclosed in a cultured and warmly welcoming little world. She had come exactly at the beginning of the social season. The anonymous author of *Canadian*

Letters wrote, "Cut off from communication with the rest of the world, the good people here [Quebec] find resources within themselves, to mitigate the severity of the climate. About the close of October, all the ships have departed for Europe. Business is then at an end, and pleasure becomes the general object.... In winter, all is dance and festivity."[1]

Mrs. Simcoe was amused to see dogs pulling loads of wood, and she liked to walk to Cape Diamond with her husband, to watch skaters or one-horse carrioles on the ice of the river, and to drive to Montmorency, but the social round claimed her heart.

There was Mme. Baby, soon her great friend, who took her to inspect the Ursuline Convent and to services in the cathedral, and invited her constantly to dine and sup. The Honourable François Baby complimented her on her French, and at the Babys' house she first ate that very Canadian delicacy, moose muffle.[2]

Just as attentive was Mrs. Caldwell, wife of the colonel who had served under General Wolfe in 1759. Every few days Mrs. Simcoe drove to Belmont, the Caldwell house four miles out of Quebec. A very indifferent house to look at, she wrote, but comfortable inside except for the heat. All drawing rooms that winter she found too hot; in the hard-frozen Quebec winter she would sit as far as possible from the red-hot stoves, fanning herself and eating ices. She often stayed overnight at Belmont; the ladies breakfasted and rode in carrioles and drank tea together. Prince Edward's[3] band gave concerts, the Prince himself came to dinner. The officers put on plays but Colonel Simcoe refused to attend, thinking the activity beneath their dignity. Indeed he complained that there were "few men of learning or information" in Quebec. But his aide, Thomas Talbot, arranged Mrs. Simcoe's dinners and dances, and out of her intensive social round she wrote happily that she found Quebec a delightful place, "everybody I see assiduous to please me."

On a later visit, Mrs. Simcoe found Lady Dorchester herself most attentive. "Uniformly polite and obliging," Lady Dorchester, whether to make some amends for the constant friction between the two husbands or out of simple kindness, walked with Mrs. Simcoe on the "heights of Abram," drove her about, invited her almost every day to dine or take tea or dance at the Château. Lady Dorchester was the only person in Canada whose attentions could flatter Mrs. Simcoe; she noted that it was very unusual for anyone to be entertained at the Château as she had been without a formal introduction. She liked "excessively" parties at the Château where in an all but royal progress she walked round the rooms speaking briefly to everyone.

Much as she enjoyed the social winter at Quebec, Mrs. Simcoe was glad to begin the journey inland. The movement of the bateau pleased her, as later the effortless gliding of her canoe. All the way from Quebec to Montreal log houses stood close to the river, lit by the tin-covered spires of village churches bright as candles.

Montreal was a smaller city where fur was still king; the fur baron Joseph Frobisher sent his phaeton to bring Mrs. Simcoe into the city. Here she dined at Mr. Frobisher's house and with the Baroness de Longueuil before going on up the river.

Now at last, in that summer of 1792, they were in Upper Canada, where settlers all lived along the water's edge — the Front — backed by unbroken forest. When they approached Glengarry, where Colonel John Macdonell was building his new house, a piper came to meet the new governor. Captain Munro lent Mrs. Simcoe a horse so that she could ride past the Long Sault rapids. At Cornwall she counted fifteen houses; at Kingston she saw fifty, one of them built of stone. And at Kingston Colonel Simcoe took the oath of office, becoming officially the lieutenant-governor of Upper Canada. A little over two weeks later, from the deck of the *Onondaga*, Mrs. Simcoe "saw the spray of the Falls of Niagara rising like a cloud."

The Onondaga, *an armed schooner of twelve guns and eighty tons burden, was one of several armed vessels belonging to the provincial government, thus constituting part of a "provincial navy." This reproduction was taken from a drawing by Mrs. Simcoe.*

"My dear Charlotte," the governor wrote from Niagara to his little daughter at home, "here I am & Mamma sitting in a very large Bower, fronting upon a fine River, & as high above it, as the sand cliff above the Shrubbery, with Sophia sitting upon the Table, little Francis with his bald Pole [poll] laughing & eating Bilberries."[4]

Mrs. Simcoe liked at once the "Beautiful view of the river" and added that "the poorness of the building is not remarked at this distance." Arriving on July 26, 1792, they found Navy Hall not ready for their occupancy and settled in three marquees pitched on the hillside. The governor was less complaisant. He wrote to James Bland Burges in August: "I am miserably off for accommodation in this country and I am fitting up an old hovel that will look exactly like a carrier's alehouse in England when properly decorated and ornamented."[5]

"Nothing can be conceived more dreary," wrote the author of *Canadian Letters,*[6] "than the united view of Niagara and Newark in the depth of winter — the river and mouth of the lake, choked up — all communication frequently cut off between the two places by drifting ice, wood on one side and the extensive water on the other." As for Newark, "a poor, wretched straggling village with a few scattered cottages erected here and there as chance, convenience or caprice dictated. The governor's house is distinguished by the name of Navy Hall. A family accustomed to the conveniences of England must have found this a most uncomfortable abode."

Governor Simcoe wrote to the Duke of Portland in 1794 that he had found "a Town laid out on the King's side of the strait of Niagara opposite the fort which consisted on my arrival of only one or two houses now containing upwards of fifty and rapidly increasing."[7] Streets were laid out, and people were building houses of square timber or logs, clearing land, and planting their fields and orchards.

Elizabeth Russell, who had accompanied her brother Peter, the receiver general, wrote in that first autumn of 1792: "We live in a log House consisting of only two small rooms on the ground floor which my brother bought being the only one that could be got at any rate. It is quite a poor cottage but it is much better than it was when we first came as then it did not keep out the Weather."[8]

A year later she described their new house (her brother complained bitterly of its cost — his *Dear* house, he called it): "We are comfortably settled in our new House and have a nice little Farm about us. We eat our own Mutton and Pork and Poultry. Last year we grew our own Buck weat and Indian corn and have two Oxen got two cows with their calves with plenty of pigs and a mare and Sheep. We have not made Butter yet but hope soon to do so. I must act the part of dairy maid as I have not got a female servant yet.'"[9] But the little farm was three-quarters of a mile from town, she sighed, and she had been unable to go to balls.

Servants were all but impossible to find. Hannah Jarvis, the wife of William Jarvis, the provincial secretary, wrote in her vigorous style, "This is one of the worst places for Servants that can be — they are not to be on any Terms ... We cannot get a Woman who can cook a Joint of Meat unless I am at her Heels — and at the price of seven, eight & nine Dollars per Month.... I have a Scotch girl from the Highlands, Nasty, Sulky, Ill Tempered Creture."[10] This girl struck another servant with the tongs and very nearly killed her.

Everyone suffered to some degree from the ague. "The place is pleasant but very unhealthy," wrote the gentle Miss Russell, "the Inhabitants being affected two thirds of the year with the fever an Ague." Hannah Jarvis wrote, "A vast number of Persons have died particular among us." All her family had "feavor." She wrote, "We have not had one Night's Sleep for this Month Past ... Mrs. Simcoe is far from well, she looks like a walking skeleton, in fact few have their health in this place." As for the governor, "his health is much impaired, and his eyes and skin are as yellow as saffron and he is peevish beyond description."[11]

Everything was expensive; Mrs. Jarvis constantly wrote to England for shoes for herself and the children, for dark strong printed calico not too fine, narrow striped red and white cotton for the little girls' gowns — there was none in Newark or even in Montreal under six shillings a yard. She wanted Britannia metal dessert spoons for the children to use to save her silver ones, castor oil, sulphur, camomile flowers, and James's powders, and asked her eighteen-year-old brother to send her "some Country Dance Books — you will get them for a shilling a Piece — let them be the Newest & Pretty."

Dancing at Niagara, as at Quebec, was the popular entertainment, and though the number of dancers was much smaller the residents took care to point out that the standards of dress and deportment were just as high. Mrs. Macaulay, wife of the surgeon attached to the Queen's Rangers, described to Mrs. Simcoe soon after her arrival the balls with wax candles, gauze dresses, and supper as well as tea. Mrs. Jarvis referred sarcastically to the ornaments piled high on the ladies' caps, and the author of *Canadian Letters*, surprised at the gay and well-dressed assembly, asked himself, "Can I be at the extremity of Lake Ontario? Many of them are very pretty women, and, after having figured at a ball, return home with renewed cheerfulness to the performance of their household duties, which are so peculiarly necessary in a colonial life."[12]

The opening of the legislature in 1795 was described by the duc de la Rochefoucauld-Liancourt: "The whole retinue of the Governor consisted in a guard of fifty men of the garrison of the fort. Dressed in silk, he entered the Hall with his hat on his head, attended by the Adjutant and 2 Secretaries."[13] Salutes were fired from Fort Niagara and the soldiers drawn up in order — the garrison in their red coats and the Queen's Rangers in their dark green coats and white pipeclayed breeches, the men with their hair powdered and drawn back into a queue below their helmets in the fashion of the time. The ladies watched, along with a group of Natives in their deerskin and beadwork. Flags waved, the band played.

We have two first-hand accounts of the same ball, given on June 4, 1793. General Benjamin Lincoln, one of the United States commissioners to meet with the Natives, gives a full account:

> The King's birth-day; to all the ceremonies of which our duty required us to attend. At eleven o'clock the Governor had a levee at his house, at which the officers of the government, the members of the legislature, the officers of the army, and a number of strangers attended. After some time, the Governor came in, preceded by two of his family. He walked up to the head of

the hall, and began a conversation with those standing in that part of the hall, and went around to the whole, and I believe spoke with every person present. This was over soon, and we all retired. At one o'clock there were firings from the troops, the battery, and from the ship in the harbor. In the evening there was quite a splendid ball, about twenty well-dressed handsome ladies, and about three times that number of gentlemen present. They danced from seven o'clock to eleven. Supper was then announced, where we found every thing good and in pretty taste. In all this there was not any thing very particular; the music and dancing were good, and every thing was conducted with propriety. What excited the best feelings of my heart was the ease and affection with which the ladies met each other; although there were a number present whose mothers sprang from the aborigines of the country. [These were the daughters of Sir William Johnson and Mary, sister of Joseph Brant.] They appeared as well dressed as the company in general, and intermixed with them in a manner which evinced at once the dignity of their own minds and the good sense of others....

Governor Simcoe is exceedingly attentive to these public assemblies, and makes it his study to reconcile the inhabitants, who have tasted the pleasures of society, to their present situation, in an infant province. He intends the next winter to have concerts and assemblies very frequently. Hereby he at once evinces a regard for the happiness of the people, and his knowledge of the world; for while people are allured to become settlers in this country, from the richness of the soil, and the clemency of the seasons, it is important to make their situation as flattering as possible.[14]

Hannah Jarvis wrote of the same ball:

At six o'clock we assembled at the Place appointed — when I was called on to open the Ball — Mrs. Hamilton not choosing to dance a minuet — this is the first assembly that I have been at in this country that was opened with a Minuet — not one in the Room followed my example — of course Country Dances commenced — and continued till Eleven when supper was announced — Mrs. Simcoe being ill Mrs. Hamilton was Lady President — Mrs. Secretary second in command — supper being ended the Company returned to the Ball Room when two Dances finished the Night's entertainment with the Sober Part of the Company. The rest stayd untill Day light & wd have stayd longer if their Servants had not drank less than their Masters. We had twenty Ladies & 20 of Gentlemen — the Commissioners from the States, who are so far on their way to treat with the Indians were there — the Council the Upper & Lower Houses were all there.[15]

Contemporary letters and diaries show a social life so close-knit as to be stifling. People dined, supped, took tea, played whist with each other every day in scarcely varied combinations. Mrs. Simcoe's diary is full of the to and fro of her small circle. John White, the attorney general, in his laconic diary is witness to this claustrophobic closeness. Day after day the entries repeat —

Dined at the Governor's, Supped at the Governor's, Breakfasted at the Governor's.

Dec. 25, 1792 Christmas day. Went to church. Dined and passed the evening with the Governor.

Dec. 27 Went to the Ball with the Governor and Chief Justice. Passed a tolerable evening.

Jan. 1, 1793 This being the 1st day of New Year the Governor had a Levee, at which a great many attended.[16]

A few weeks later: "Dined at Mrs. Simcoe's where met Dr. & Mrs. Macaulay, Captain Russell and sister and Mr. Pilkington.... At home all the morning. In the evening Mrs. Simcoe, Mr. & Mrs. Macauley to cards and supper."

He "walked with Captain Russell and sister to the New House," "Dined with Dr. Holmes and returned very tipsy. N.B. To dine less often at the Fort." The life of a man without his family was particularly dependent on others but scarcely more affected by homesickness.

A reproduction of a drawing by Mrs. Simcoe of Navy Hall in Niagara as seen from the river in 1792.

Mrs. Simcoe often records her joy at receiving letters from home. Letters and diaries ring with complaints —"it is now six months — it is now a year — since I heard from you. Are you ill — have you written." The arrival of ships is eagerly recorded — the *Onondaga* is in, the *Mississaga* is in — for during the summer and early autumn ships brought the mail. In winter, thoughts turned to the winter express brought by men on snowshoes. Letters received were excitedly read and answered in haste so as to catch the returning express. Or letters might be sent by a traveller going to Montreal or New York. At the news that someone was going east — and news passed from house to house with unbelievable speed — pens were hastily taken in hand to send off as many letters as time would permit. "An Indian goes," Mrs. Jarvis began a letter, and at its conclusion added, "the Indian did not go," and wrote a page more.

The settlers felt lonely and isolated, yet the little town was in the main line of communication between the United States and Canada and the Simcoes were constantly in their primitive quarters receiving distinguished guests. The Duke of Kent visited them almost before their trunks were opened, soon followed by the United States commissioners, come to treat with the Natives, the emigré duc de la Rochefoucauld-Liancourt and his party (though one of them "kept a shop"), army companions of the governor, Alexander Mackenzie fresh from the Pacific bringing sea otter skins, and a steady flow of observant travellers and intending settlers. Then there was the lively, picturesque life of Niagara: soldiers and Negro slaves, British officers, American backwoodsmen in homespun, Natives in full regalia, Detroit merchants in broadcloth, half-breeds, sailors from the lake boats, fur traders.

But the officers of the colony, thrown constantly into each other's company, especially in winter, were intensely critical of the country itself, of each other, and above all of the governor and his wife. Elizabeth Russell mourned, "I long to go to England for I grow tired of this country so little comfort is there compare to what I have been accustomed to."[17]

Hannah Jarvis called it "this Grim country." "Towns are rising in Idea fast," she wrote, "are laid out on Maps very fine — but rise slowly in reallity. This Town increases very rapidly, will in a short time be a very Pretty Place. We have a Jail built with Logs a Court House framed upon it two stories High — as yet that is all it remaining with its ribs only."[18]

They watched and talked about each other — Hannah Jarvis refers to nameless scandals "that make the Hair of an Honest Man stand Strait." But for the most part they watched the Simcoes. Everyone knew that the governor wanted a capital on the La Tranche River and that he was constantly at odds with Lord Dorchester. Many described him — the author of *Canadian Letters* wrote that he was "in figure tall, strong rather than elegantly formed, an open countenance & an eye not void of intelligence. The gentleman is plain & unaffected in his manners. The opinion, however, impressed in general by his appearance was that he was a man of apathy."[19] John White said that "Col. Simcoe (a most upright man) is wholly military, he cannot hear any thing like civil inquiry or proceeding." The result was that they had "decision without enquiry and promptitude without deliberation."[20]

Serious difficulties arose from the governor's frequent absences from the little temporary capital at Newark. After complaints of delay and confusion White added, "The absence of our Governor who is never here above 3 or 4 Months is the cause of all." Papers had to be sent to York to be signed and then returned. Hannah Jarvis wrote in November 1793 that the governor was at York, the chief justice, attorney general, receiver general, and secretary at Newark, and the acting surveyor general at Niagara Fort —"thus our government is to spend the Winter at respectable distances."

William Jarvis wrote that Governor Simcoe was very unwell "and if he has a good shake with the ague I think it will be but justice for his manners in dragging us from this comfortable place

[Kingston] to a spot on the globe that appears to me as if it had been deserted in consequence of a plague."[21]

Opinions of Mrs. Simcoe were often favourable at first. Elizabeth Russell on first meeting the Simcoes when she arrived in Quebec in June 1792 wrote, "I like the Governor and his lady very much. She seems a very agreeable woman without the least Pride or Formality." Yet pride and formality were later the chief accusations against her. The author of *Canadian Letters* described her:

> Mrs. Simcoe is a lady of manners, highly interesting, equally distant from hauteur or levity. Accustomed to fashionable life, she submits with cheerfulness to the inevitable inconvenience of an infant colony. Her conduct is perfectly exemplary & admirable conforming to that correct model, which ought to be placed before a people, whom a high pattern of dissipation would mislead, of extravagance would ruin.[22]

Hannah Jarvis was in general hostile. The governor, she wrote, had up to then given two public balls: "Mrs. Simcoe has been ill on both occasions — the first in childbirth the second in a Fevor as *reported* — I believe she would wish to be ill in order to avoid Expense — this entre nous. I am sorry the Governor did not come out solo as the People seem not to like Petecoat Laws."[23] She blamed Mrs. Simcoe for everything. "Our trunk of Linnens & sheeting much mildewed — Mrs. Simcoe's things escaped." When the Simcoes left Upper Canada in 1796 she wrote, "I hope they will detain him in England and his Wife also — let us have a Man who is fond of Justice."

There was a feeling expressed in *Canadian Letters* and often referred to by Mrs. Jarvis that Mrs. Simcoe's money and connections had some relation to her husband's appointment. "With this lady he received a handsome fortune. Col. Simcoe was considered an officer of merit, & served with reputation, but whether the Government was intended as a recompense for his services, or its attainment to be referred to the interest of Mrs. Simcoe's relations, opinions are various."[24]

How far was Mrs. Simcoe aware of this floating cloud of rumour and criticism? It is perhaps significant that she scarcely mentions the Jarvises or John White and seldom speaks of Elizabeth Russell. One day she tasted Miss Russell's preserved cherries, pronouncing them very good, and she admired Miss Russell's method of pressing plants in books —"I wish I had thought of doing so." And she rode with Mr. and Mrs. Jarvis to call on Mrs. Powell. But her time was taken up with her own small and devoted circle.

Mrs. Macaulay, wife of the garrison surgeon of the Queen's Rangers, whom Mrs. Simcoe found "very agreeable," drank tea with her, played whist, and went with her to Queenston landing for a picnic. Mrs. D.W. Smith, "a beautiful Irish woman," kept two tame raccoons, which intrigued Mrs. Simcoe. When she was ill she stayed with Mrs. Smith, who later, a week after her little boy was born, went with Mrs. Simcoe by boat to dine with Mrs. Hamilton.

The wife of the Queenston merchant Robert Hamilton was a frequent companion of Mrs. Simcoe's. They dined together and went to see trees on fire, "a beautiful effect," drank tea, and watched the Seven Nations, as Mrs. Simcoe called them, pass in their regalia. They played whist evening after evening and Mrs. Hamilton took Francis home to nurse him when he caught cold. Her husband, the merchant, was almost the only person for whom Hannah Jarvis had a good word. "A pleasant Intelegable Man," she called him, "a Gentleman in Words and Manners."

There was Mrs. Powell, wife of Judge William Dummer Powell, "a very sensible, pleasant woman" with whom Mrs. Simcoe drank tea and dined. And Mrs. Tice at whose house she stayed because it was higher and cooler than Navy Hall.

A good deal of the restlessness and acerbity evident among the settlers at Newark was due to uncertainty as to the future of the colony. William Jarvis resented having to leave Kingston and he was soon just as much irritated at the prospect of having to leave Niagara. "People here only live from hand to mouth," he wrote, "as if they were to be gone tomorrow."

Rejoicing in one sentence that she and her brother had moved into their new though very expensive house, Elizabeth Russell went on, "but this is not an End of it for he will in two or three years or perhaps must sooner be obliged to be at the same or a greater expence in Building another House at Toronto (now called York) which place is only to be the Temporary seat of Government where we are to be moved after that Heaven only knows."[25]

"We expect to be ordered to York," wrote John White in 1796, summing up his anxieties and distresses of the last four years, "— where I must build a house — but how and in what way is at present a mystery — unless something better turns up I am afraid it will be impossible. Look at me — cut off from that society that alone makes life desirous — the Society of those that we love. Banished — solitary — hopeless — planted in a desart, surrounded by savages — disappointed — and without prospect."[26]

White was unusually gloomy even for him, but the feeling of concern and instability was a general one.

"I still distinctly remember the unnamed aspect which the country exhibited when first I entered the beautiful basin," Joseph Bouchette wrote years later about Toronto harbour, which he surveyed in 1793.

Dense and trackless forests lined the margin of
the lake, and reflected their inverted images in

its glassy surface. The wandering savage had constructed his ephemeral habitation beneath their luxuriant foliage, the group then consisting of two families of Mississagas, and the bay and neighbouring marches were the hitherto uninvaded haunts of immense conveys of wild fowl. Indeed they were so abundant as in some measure to annoy us during the night.[27]

The Queen's Rangers, who had arrived a few days before the Simcoes, were felling trees and building themselves huts on the site of the present Old Fort York. The governor had brought his own quarters with him. The picture of a lieutenant-governor and his family spending a Toronto winter in a tent has intrigued imaginations ever since, and the canvas house aroused comment at the time. When he was first appointed, Simcoe had asked for "a Canvas House similar to that sent with the Governor of Botany Bay — as it might be highly convenient if not necessary, in various expeditions 'twill be proper I should make."[28] One was bought at a sale of the effects of Captain Cook, the one apparently occupied by Cook himself, who had, oddly enough, been master of the *Pembroke* under Simcoe's father. The canvas was laid on a wooden framework and boarded up outside for the sake of warmth.

Joseph Bouchette wrote of the canvas house, "Frail as was its substance, it was rendered exceedingly comfortable and soon became as distinguished for the social and urban hospitality of its venerable and gracious host, as for the peculiarity of its structure."[29]

A year later at Niagara the canvas house made a great impression on General Hull, who had come to treat with the Natives.

On my account the Governor ordered supper in his canvas-house, which he brought from Europe. It was joined to his dwelling-house. It is a room twenty-two feet by fifteen, with a floor, windows and doors, and warmed with a stove. It is papered and painted, and you would suppose you were in a common house. The floor is the case for the whole of the room. It is quite a curiosity. About eleven o'clock I was conducted to my chamber. Perceiving me so much pleased with the canvas-house, the Governor ordered breakfast in it.[30]

Elizabeth Russell wrote sympathetically:

The Governor with his family & Redgiment has been there [at York] about where they mean to stay the winter himself & family have only a Canvas House to cover them from the inclemency of the weather. The Officer in tents & huts. I very much pity the poor Women who are with their Husbands. It is surprizing how Mrs. Simcoe who is a very Delicate little woman (about the size of Mrs. Boston) can support the fatigue she does. For my own part I am determined to stay where I am till there is a comfortable Place there to receive me for I never will be exposed again to the fatigue and uncomfortable Habitation as I have been here.[31]

Her brother, Peter Russell, wrote to her from York:

The Governor and Mrs. Simcoe received me very graciously — but you have no conception of the Misery in which they live — The Canvas house being their only residence — in one room of which they lie and see company — and in

the other are the Nurse and Children squalling
— an open Bower covers us at Dinner — and a
Tent with a small Table and three Chairs serves
us for a Council Room.[32]

In the same month Mrs. Jarvis wrote from Newark:

The Governor and Family are gone to Toronto
(now York) where it is said they Winter — and a
part of the Regiment — they have or had, not
four Days since, a Hut to Shelter them from the
Weather — in Tents — no means of Warming
themselves, but in Bowers made of the Limbs of
Trees — thus fare the Regiment — the Governor
has two Canvas Houses there — Everybody are
sick at York — but no matter — the Lady likes
the place — therefore every one else must —
Money is a God *many* worship.[33]

Meanwhile Mrs. Simcoe, with her gift for enjoying the
present moment and the scene before her, was living quite happily
in her canvas house and bower of branches. St. Jean Rousseau,
the last of the French traders, still lived at the mouth of the river
called after him St. John's River (later the Humber). A few farmers
like Coon, Playter, and Scadding were beginning while the
Simcoes were at York to clear land. Mrs. Ashbridge in her house
across the Don gave Mrs. Simcoe seeds for calabashes and told
her how to grow them. Loons floated on the bay uttering their
uncanny cry, salmon abounded in the rivers and deer in the
woods, and wolves howled on winter nights.

Thomas Talbot, who was later to found the Talbot settlement,
acted as Governor Simcoe's aide and often walked or rode with
Mrs. Simcoe when he was not travelling with the governor. At
York he was particularly useful; he and Mrs. Simcoe raced on

horseback on the peninsula and she watched him skate on the frozen bay while the Shaw children ran about and set fire to the long grass.

At the same time Talbot was writing to Colonel McKee from York: "Col. Simcoe and the Queen's Rangers are encamped here and preparing huts for the winter. The foot of the rapids [of the Miami in Ohio] is quite London to this spot. However, I fear it will be my fate to pass some months here. There is a most magnificent city laid out which is to be begun in the spring."[34]

Mrs. Macaulay came over from Newark and the ladies were mustered to dance reels. Mrs. McGill came too with her sister, Miss Crookshank, who later became the second Mrs. Macaulay. They dined and drank tea and rode three miles to Mr. McGill's lot; another day they walked to Dr. Macaulay's lot (which began at the northwest corner of the present Queen and Yonge streets) and picnicked there in the woods.

Another friend, Mrs. Richardson, who was the newly married wife of the surgeon and sister of Mrs. Hamilton, breakfasted with Mrs. Simcoe and as it was raining they "played at chess all day." When Mrs. Hamilton came from Newark to see her sister the three ladies drank tea in the arbour till a violent thunderstorm drove them into the tent. Twice in a week "Mrs. Richardson spent the day with me," and the ladies went to see how Castle Frank was getting on and found the floor not laid and the carpenters building a hut for themselves.

At York, where there were few ladies and no social tradition, Mrs. Simcoe quickly invented a new kind of entertainment. She drove with her friends to Castle Frank, which with its tree-trunk pillars was slowly taking shape. Here they toasted thin slices of venison on sticks over the camp-fire, dining happily in the open air, and none of the ladies caught cold. Life at York was to Mrs. Simcoe a kind of rustic interlude between the close-textured society at Niagara and the more cosmopolitan and sophisticated entertainments of Quebec.

★ ★ ★

The duc de la Rochefoucauld-Liancourt wrote of Mrs. Simcoe while he was visiting her husband at Niagara:

> Mrs. Simcoe is a lady of thirty-six years of age [she was actually twenty-nine]. She is timid and speaks little, but is a woman of sense, handsome and amiable, and fulfils all the duties of a mother and wife with the most scrupulous exactness. The performance of the latter she carries so far as to be of great assistance to her husband, her talents for drawing the practice of which to make maps and plans enables her to be extremely useful to the Governor.[35]

The duc could not know that his timid hostess was just then writing in her diary of himself and his party, "Their appearance is perfectly democratic and dirty.— I dislike them all."

She fulfilled her duties not only with exactness but with a relentless zest and usually enjoyment. She liked her horse to leap over logs in the path, and every few days, if no longer journey offered, she was away to see a waterfall, a hill, or any "fine view."

For there was something picturesque at every turn and all her life she had been drawing pictures and looking for suitable "scenes." She had, as she wrote, "the picturesque eye." She drew everywhere, going down the St. Lawrence rapids or sitting so close to Niagara Falls that the spray wetted her paper. Through her words we see scenes that delighted her: the "seigneuresse" of a village near Quebec sitting in the churchyard and reading to her assembled "peasants" some handbills of a candidate for the next election; the regimental band playing before her log hut in the evening after dinner; Francis sitting on a rock to watch an Indian washing clothes in the lake.

She had always loved the out-of-doors and here there was little else. Nature as she found it was not always pleasant; she complained bitterly of the heat in summer and in stove-heated rooms in winter. Mosquitoes made her miserable but like most Europeans she was intensely curious about rattlesnakes and pleased when two live ones were sent to her in a barrel so that she could hear their weird rattle. There were other strange creatures — moose, fireflies, and flocks of wild pigeons darkening the sun.

She resembled the lady settlers of a generation later — Mrs. Traill, Mrs. Moodie, Mrs. Stewart — in her keen interest in plants and her knowledge of them, though she was most unlike those ladies in her commanding social position and her prosperity. Like Mrs. Traill, she tirelessly collected native remedies — calamus root for a cough, sweet marjoram tea for headache, sassafras tea for the ague.

The tents and bowers in which she slept she accepted with equanimity; they were picturesque; they were temporary expedients. Also, the deeper reason, she was supported by her profound conviction of her husband's and her own importance. He was the governor and the lustre of his position transformed tent and hut; wherever the governor sat was the head of the table.

It is perhaps not surprising that she was disliked by some of the people around her. She was young, wealthy, demanding, and very proud of her position in the colony. But she had her terrors as well. She dreamed of being fired on by enemies hidden in a wood through which she was walking with the governor and Lieutenant Talbot. This fear weighed on her; yet she reflected that if she were at home in England her anxieties would be even greater, for her husband would be involved in the apparently endless European war.

It was the Americans who menaced her world, never the Indians. In her condescending way, Mrs. Simcoe took a mild interest in farmers and arriving settlers, but her real enthusiasm was reserved for Indians, their "superior air," their "impressive action"; they "look like figures painted by the Old Masters."

She had a link with the Natives in her little son Francis, who, she said, was rude to guests but always polite to Natives. Francis, for whom Castle Frank was named, must have been a charming little boy. We see him at his third birthday party dressed as an Indian, and when a royal salute was fired at the naming of York, an Ojibwa chief "named Great Sail took Francis in his arms, & was much pleased to find the child not afraid but delighted with the sound."

Elizabeth Simcoe's drawing of the Ojibwa chief Great Sail.

Sophia is named only twice in the diary and the existence of Katherine is not mentioned at all. This sixth daughter was born at Niagara in January 1793 and died and was buried at York in April 1794.

We get some side glimpses of the children in their mother's letters to Mrs. Hunt and in the brief original diary that Mrs. Simcoe wrote every day, on which her final diary was based. In this original diary she wrote on October 28, 1794, that she had "sent Sophia to school." On November 17, she "found Sophia had a rash, returned in the open Carriole with Francis to Belmont least he might catch it"; and on November 21, Sophia was "quite well & goes to school tomorrow." Neither Sophia's school nor the rash makes any appearance in the final diary. Nor were the four little daughters at home mentioned in the diary, but only in surviving letters to them and to Mrs. Hunt.

The governor and his wife were happy in their marriage. Mrs. Simcoe watched over her husband's health and nursed him with assiduous care in his frequent illnesses. If her diary and the comments of their friends lead one to believe that she dominated him there is no doubt that he was devoted to her. The governor was addicted to writing poetry, and copies survive of many of his efforts, ranging from "The Veal-Pye's Tragedy" to "An Epilogue to Addison's Cato." A small piece of paper is fastened to a page of Mrs. Simcoe's diary with a rusty pin. On it is a poem Governor Simcoe wrote while he waited for his wife at Kingston on her return from Quebec. It is dated January 1, 1795.

> Twice six revolving years the Sun his course
> Thru yonder azure plains, diffusing joy
> Gladness and light, has discontinuous moved
> Since thou, Eliza, ever flowing source
> Of happiness domestic, dost employ
> My wedded thoughts, most honoured & most
>   beloved!
> And if the gathering clouds of fleeting Life
> Arise, thy presence soon illumes the Scene
> And pleasure draws from elemental strife!
> And now when night & absence intervene
> O may my wishes wing Thy speedy way
> Return thou source of Joy, return thou Source
>   of Day.

From Santo Domingo, where he was sent as Commander-in-Chief of the British forces after his return from Upper Canada, Simcoe addressed his letters to "My dear and most excellent wife,"

"My most excellent & noble wife." From Port au Prince in 1797 he wrote, "O for my dear my best Secretary!"[36]

He remained only eight months at Santo Domingo; the family took up their life at Wolford, where four more children were born — John, who died early, Henry, a second Katherine, and Anne.

A visitor described family prayers at Wolford: "It was somewhat imposing to see the maid-servants headed by the housekeeper, and the men-servants headed by the butler — seventeen in all — file into the dining room morn and eve and hear the master or the mistress of the house read and comment on the chapters selected for daily worship."

There were often ten or fifteen carriages at the door, and a servant reported with awe, "I have known three or four lords staying at Wolford at one time." A friend wrote that going to Wolford was like going to court.

The Simcoes had brought from Canada sleighs, a canoe and paddles, bows and arrows, and Native clothing, and whenever there was snow they went out in the sleigh drawn by a pony.

A few pages survive of a diary Mrs. Simcoe was keeping two years after her return to England. The governor had gone to Exeter, she wrote to Mrs. Caldwell in Quebec, and she had had a letter from her special friend Mme. Baby. Walking on the sands at Teignmouth she recorded three beautiful views: "ships about the size of those in L. Ontario lying in the River, forms a sweet picture."

Young Caroline wrote from Wolford Lodge to Mrs. Hunt in 1800: "Last Wednesday there was a fine masquerade. Every body was dressed in some character of Shakespeare. Papa was Prospero, & introduced all the company. Mamma was Mrs. Page, My little sisters acted Pyramus & Thisbe. Eliza was Thisbe, Charlotte Pyramus, Harriet represented Wall, Sophia Moonshine and Francis Lion."[37]

Simcoe was placed in charge of Plymouth and the troops in the Western District to prepare against Napoleon's threatened invasion; then in 1806 he was appointed to command the British forces in India. Mrs. Simcoe and her oldest daughter Eliza went to London to buy wardrobes for their journey. While they were gone, Simcoe, a lieutenant-general since 1801, was ordered to join the fleet off Portugal where an invasion was expected. On the voyage to Portugal he became ill and had to return immediately to England. He was taken to the house of friends in Exeter and died there on October 26.

The general was buried by torchlight in the little chapel he had built at Wolford. His monument in Exeter Cathedral has a life-size figure of a Queen's Ranger on one side and of an Indian on the other, with a bust of Simcoe between. During the bombing in the Second World War the monument was broken to pieces, but it has been skilfully reconstructed. At the bottom is an inscription commemorating Francis Gwillim Simcoe, killed at Badajoz at the age of twenty-one and buried on the battlefield.

Mrs. Simcoe entered upon forty-four years of widowhood. Now she kept only seven servants instead of seventeen. As she grew older she became more autocratic and it was even said that her daughters dared not sit down in her presence without permission; they were to remain with her, and she sent all their suitors away.

She was as restless and fond of travel as ever and she and her daughters moved constantly up and down the west country, going often to visit her son Henry, who was a clergyman settled in Cornwall. When she was on a journey she always started at six o'clock and went fifteen or twenty miles before breakfast. She was active until her death in 1850 at the age of eighty-four.

She was always eager to hear news of Upper Canada and perhaps she continued to feel the possessive affection she expressed two days after her return to England in 1796. Driving toward London, the houses, she wrote, appeared very well but the "fields looked so cold, so damp, so cheerless, so uncomfortable from the want of our bright Canadian sun."

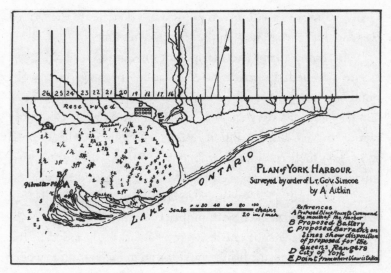

The first official plan of York (now Toronto), 1793.

The people of Ontario owe a considerable debt to John Ross Robertson, who collected historical material relating to Toronto and the Simcoes. His collection was unorganized, piled together without discrimination. The text of Mrs. Simcoe's diary in manuscript differs a good deal from the text presented to the public under Mr. Robertson's editing in 1911. But there is no doubt that he salvaged great quantities of material that would otherwise have been dispersed and lost.

Mr. Robertson visited Wolford where the manuscript of Mrs. Simcoe's diary was then kept, and not only had the diary transcribed but set artists to draw or photograph every house, church, or inn connected in any way with the Simcoe family and to copy all of Mrs. Simcoe's drawings and maps that he could find. These copies are arranged in scrapbooks in the Toronto Reference Library.

The manuscript of the diary itself, with a few letters, two or three notebooks, and a number of sketches and watercolours, some on paper and some on birch bark, are in the Ontario Archives.

General Simcoe gave fourteen of his wife's sketches to the Prince
Regent and they are now in the British Museum.

Mrs. Simcoe kept two diaries, not one. In the bateau or tent
as she travelled she made brief notations in small notebooks
bound in parchment. She noted particulars of the governor's
ailments and of letters written — "Wrote to Eliza & Charlotte,"
"wrote to Mrs. Burges, Elliott, Hunt & Gwillim," "the Express
went to Quebec, missed sending my letters." There are two
intriguing and mysterious entries — "S. 22nd pasted Flowers on
a petticoat," and "The Greeks sailed with Majesty between heaven
& earth Raphael walked with propriety on the Earth."

These on-the-spot entries were pruned or expanded in the
final diary kept in large blank books found in green mottled paper.
The ink is brown but the writing is perfectly legible, and scattered
through the text are small sketches of buildings and tiny maps.

The diary was sent in sections to Mrs. Hunt, who was taking
care of the little girls at Wolford.

A few entries from the original diary may be given for
purposes of comparison.

[November 1794]

F 7   Went to Belmont

S 8   returned home dined at Mrs. Taylor's

Sunday 9th   at church   do   do

M 10   Walked to Mrs. Ogden's.

T 11   went to the Chateau to Tea in the Morning.
I attempted to go to Belmont in the covered
Carriole but found the roads too bad.

W 12   dined with M. Baby   no letters by the
post

T 13   spent the Evening at Mr. Ogden's   Sophia
slept at school

F 14th   dined at Mrs. Winslow's

S 15   put off going to Powel place on account
of the snow & bad weather.

Now for the first time the diary has been transcribed exactly and completely. Punctuation has been added only where it seemed necessary to make the sense clear. The abundant and capricious capitalization stands as it does in the manuscript. Mrs. Simcoe was fond of quoting from memory foreign phrases, some of which are quite untranslatable. Notes have been kept under control and persons not identified in the notes are briefly identified in the index.

The staffs of the Public Archives of Canada, the Public Archives of Ontario, and the Toronto Reference Library have been, as they always are, most obliging and helpful. My special thanks go to Edith Firth of the Toronto Public Library.

MRS. SIMCOE'S DIARY

I

JOURNEY TO CANADA
September 17 to November 10, 1791

Weymouth, Saturday, 17th Sept., 1791 We arrived at Weymouth.
I walked with Lady Collier on the Esplanade in the Evening.

Sunday 18th Went to Church with Lady Collier; & to the Rooms
in the Evening. The King looked very well.

M. 19th I went to Portland Island with Lady de la Pole & went
round the island in a Cart, the conveyance usually used on those
rough roads. The sea views are very fine. There is an uncommon
aperature in the Land in one spot where we looked down as if
into a vast well and saw the waves dashing below. We drove by the
Light House. There are some buildings in ruins covered with Ivy
which have a very picturesque appearance. We stopped to take
some refreshment after the drive at one of the largest Villages on
the Island where we tasted Portland Mutton. The Inhabitants of
the Island have laws and regulations peculiar to themselves; for
instance, the sale of land is effected by the presentation of a Stick
before witnesses, no writings or Parchment used & no Lawyers
consulted. We crossed a very narrow passage to the Island but it
is sometimes very rough.

I dined with Lady de la Pole at Stacey's Hotel and went in
the Evening to see the play As You Like It, which was very well
performed. Coll. Simcoe dined with Lord Grenville.

T 20th I was tired with writing and did not go to the Ball.

W. 21st   The Chancellor [Lord Thurlow] is gone into Flintshire. The Sealers [officials who prepare documents for sealing] are following with Gov. Simcoe's Commission but not having yet overtaken him we are detained here and complaining of losing a fine E. wind. We give 2½ guineas a week for a very small Lodging. I could not go to Lullworth today lest the Commission should arrive in which case we are to sail immediately.

T. 22nd   Intelligence is received that the Chancellor is gone to Cumberland.

F. 23rd   I was pleased with a Camera Obscura I saw fixed in the top of a Room. I bought a wooden Pentograph. Misses Rolles are here and very civil to me. I went 5 miles with Lady Poulett and her Children in her Sociable [a carriage] and dined with her.

In the Evening we walked on the Esplanade. The Royal family came and spoke to Lady P. and the Princess Royal carried Lady Mary a heavy child three years old the whole length of the Esplanade.

S. 24th   I walked on the Sands with Coll. Simcoe before breakfast. We met the King. He asked me whether I left my Children at school, how I should like being at Sea, etc. I was not well and dined at home. Sir de la Pole sent me landrails [corn-craiks]. My french Cook dressed them without taking out the inside and I found a sea shell as large as a nut in one of them. I thought they lived by suction — how could this be?

Sunday 25th   I was at the Rooms tonight, Capt. Sydney Smith was there & wore a handsome Star given him by the King of Sweden in whose service he distinguished himself. He is thought to be like Charles the Twelfth. His countenance reminded me of pictures of some great men in Elizabeth's reign — a marked countenance expressing the reverse of a trifling character.

The whole of this day it blew so heavy a gale that the Triton was obliged to go out to sea, it being dangerous to remain at anchor. From Lady de la Pole's windows (where I dined) the waves looked tremendous. The scene was grand but as the Queen [Charlotte] observed this Evening, was mixed with too much horror to be pleasing.

I dined yesterday at Sir G. Collier's with Capt. Murray of the Triton who appears a very gentlemanlike man, and his having the reputation of being an excellent Officer is a great consolation to us who are about to sail at so late a Season for a Northern Climate. Sir J. Jervoise is the only man who tells Coll. Simcoe that he is certain of making his passage at this time of year. Others think it too late but he is a man of nautical affairs & therefore his opinion is to be trusted to.

The King asked Capt. Murray about his Sea Stock [of provisions] and hoped he had prepared for making my passage as comfortable as possible to me.

M. September 26th, 1791   Wind E, blowing fresh fine and clear. It became calm this morning & at one o'clock p.m. we embarked on board His Majesty's frigate Triton 28 Guns, Captain G. Murray. Capt. Stevenson accompanied us & Lt. Grey a son of Sir Charles Grey's, for whom Coll. Simcoe requested a passage, who is going to join the Fusileers of the 7th Regt. at Quebec.

I became giddy as soon as I entered the ship and went to my Cabbin, an apartment just large enough to swing a Cott which I immediately got into. In going through the Race of Portland, one of the Port hole Windows was stove in & the Gentlemen at dinner were quite wet.

T. 27th   E. fresh and fine. Went before the wind 9 notts an hour.

W. 28th   E. fresh and fine. Went upon the Deck. Our hours are early we breakfast at 8 dine at two & never take any supper.

Sunday Oct 2nd   Calm.

M. 3rd   Rough.

T. 4th   I got the better of my sickness yesterday but there blew so strong a gale of wind that I was obliged to remain in my Cot or in a corner behind the Stove in the great Cabbin, to secure myself from falling. It was by persevering to go on the Deck & by eating salt beef covered with Mustard, that I so soon became well & as my health amends my spirits rise & I am rather diverted at the difficulties we meet with at dinner, when in spite of all care the dishes are often tossed to every corner of the Room. The Ship not having sufficient Ballast makes her Roll so unreasonably. I think I have great merit in beginning to write to you[1] thus early, in spite of rough weather. The Children are well but never appear to me safe but when in their Cotts, for the Nurses are much undisposed & have very indifferent sea legs. I am learning to walk on deck, but cannot do it without leaning on a Gentleman. Capt. Murray who has been in France plays at Reverse with us. Sophia's amusement is seeing the Poultry on deck where a little midshipman carries her every day. The wind has for some days driven us to the southward of our Course. It begins to blow hard again so I must retire to my Cott.

W. Oct. 5th   Calm. Went five notts an hour.

T. 6th   Went six notts an hour.

F. 7th   We saw Porpoises.

S. 8th   Calm and fine. It is expected we shall see the Western Isles tomorrow night.

Sunday 9th   Hot and fine. We rose from dinner at 3 o'clock to see a Ship pass. She was the Minerva of London from New York to Malaga. I admired the sight as she sailed close to us. She did not give us any intelligence. At 10 p.m. an Island was seen.

M. 10th   Fine, very hot. The heat was so excessive I could not sleep & rose at 6 to look at the Island which was Corvo [one of the Azores]. The mist presently dispersing we saw Flores but the atmosphere far from clear. Corvo is extremely high land, lat. 39, Corvo S. S. E., 3 leagues.

Coll. Simcoe has been reading in Charlevoix[2] that Corvo was discovered by a Portuguese who found it uninhabited, but saw an Equestrian Statue on a Pedestal of what Metal made he knew not but there was an inscription on it which was not legible. The right hand of the figure pointed to the West.

The Western Isles are inhabited by Portuguese who are fond of buying black cloathes whenever Ships call there, which they frequently do to take in water & which we should have done, had not the lateness of the Season in which we quitted England made it necessary not to lose an hour on the passage as we are doubtful of reaching Quebec before the St. Lawrance is filled with Ice.

I should have like to have gone on Shore here, as the Climate is said to be delightful & the Islands abounding in Grapes, Oranges, Melons, Chestnuts etc. No boats came to us with fruits & they rarely fish beyond their harbour on account of the heavy squalls to which the Coast is subject which endangers their being blown out to sea. From the description of the Islands I would like to make a voyage here instead of going to Tunbridge or other watering Places, where people frequently ennuyer themselves. The scheme would be more enlarged & I believe much more amusing. Being at Sea in good weather is delightful, & there is no occasion to execute such a voyage in the Equinoxial season.

T. 11th   Wind light & contrary, very hot. A ship on her larboard tack was seen last night but we being on starboard did not speak

55

with her. I rose this morning at 3 & looked at Orion in great brightness. The heat is excessively oppressive tho we have the windows open all night.

W. 12th I copied some prints of Ships Capt. Murray lent me. An American Vessel was seen.

T. 13th Fine. A sail passed this morning supposed to be an English 44 [guns]. At noon a Portuguese Vessel was scene.

F. 14th Very hard gale this Evening. The Sea ran mountains high. I sat on Deck & saw the men reefing the Sails. Their situation appeared tremendous. Mr. Benge the purser gave Coll. Simcoe an account of his having been twice wrecked on the 14th of October which made him rather distrust his safety on this anniversary. He was in the Deal Castle when she & 17 ships were lost on the Spanish main. She was carried by a violent gale of wind over a High Rock and stuck on the Sands. At 2 in the morning her bottom stove in, but she did not sink till after day light when all the men except 17 got on shore on Rafts. The account of such perils during such weather was not very amusing to me.

S. 15th Wind N.W. hard gale, cold. This hard gale did not cool the Cabbins which had been so extremely heated; I was therefore glad to be on Deck to get rid of the headache notwithstanding the weather was so rough that I was obliged to hold fast by a Cannon. The waves, rising like mountains, has the grandest and most terrific appearance & when the Ship dashes with violence into the Sea & seems to lose her balance as much as a Chaise in the act of overturning, it is surprizing that she rights again. I viewed this tempestuous scene with astonishment.

Sunday 16th A very stiff gale. Fine weather makes me very happy but when it blows hard this sejour is certainly horrid beyond the imagination of those who have not experienced it. The noises on board a Ship (till one becomes accustomed to them) almost deprive one of one's senses; in bad weather they are doubled; every place wet & dirty, besides being bruised by sudden motions of the Ship & half drowned by Leaks in the Cabbin. The gale has today been stiff & contrary. 2 days since we expected to have been ere this catching Cod on the banks of Newfoundland, & now we are far off. Those who are of a sanguine temper think we may get to N. York — others forsee that we shall be driven to Barbadoes, where we must pass the winter and in May sail for Antigua to refit.

Coll. Simcoe is the only person who supposes it possible to reach Quebec. It will be so late before we come into the River St. Lawrance that the Pilots will probably have quitted the Isle of Bique & the Master of the Triton cannot carry her up without a Pilot. In this case we must return to the Gulph, and the Season being too severe to keep a Northern Latitude, we must steer for the Barbadoes, & there shall meet with millions of those black Beetles I so much detest, those verdaderos ninos d'esponomon — lizards, centipedes & scorpions besides! Desdichada de mi que tengo de hazer?

After being amused during the day by a description of those vile reptiles, the Evening proved so rough & dismal that everybody sat melancholy & unoccupied. I learnt a hymn in the Spectator happening to open the book where there was one applicable to our present situation.

I then sat myself down to copy [pictures of] Ships and by perseverance & determined opposition to unfavourable circumstances I finished six pretty correctly. My Cott striking against the side of the Cabbin most uncomfortably Coll. Simcoe thought of the method used by the Ancients to lessen the force of Battering Rams by hanging up feather beds to receive them. This device made the Cot slide up and down very easily.

M. 17th   Pleasant weather. We saw Porpoises.

T. 18th   A pleasant morning. At 12 a sudden gale of wind arose & while I was engaged in a game of Piquet with Capt. Murray, a lee lurch threw me to the side of the Cabbin against the fender. I was vexed at the accident though not hurt having piqued myself on having been so expert as always to have avoided falling.

W. 19th   A brig seen. A Shag [cormorant] with a Red Bill was seen. Wind variable.

T. 20th   Wind moderate. We are 130 leagues from Newfoundland. This distance we have kept these last five days. I began to draw a map of the Genesee Country.[3]

F. 21st   Very hard gale. A tempestuous night it rained upon my bed, but a thick great Coat covered me & I slept well. This Ship is a good Sea Boat but so leaky in her upper works that the floor of my Cabbin is scarcely ever dry and the Baize with which it is covered retains the wet, therefore I always wear clogs. Some shrouds were lost in this gale of wind.

S. 22nd   N.E. hard gale.

Sunday 23   Wind N.E. Whales seen near the ship & many Birds which are signs of being in soundings tho none can be obtained. As the Sun has not been seen for some days no observation can be taken, & the Compass is so bad a one that it traverses to all points in a gale of wind, so that the Master knows not where we are or (in bad weather) what course we are going.

M. 24th   Wind N.E. Cold & clear. Numbers of gulls shear-waters & Mother Carey's chickens flying about. The latter always are the forerunners of bad weather, they are a pretty brown bird with white spots, rather larger than a Sparrow. At 12 we were in 75 fathom water. Cod, Haddock & Halybut were caught. A very cold night & rained into my cot.

T. 25th   N.W. Wind, excessive cold. No soundings since 12 last night. It is extraordinary to be out of them so soon. It is hoped we shall keep clear of Sable Island which is frequently envelloped in fog & therefore very dangerous. No trees grow on it, but there is plenty of wood from the frequent Wrecks that are driven on its shores. It abounds with Rats, Snipes etc.

W. 26th   Wind N.W. So extremely cold that I could not stay upon Deck without a fleecy hosiery Great Coat on; a bird like a Linnet & a Cross Bill's Bill alighted on the Rigging. It was out of the reach of land. I hoped to have it in my Cabbin but it soon died.

T. 27th   Wind moderate. A beautiful owl olive colour with white spots and black about his face was caught today. He was not larger than a thrush & not wild; also a bird the size of a Lark.

F. 28th   Wind N.E. A fine morning and we fortunately made the Isle of Sable thirteen leagues N., only 8½ fathoms water before 12 o'clock, when a very thick fog came on.

If it blows hard till tomorrow we hope to go through the Gut of Canso, a beautiful passage between high rocky shores and the shortest way to the Gulph of St. Lawrance. I am now reconciled to being at Sea. I am well enough to work, write or draw; & moving at the rate of 10 miles an hour without fatigue or trouble (which in this good weather is the case) is very pleasant. I should like to embark in summer, see various Coasts, look into the harbours, and pass 2 or 3 months in this way, for example, come to Spanish River where we hope shortly to be, & I am told is a pretty place, & I hope to visit Mrs. McCormick [wife of the governor of Cape Breton Island] there tomorrow.

S. 29th　Wind N.W. The wind against our going through the Gut of Canso. At 8 today we saw the Coast of Nova Scotia, at 12 observed White Island & saw American Schooners. The white Sails appeared very pretty to us who had been so long without seeing any objects & the breakers along the coast contrasted with some dark shores had a good effect. We saw the Gut of Canso at a distance. At 4 we saw Richmond Island in some charts called Isle Madame which we were very near. It is a bold perpendicular dark Red rock, shaded almost to black, & covered with Pine which looks richer than Oak, and the conic shape when in large Masses looks well. Some large, blasted Pine quite white had a wild fine effect. At the end of this island are Rocks under water which form fine breakers dashing up to a great height & sinking beneath the blue tide. A little distance from Richmond lies Green Island a small, low, smooth, olive-coloured strip of land. Behind Richmond is Arichat Harbour from whence we saw a schooner coming. Within half an hour she came up with us, but could not Pilot us into Arichat Harbour or we should have anchored safely there & waited for an E. wind to carry us through the Gut of Canso.

Coll. Simcoe quotes "there is a tide in the affairs of men" & says our losing the opportunity of going thro the Gut of Canso makes him for the first time doubtful of reaching Quebec. He is particularly disappointed at not seeing this passage as his father proposed to carry large ships thro it & would have gained much time by so doing. This advantage was lost, as his proposal was objected to by the officers, who were afraid to risk the Passage. We are now beating about, not making much way or venturing to make more sail than will carry us 5 notts an hour during this night, lest we get among the numerous breakers hereabouts.

Sunday, October 30th　Wind W. clear & cold. Lat. 45¾ Lon. 42½ Passed Louisbourg at 7 this morning. Coll. Simcoe was very sorry he had not seen that harbour so often mentioned in his father's papers. At 10 we passed the Isle de Scatari. Then saw Cape Breton.

At eleven made Flint Island & Cape Perce. We passed Spanish River at 6 in the Evening. I did not see it. Gov. McCormick lives there & has a brig in which he goes to England.

M. 31st   Wind N.E. Snow. At eleven we passed Niganiche Island. At 12 Cape Nord which is broken into Rifts & Chasms, a very bold Coast. There was a good deal of snow on the Trees, & as it is still falling together with fog I saw but little. It had a wild appearance. This place abounds with Ducks. Lat. 47 Lon. 42½.

T. Nov. 1st   Wind N.W. Cold. We saw the Magdalen Islands. They are uninhabited & in summer frequented by Sea Cows. There is good Duck shooting on them, and Cod fishing near them, for which purpose an American Schooner is now at anchor off one of them. At 12 saw Amherst Island & afterwards the Island Entry.

W. 2nd   Wind N.W. Very cold. I saw Amherst Island in another point of view; also Deadman's Isle, which appears like a Barn. We met the Liberty of Whitby, bound to Portsmouth from Miscou in the Bay of Chaleur, laden with Plank. The Liberty informed us that the Alligator with Lord Dorchester on board had put into Hallifax the 7th of September having sprung her Bowsprit, and the Penelope was nearly being lost at the same time. Capt. Murray sent a boat on board the Liberty with letters for England. During the time we lay to, several Cod Fish were caught. I like the Chowder made of them very much. Coll. Simcoe has the gout in his hand.

F. 4th   Wind N.E. Dreadful gale & snowstorm; several men frost bit during the last night, which was the worst weather we have had. The Ship pitched her forecastle under water continually. In the morning the Isle Bonaventure was seen, but the wind being contrary they tacked all day & lost ground. We were under single Reef courses the whole day. Coppers are kept boiling night & day to thaw the tackle & Ropes which are continually freezing. The

Sailors have no cloathing more than they would have on a West India voyage & suffer severely. Had we been 8 leagues more to the northward this wind would have served to carry us up the River.

S. 5th   Wind N.W. moderate during the day but at night the wind came S.W. & we ran our course at the rate of 8 notts an hour. Isle Bonaventure was seen again.

Sunday 6th   Wind N.W. Passed Cape Rosier in fine weather but at 12 o'clock a most heavy gale of wind came on which lasted till 12 at night, the highest sea & the roughest weather we have had. Two Reefs in the Foresail. Tacked all day & lost much ground. If this weather continues many hours we cannot weather it but must be blown out of the River & go to N. York if we can, more probably be blown to the W. Indies, the men being so disabled by the frost & so many on the sick list that there is not enough to work the ship against adverse winds. The dinner overset, the Tea things broke, but I eat broth without spilling it.

M. 7th   Wind moderate. Anticosti Island seen.

T. 8th   Wind moderate, N.W. hard frost & clear. We saw part of the Nova Scotia Coast called in the chart Les Vallees. Tacked all day & made some way.

W. 9th   N.E. Clear & moderate. Saw Mons Camille & Riviere Matteaux.

I walked two hours on the Deck this afternoon & saw a fine sunset behind Bique. When we came within sight of Bique Capt. Murray fired a Gun for a Pilot & one very soon after the signal came on board. He had arrived from Coudres this day to attend a dance at Bique which latter place he had quitted a week before, not expecting any ships from England at so late a Season. Tomorrow he would have returned to Coudres, & we must have left the

River for want of a Pilot. Our arrival this day was therefore most fortunate. I copied some of Des Barres' Charts this morning. The wind was so fair that all the sails were set, even the Sky Scrapers & the ship went so steadily that I did not feel any motion.

T. 10th   N.E. Rain & mild. We saw 3 Ships on their way to England anchored off the Brandy Pot Islands. Passed Hare Island & the Kamouraskas. I feel the air much heavier since we have been so near the land. We expect to be at Quebec in the night; the Island of Orleans reaches from nearly opposite Cape Tourmente to within a league & ½ of Quebec. It is 7 leagues in length & 3 in width. As Baron la Hontan[4] says "north of the Isle of Orleans the River divides into 2 branches; the Ships sail thro the south, the north channel being foul with Shoals & Rocks."

2

A WINTER IN QUEBEC
November 11, 1791, to June 5, 1792

Nov. 11th 1791 The Triton anchored at Quebec at one this morning. At 7 I looked out of the Cabbin window & saw the Town covered with Snow & it rained the whole day. Coll. Simcoe & Capt Murray dined with Genl. Clarke[1] to meet Prince Edward.

I expressed so much concern to quit the ship that Capt. Murray said he was almost afraid to dine on shore lest I should order the ship under weigh to sail on a further voyage. I was not disposed to leave the Ship to enter so dismal looking a Town as Quebec appeared through the mist sleet & rain, but at 6 o'clock Lt. Talbot[2] went ashore with me, & Genl. Clarke's covered Carriole (a small Post Chaise on Runners instead of Wheels) was ready to carry me to the Inn in the Upper Town to which we ascended an immensely steep hill through streets very ill built. The Snow was not deep enough to enable the Carriole to run smoothly so that I was terribly shaken & formed a very unpleasant idea of the Town to which I was come & the dismal appearance of the old-fashioned inn I arrived at (which, I could suppose, resembled my idea of a Flemish house) was not prepossessing. My rooms were all on the first floor and a large Kitchen adjoining the sitting room. I did not suffer from cold, for it was heated by Poils or Stoves, which were so well supplied with wood, that I found it sometimes necessary to open the Finettes or sliding panes of glass in the windows. I met with fine partridges & excellent Apples called Roseaux, pink throughout, & they had a flavour of strawberries — a very early apple & they do not keep.

Sunday 13th   Captain Murray sailed for Hallifax. I sent letters to England by a Merchant Vessel. I was amused by seeing dogs of all sizes drawing traineaux with wood. Mastiffs draw loads of Provisions, and very small dogs Carrioles with Children in them.

F. 18th   I walked with Coll. Simcoe to Cape Diamond which is fortified by many works & from whence there is a very grand view of the Town, shipping, distant mountains as far as Cap Tourmente near the mouth of the River. The inhabited country near Quebec is embellished by the Villages of Montmorency, Charlesbourg, Lorette, St. Foix. It seemed very perilous walking over acres of ice, but cloth shoes or coarse worsted stockings over shoes prevents slipping.

S. 19th   I went to the House we have hired in St. John Street, which is a very moderate one, but the only one at present to be let. There is a Poil in one parlour, & a fire place in the other.

M. 21st   I went to a Subscription Concert. Prince Edward's Band of the 7th Fusiliers played and some of the officers of the Fusileers. The music was thought excellent. The Band costs the Prince 8 hundred a year.

S. 26th   A Mr. Hazzeel who is lately come from River la Tranche [the Thames] dined with us & confirms the favorable opinion we have entertained of the Country on its banks. We supped at Major Watson's. Mrs. Watson appeared pleasing. Mrs. Caldwell[3] was there.

Sunday 27th   I went to Church. The Service is performed in a Room occasionally used as a Council Chamber. Prince Edward always goes to Church and his band plays during the Service. On the death of two Jesuits the Recollet Church will devolve to the English, & as these Men are very old the English Government do not think it necessary to build a Church for the use of the

Protestants; indeed the French allow us to use the Recollet Church between the hours of their Service, but as they will not admit of fires in it, the Council Chamber is generally used as a Church in the Winter.

M. 28th   I went to a Concert and afterwards to a dance at the Fusileers' Barracks.

T. 29th   I supped at Major Stewart's & met Mrs. P.V. the most unpleasing woman I have seen in this place. She is just arrived from London.

W. 30th   St. Andrew's Day. Coll. Simcoe dined with Dr. Mabane at Woodfield, he was an Army Surgeon, came into the Council at Quebec, amassed money & lives what is called most hospitably, far beyond his fortune.

T. 1st Dec.   A fine clear cold day. I walked near 3 miles to Major Holland's where I saw some fine Prints of Italy & Mount Vesuvius.

Observing that the Stoves are generally heated to an excessive degree, I was told that in this house they are always moderate. I looked at Fahrenheit's Thermometer in the Room & it was 74. They said that it had been 86 at Chief Justice Smith's a few Evenings ago.

From hence I went in an open Carriole (which is a sort of Phaeton body on a sledge or Runners, shod with iron instead of wheels) to Woodfield to call on Dr. Mabon's sister. It is 3 miles from Quebec, a beautiful situation among woods on the steep & high banks of the St. Lawrance & within a mile of Wolfe's Cove, the spot where Genl. Wolfe landed. From hence I went to Sans Bruit a house of Coll. Caldwell's let to a Mr. Toozey, a Clergyman from Sussex, of whose skill in farming Mr. Young the agriculturalist has written so largely. I walked from hence to Quebec 2 miles. It is fatiguing to walk on snow when not perfectly frozen & my half boots were heavy with Icicles.

F. 2nd   We dined at Belmont 4 miles from Quebec, Coll. Caldwell's, a very indifferent House in appearance, but comfortable within. I nearly fainted with the heat this Evening & was told that Fahrenheit's ther. in this Drawing Room had one Evening been at 100. I eat part of a metiffe, a bird between a wild goose (the outarde) & a tame one. It was much better than a tame Goose. I found it so cold coming home after supper in a covered Carriole that I wore one of the fencing masks lined with fur which Capt. Stevenson gave me.

S. 3rd   Coll. Simcoe set out for Montreal accompanied by Capt. Stevenson, they wore large Beaver Coats, & the Carriole was filled with Buffalo Skins. I copied some views of Italy Major Holland lent me.

Sunday 4th   Mrs. Toozey carried me to Church in a Carriole like a narrow Coach which from its length was much easier than those usually used, but too heavy for one Horse to draw with ease, therefore seldom used.

M. 5th   A thaw today; the air Raw and cold, and the roads full of Cahots, but it did not deter the Prince & a Party from driving 8 miles to Lorette. It is the custom here to make parties to dine in the Country at a distance of 10 miles. They often carry a cold dinner & return to a dance in the Evening & this in the severest weather which seems as much relished by the English as the Canadians. Their partners must be very agreeable or they could never have liked these parties. I drank tea with Mrs. Watson. A slight shock of an Earthquake was felt in Port Louis Street this Evening.

   Quebec is divided into Upper & Lower town. The latter is inhabited by Merchants for the Convenience of the Harbour &

Quays. They have spacious Houses 3 stories high built of dark stone, but the streets are narrow & gloomy. In the suburbs of St. Roc are Ruins of the Intendant's Palace which was a very large building. The Upper Town is more airy & pleasant though the Houses in general are less.

The Chateau, the Residence of the Governor, contains some very good Rooms built by Sir Frederick Haldimand.[4] The situation is very high & commands a most noble prospect down the River. The old Chateau is in a ruinous state but is used for publick offices & convenient for the Gov. as being so near his own Residence that there is only a Court Yard between them.

W. 7th   Genl. Clark's servant threw himself from the Chateau into the Lower Town 600 feet without breaking a bone, or being killed. I received a Letter from Coll. Simcoe, who travelled in the Carriole to 3 Rivers 100 miles where he found the River open & was obliged to cross it in a boat & proceed the remaining 100 miles to Montreal in a Calash (a Carriage like a Gig with a seat in front for a driver). He reached Pt. au Trembles which is within 3 leagues of Montreal, the second day from Quebec.

Sunday 11th   I dined at Coll. Caldwell's & soon after I returned home Coll. Simcoe arrived from Montreal which place he left yesterday & brought with him Mr. Talbot of the 24th Regt. a relation of Lady Buckingham, who was Aide-de-Camp to the Marquis while he was Ld. Lieutenant of Ireland & at whose request Coll. Simcoe takes Mr. Talbot into his family.

15th   We walked to the Provision Store, a road by the River side below Cape Diamond always sheltered & well beaten.

18th   We dined at Belmont.

M. 19th   Dined & supped at Madame Báby's,[5] & eat part of the

Moufle of the Orignale or Elk. They are sometimes shot by the Indians, & much esteemed. It is a very rich dish with an excellent sauce. I am told the lip of the Ox is sometimes sold for it. A pie made of crete de coys is also a very favourite dish among the Canadians & easily procured as a quantity of Poultry are killed in the beginning of the winter & kept hung up in a frozen state. The Poultry eat dry, but when preserved in Barrels of Snow as is the custom at N. York they retain the juices much better.

T. 20th   We supped at Mr. Ainslie's.

W. 21st   We dined with Mr. Williams, the Clerk of the Council. The supper was very elegant. Mrs. Williams is a very genteel woman & paints beautifully, & dresses very well. She has not been here above two years having been educated in London.

22nd   I had an order from the Catholic Bishop for admittance to the Convent des Ursulines, where I went today with Madame Báby. The Superieure is a very pleasing conversible woman of good address. Her face & manner reminded me of Mrs. Gwillim [a relative]. The Nuns appeared chearful, pleased to see Visitors & disposed to converse & ask questions. Their dress is black with a white hood & some of them looked very pretty in it. They carry cleanliness & neatness to the greatest pitch of perfection in every part of the Convent, & are industrious in managing a large Garden.

They educate Children at this Convent, taking both pensionnaires & day boarders. They make many decorations for their altars & Church, & gild Picture frames. They shewed a fine piece of Embroidery worked by an English Nun, since dead. Some of them make boxes & pin cushions of birch bark worked with dyed hair of the Orignale. It is so short that it must be put through the Needle for every stitch which makes it tedious. All sorts of Cakes & Sweetmeats are made here & all the Deserts in

Quebec are furnished by the Nuns. They dry apples in a very peculiar manner, they are like Dried apricots. All these things are of use to maintain them, their finances being very moderate.

Another Convent is called the Hotel Dieu for the reception of the Sick, whether French or English. It is attended by the Medical Men on the Staff, who speak highly of the attention payed by the Nuns to the Sick people. The General Hospital is a Convent a mile out of Town, where Sick & Insane people are received.

The Great Church or Cathedral stands in the Centre of the Town & appears to be filled with People at all hours of the day. It is a handsome building. Near to it is a Seminary where boys are educated, & some of the Catholic Clergy reside there.

The Jesuits or Recollet Church is a handsome building ornamented with some pictures but no fine paintings. Two models of ships are suspended in it, placed there in commemoration of the arrival of some of the first Settlers from France. The only two Jesuits living have spacious Apartments near the Church & a Good Library & Large gardens. I went to a subscription Ball this Evening. There were three Rooms well lighted & the company well dressed.

S. 24th   Doctor Nooth says a great light was observed last night in the air in a direction N.E. beyond St. Paul's Bay which is 30 leagues below Quebec in the St. Lawrance. He supposed an irruption had taken place from a Volcano, which is believed from the reports of Indians to be in those parts, & a fresh irruption might have taken place there, Occasioned by an earthquake which was severely felt a few days since near St. Paul's Bay. However, there is much of conjecture in the supposition about the Existence of this Volcano.

Sunday 25th Christmas day   I went with Madame Báby at 5 in the morning to the Cathedral Church to see the illumination of the Altar, which to those who have not seen the highly-decorated

Roman Catholic Churches in Europe is worth seeing. The singing or chanting was solemn. The Church was crowded. I was wrapped up very much, and wore a kind of Calech lined with eiderdown, a very comfortable head-dress; but the cold was intense for the Roman Catholicks will not admit of fires in their Churches lest the Pictures should be spoiled. I saw no fine pictures.

M. 26th   This day the Division of the Province into Upper & Lower Canada & the new Constitution given to the former was announced by Proclamation. There were dinners at the Hotels & illuminations at night to commemorate this event.

W. 28th   I was at a very pleasant Ball at the Chateau, & danced with Prince Edward.

T. 29th   We drove to Woodfield & admired the beautiful scenery around it.

S. 31st   We drove to Belmont. We saw two Indians from Lorette who had mocassons to sell, a kind of leather shoe made of untanned Deer Skins which I was glad to buy for the Children on account of their softness. These Lorette Indians were originally Hurons converted (but reluctantly) by the Jesuits. They speak french & are so intermixed with that people that they scarcely appear to differ, but in dress. They wear Shirts, Leggings & Blankets, & the men wear fur or cloth caps.

I walked this Evening at nine o'clock to Fort Louis Gate. The moon shone bright & however intense the cold is here, it is so extremely still at night that it is less felt than in England where a less degree of cold is attended with wind. There is little wind here except with a snowstorm. The french call it poudré & to travel with that blowing in one's face is very disagreeable. The Canadians wear scanty thick woollen coats (and sometimes leather ones) with hoods to them, over a Bonnet Rouge & their coats are tied round with a coloured worsted sash. They have always a pipe in their mouth. The french women wear long thin linnen Cloaks, sometimes hoods lined with eiderdown but often walk in the street with only a Muslin Cap.

There was an anniversary dinner today, attended by those Gentlemen who particularly distinguished themselves in the defence of the Town, when attacked by Montgomery on 31st December, 1775. Coll. Caldwell was among the most active persons on this occasion.

This day five years since the air became in a few hours so dark that it was necessary to light candles at 3 o'clock, black clouds were continually rolling onwards from the S.W. The darkness continued the whole of the next day when a person could not be discerned on the opposite side of the Street. It was supposed to be occasioned by the irruption of a Volcano. Pere Gravé believes the report of Indians who assert that they have seen a burning Mountain to the N.E. of St. Paul's Bay.

Accounts received from Montreal of the defeat of 2000 of the people of the U. States about 20 mile from the Miami Fort, by 1400 Indians. They had barricaded their Camp with flour barrels etc. The Indians attacked them, beat them, & took 6 pieces of Cannon, all their provisions, new cloathing etc., killed 1200 men, Coll. Butler & other officers among whom it was supposed St. Clair fell. The Indians lost only 50 men. The remaining Troops retreated & were pursued by 400 Indians, who probably would have destroyed them all if they had not stopped to plunder.

January 1792 6th Le Jour des Rois. I went with Madame Báby to the Cathedral & heard Mons. du Plessis the Bishop's Chaplain preach a most excellent Sermon on the subject of the Kings of the East seeking Jesus Christ. His action was animated & the sermon impressive. The Bishop himself was present, he wore a white muslin dress & a rich mantle embroidered with gold, blue silk gloves worked with gold; his mitres were pink & silver &

blue & gold, he changed them two or three times during the Service, which had a theatric, poor & unfit appearance.

S. 7th   Fahrenheit's thermometer 23 degrees below 0. I rub silk gowns with flannel to see the beautiful streams of fire which are emitted with a crackling noise during this cold weather.

T. 10th   I bought an Eiderdown quilt which cost £4 16s. I walked today.

12th   I drove out in a covered Carriole.

W. 18th   A Ball at the Chateau, this being the Queen's [Charlotte] Birth night, there were near 300 People. The Ladies were well dressed.

21st   Miss Johnson dined with me & we went to a dance in the Evening at the Fusileers' Mess Room — very agreeable. The Thermometer 24 degrees below 0. In the N. York Paper I read of "a leaf imported from Botany Bay which when dried goes off by the application of a match with an explosion like gunpowder & the air is agreeably perfumed."

24th   I gave a dance & supper to a dozen of the Fusileers & as many young dancing Ladies. My Rooms being small obliged me to invite so few & only those who danced.

29th   Drove in a covered Carriole towards the Isle of Orleans. The Ice was so rough & Snow uneven that I was almost Sea Sick.

30th   I went in an open carriole to see the Falls of Montmorency. The River Roars over a rocky bed among woods before it reaches the precipice, over which it falls 280 feet, the Rocky sides are covered on the summit with wood. Sir F. Haldimand built a

Summer House projecting over the water supported by beams. We descended to it by steps cut in the rock & from it had a fine view of the fall. Sir F. Haldimand built a good House near the Bank of the River & commanding a fine prospect. I should like to spend a summer there very much. Prince Edward hired it last year but as he went to Quebec every day found the stony roads prejudicial to his horses' feet. There is a road from Quebec which leads below the fall, at the bottom of which a Cone of Ice is formed in winter.

31st   A very pleasant dance at the Chateau this Evening.

February 7th   At two o'clock the Kitchen Chimney was on fire. It was soon extinguished as the people here are expert in using fire Engines. The Houses being covered with shingles (wood in the shape of tiles) fires spread rapidly if not immediately put out. The Prince, General Clarke etc. dined with Coll. Simcoe & this accident retarded the dinner, so I went to bed before dinner.

8th   Supped at Mrs. Smith's.

9th   Coll. & Mrs. Caldwell & Major & Mrs. Watson dined with us. We went to the Assembly, where an account was brought of our House being burnt down. Coll. Simcoe went home & found it was only the chimney on fire. I was not told of it tho an officious man afterwards assured me he would have informed me had he known it.

11th   We supped at Madame Báby's, but not till 12 o'clock it being a fast day. Then there was a grande manger.

Sunday 12th   Walked to l'Ance de Mer.

M. Feby 13th We walked to the Provision Store before breakfast; dined at Belmont. The thermometer 3 degrees below 0.

Quebec Febry 13th 1792
My Dear Mrs. Hunt★

[★Note: This letter (not part of the diary) was actually mailed to Mrs. Hunt at Wolford, where it was preserved. It is included because it expands the interest of the diary. The same applies to the letters starting on pages 85, 118, 121, and 161.]

I was disappointed at not hearing by the November Mail from Wolford but doubt not that you thought (as I did when in England) that there was no communication with Quebec but in summer; however I hope the Dec. Mail which we daily expect will bring me some news of you & my friends at Wolford.

Though I anxiously think of, & wish to see the Children, I am glad they are not here, as it would be utterly out of my power to have as much of their company as would be necessary. You cannot think what a gay place this is in winter, we do not go to half the amusements we are invited to, & yet are few days alone; a week without a Ball is an extraordinary thing & sometimes two or three in that time; there are no parties without suppers which disturbs me greatly as I do not like late hours, however the dry cold air is so invigorating that it prevents the ill health I should without it acquire with so much sitting up. I never was so free from colds as I have been this winter tho' I dance a great deal & leave hot rooms without wrapping myself up, as is the way here. It is an expensive place this, we buy water, & wood is a *very* dear article from the quantity consumed, it costs us near four shillings a day. The stoves & dancing spoil ones Cloaths as soon as at Bath, & they give great dinners tho' the Cooks are not so good as in England & the provision being all froze is not so good & does not go so far as in England.

I should be quite ashamed of seeing you & Mrs. Burges, for I am much too dissipated to spend my time in those rational amusements in which you both so much excell, & if I travel much in summer I shall not then have time for sedentary employment.

The extreme dryness of the climate makes it very pleasant, & it is never windy; tho the Thermometer is but a few degrees above zero. I was yesterday morning walking at eight o'clock, with nothing more than a shawl & furr Capp & tippet. I see beautiful stars every night & am wretched not to have you & Mrs. Burges to tell me what they are, which I have no chance of knowing, for the women here are illiterate, & if the Men were otherwise I could not ask them. I know Orion perfectly who is always before my window & I think of Procyon, Gemini & Syrius. I talk a great deal of French, which as few other English Ladies here do, pleases the French people much.

I am excessively impatient to hear from you whether the Children have the whooping cough, as the Physician here thinks the little Boy has it, but I am fully convinced it is Worms, for which he has just begun to take Medicine & is I hope getting better daily. We now think of staying here till May because we cannot proceed further than Montreal untill the Ships come from England. We are going to change our House for the chimneys of this being bad, the House has been on fire twice; the other night we were at a Ball, & Mr. Talbot was sent for in haste to go & try to save the papers for the roof of the House was falling in, however it proved nothing of any consequence & they did not tell me till it was extinguished, so I escaped the alarm. The other time it happened when the Prince & all the beau monde were coming to dinner & spoilt part of it. The pleasantest thing I know here is that we being too great to sit at the top & bottom of our table, the Aid de Camps (or Gentlemen of our Family, or suite) sit there, & we about the middle of the Table which is the post of honour; & that saves a great deal of trouble.

My best wishes to Mrs. Hunt, how much I wish to hear from her. The communications with England are vastly more frequent & easy than I thought they were. England does not seem half as far from Canada, as Canada did from England; the fewer mile stones there are on the road, the shorter the road appears, & it is just as in crossing the Atlantic there are so few objects to date the time by, that it flows unperceptibly, & had not my judgment & reason told me otherwise my fancy would have persuaded me that I had been at Sea for eight days only.

Servants need not have been afraid of coming to this Country — they have here immence Wages are well treated & work very little. This climate I am sure is healthier than England it is so dry; at least I find it agree better with me than the damp weather.

The Officers act Plays. I think of you as I know it is your favourite amusement indeed I think there are more amusements & gaiety here than a winter at Bath affords & that you would not expect in so remote a Country. The Prince's Band cost him near five hundred a year being a selection of fine performers so you may suppose the Concerts are not to be despised.

Do not let me be disappointed of hearing from you, had I as much leisure I would write much more, believe me your Affect. Friend

E. Simcoe

14th Supper at Major Stewart's. The Prince was there. During the winter large Masses of Ice float down the River & the people who come to market from the opposite shore pass in Canoes which they quit when they come to one of these large bodies of Ice & carry their Canoes across the Ice on their Shoulders & launch it again in the water & this is repeated several times before they reach Quebec where they sell a fat Turkey for 15d. & provisions of all kinds in proportion. The mode of passing the River appears so difficult & dangerous that is seems hardly credible till it has been seen. This Evening it was announced that, "le Pont est pris," that is there is now a compleat body of Ice filling up the River & Canoes will no longer be used, as Carrioles will drive across, which is very useful for the Peasants & very pleasant to those who drive for Amusement & this year the weather having been calm & the wind with the tide when it froze, the Ice is very smooth. It is seven years since a Pont was formed.

15th   Coll. Simcoe & I were going to walk on the Pont. As there was a narrow space containing water between the land & the Ice, a plank was laid across, which Coll. Simcoe had passed, & stepping back to give me his hand he slipped into the water, but luckily caught hold of the plank which supported him until the Canadians who were near & on my screaming out "Au secours" assisted him out. Had the plank given way he must have gone under the Ice & it would have been impossible to have got out. We walked to Monsr. Báby's, & I ran home to order dry clothes to be brought there.

17th   I went to the Ball at the Chateau. There was also a dance at the Barracks tonight.

S. 18th   One of the Casmettes near Fort Louis Gate has been fitted up for a Theatre. Some Canadian Gentlemen represented Le Medecin malgre lui & La Comtesse d'Escarbagnas. I was surprized those people unused to see Theatrical Representations could perform so well as they did & I was much amused. The Fusileers are going to act Plays but as Coll. Simcoe does not like to see Officers so employed he does not intend to go to the Theatre again.

I went across the River to Point Levy yesterday. The Ice was excellent & the Sun excessively hot. We walked as far as the Church. The firs looked beautiful among the Snow this bright day. We met the Prince en Carriole. I gathered bunches of berries from a low shrub Dr. Nooth called a Clithera. People cut holes in the Ice & catch many fish thro them. Poisson d'ore pickerel are the most esteemed fish.

Sunday 19th   Dined at Monsr. Báby's. Met Madame Tonancour. Salaberry etc.

M. 20th   The Heads of the French Clergy dined with Coll. Simcoe — the Bishop, Monsr Gravé, Père Barré etc. (Pere Barré quite an Irishman & too jocose for his station).

T. 21st   Madame Báby, Salaberry etc. dined with us & stayed till 2 in the morning. Ther. 26 degrees below 0.

S. 25th   Walked to the Provision Store. The Scene on the River is now a very gay one. Numbers are skating; Carrioles driven furiously (as the Canadians usually do) & wooden huts are built on the Ice where Cakes & Liquor are sold, & they have stoves in their hutts.

T. March 1st   Walked to Pt. Levy.

F. 2nd   I gave a dance to forty people. The Prince was present. We have left the House we had in St. John Street & taken one the back Rooms of which look into the Ursuline Gardens. By removing a wooden Partition up Stairs we have made a Room 45 feet long with a tea Room & Card Room adjoining, which makes a good apartment for a dance, with a supper Room below.

The Fusileers are the best dancers, well dressed & the best looking figures in a Ball Room I ever saw. They are all musical & like dancing & bestow as much money, as other Regts. usually spend in wine, in giving Balls & Concerts which makes them very popular in this place where dancing is so favourite an amusement, that no age seems to exclude people from partaking of it; & indeed I find giving Dances much the easiest mode of entertaining company, as well as the most pleasant to them. Mr. Talbot manages all the etiquette of our House, is au fait in all those points which gave weight to matters of no moment [he acted as a social secretary].

Sunday 4th   Capt. Shaw[6] of the Queen's Rangers & 4 other gentlemen arrived from Frederickstown in New Brunswick which is 370 mile from hence. They walked on Snow Shoes 260 miles in 19 days, came up the River St. Johns & crossed many small Lakes. Their mode of travelling was to set out at daybreak, walk till twelve when they stood ten minutes (not longer because of the cold) to eat. They then resumed walking till ½ past four when they chose a spot where there was good firewood to Encamp. Half the party (which consisted of 12) began felling wood, the rest dug away the snow till they had made a pit many feet in circumference in which the fire was to be made. They cut Cedar & Pine branches, laid a blanket on them, & wrapping themselves in another found it sufficiently warm with their feet close to a large fire which was kept up all night. Capt. McGill who set out with them cut his knee in felling wood & was forced to stay at the Madawaska Settlement.[7]

One of the attendants a frenchman used to the mode of travelling carried 60 lb. weight & outwalked them all. They steered by the Sun, a River & a Pocket Compass. Capt. Shaw is a very sensible, pleasant Scotchman, a highlander. His family are to come from N. Brunswick to U. Canada next Summer.

Capt. Shaw gave me a description of the Moose Deer which they call here Orignale & of which we eat the moufle. Their legs are so long & their bodies so heavy that they step to the bottom of the Snow, but they are so strong that they notwithstanding trot 10 miles an hour & travel through the most unbeaten country, subsisting on the moss of trees & young boughs. They travel in droves, the strongest going first & when they come to a good place for browsing stay till they have taken all the tender boughs & then seek another station. They may be tamed, but if several are not kept together, in the spring they will probably return to the Woods. The Moose Deer is frequently met with in New Brunswick & the Caribou which is so light an animal as scarcely to break the Snow. I have seen a caribou at Mr. Finlay's. It was like an English Fawn.

T. 6th   We dined & supped at Mr. Finlay's the Postmaster-General.

W. 7th   Drove in an open Carriole to Coll. Caldwell's. I gave a dance to 30 people this Evening. I was this week in a Covered Carriole driving towards the Isle of Orleans, but part of the River having frozen when the tide was coming in fast & blowing fresh the Ice was so rough that I was quite Sea Sick in the Carriage. As we passed the furrows of Ice, the large heaps collected in some places many feet high, formed an extraordinary sight.

F. 9th   Chief Justice Smith dined here. The Fusileers acted The Wonder tonight.

T. 13th   Supped at Mr. Ogden's.

W. 14th   Supped at Mr. Coffin's.

T. 15th   Went to a musical party & a dance at the Barracks which was very pleasant. The Fusileers all dance as well as Count Schernischoff or any famous Russians.

Another mail arrived and no letter from you, my dear friend Mrs. Hunt. How is it that you I esteem so wise, should not have had observation enough to have found out by the news papers that Packets go to N. York & Halifax every month & are immediately forwarded from thence here? Do you not remember Lake Champlain & Lake George & all that route from N. York to Quebec which you have so often drawn & which is passed constantly & in a rapid manner when the lakes are frozen? This Town is now supplied with fresh Cod in a frozen state from Boston distant 700 miles & it is sold at 6d per lb. So you have proof that we are not excluded from communication with the rest of the World, or destitute of Luxuries.

We have had some excellent Venison from the township of Matilda above Cataraqui. I daresay you remember that name on the Map above 400 miles from hence. I find our Maps to be little better than Sketches, little of the country being surveyed. The Surveyors draw slowly & I am told when they want to suit their map to the Paper do not scruple cutting off a few miles of a River or adding to it.

Coll. Simcoe has had a letter from Capt. Murray from Hallifax, which place he compares to Capua. Coll. Simcoe makes the same complaint of Quebec where he finds few men of learning or information; Literary Society not being necessary to the amusement of Ladies I am very well off amongst the Women & really find this a delightful Sejour. The Morning Coll. Simcoe & I spend together in reading, walking, etc. In the Evening I go to Balls, Concerts Suppers & when I am with french families, je fais le conversation d'une facon a peu pres parisienne (as Monsr. Báby is pleased to say) & to have everybody I see *assiduous* to please me, & to have nothing to do but to follow my own fancy, is a satisfactory mode of living, not always attainable on your side of the Atlantic. How happy I am!

I quite enjoy the thoughts of the long journey we have before us & the perpetual change of scene it will afford, but the people here think it as arduous & adventurous an undertaking as it was looked upon to be by my friends in England. It is surprizing that those who are so much nearer to a Country should esteem it as impracticable as those who are so many thousand miles distant.

Capt. Murray was all but lost in going to St. Johns & from thence to Hallifax. The day after he left Quebec the River was so full of ice his sailing would have been impossible. No ship ever left Quebec as late as the Triton. The Merchant Men sail on the 10th of October. Capt. Shaw also advises me not to believe the formidable accounts I have heard of Rattle Snakes, of which he has seen numbers in Carolina. He affirms they never bite but when trod upon or attacked, & the wound they make is cured by well-known herbs, as horehound & plantain juice.

18th of March   We walked from 7 till 9 this Morning on the heights of Abram, the plain on which Genl. Wolfe was killed. It is said he was shot from behind a fence rail by a French Priest who is still living. The Troops daily practice walking on these Plains in Snow Shoes. The Racket is made of Deer or Elk skins, the frame is of light wood an inch thick, 2 ½ feet long, 14 inches broad. We found it dry at this early hour on the Track the Troops had beaten.

M. 19th   We dined at Mr. William's. Went in the Evening to the Concert & returned to Supper, an elegant Supper in the Council Room, after which there was Music.

W. 21st   Mrs. Caldwell dined with me & we went to the Assembly in the Evening.

22nd   Walked to Sans Bruit. Capt. Fisher of the Engineers lent me his Portfolio in which was some beautiful views taken in the Island of St. Domingo; I almost regretted not to have been in the W. Indies. We supped at Mr. Ainslie's tonight.

31st   We walked to Coll. Caldwell's before breakfast & returned as far as Sans Bruit in a Carriole & dined there. The most unpleasant time of the year is now commencing. The Snow melting prevents the use of Carrioles there is still too much to use Calashes (which are a one horse Chair with a Seat for the driver) or any carriage on wheels. During the Month of April the people are from this circumstance little able to go from their Houses; besides Easterly winds which bring rain prevail very much.

T. 3rd April   We walked to Belmont before breakfast & found the road dry, but in the middle of the day the Snow was so melted by the excessive heat of the Sun that we stayed there until 8 o'clock & walked home the snow being then perfectly frozen again.

W. 4th   Mr. Fisher of the Artillery showed me some beautiful views he took of Windsor Castle for Prince Edward. His oil painting did not please me.

Sunday 8th   We walked a mile before breakfast about Cape Diamond. After Church we repaired to the lines [the town walls] with Mr. Talbot who shewed us an unfrequented terrace where Sir F. Haldimand began to make a walk on the side of this noble Cliff which is crowned by fortified Works. The Terrace commands the St. Lawrance as far as Cape Tourment & the Isle of Orleans to the East.

The Shipping & the lower Town are immediately below, & towards the heights of Abram the blue distant hills of Vermont [or probably Maine] are seen & the Spray from the fall of the Chaudière River about 8 miles off. The rocks & brushwood that adorn the precipitous side of the hill form a fine background to this grand scene, with which we were so delighted that we came to view it again in the Evening & did not return home till it was dark or rather starlight.

12th   A party of 20 at supper.

13th   Walked towards Wolfe's Cove & upon Cape Diamond. Dined with Mrs. Winslow.

F. 20th   The Prince dined with us, Gen'l Clarke, Mrs. Murray & St. Ours; a very cold Evening indeed. As the cold weather & the short days leave us people cease to be sociable, & no kind of gaiety is continued but a few dinner partys. I have been so unaccustomed to pass Evenings alone this winter, that I do not like relinquishing Balls, Concerts, Suppers & Cards.

Quebec April 26th 1792
My Dear Mrs. Hunt
      I was happy to receive your letter, which nothing but your modesty could have made you think of apologizing about. I am sure a letter from you would be always acceptable to me, even if you had not as you say so interesting a theme as the children. I think Eliza must have made a surprizing progress in French to read it nearly as well as English already. How much they have grown. I received the letters while on a visit, & was in raptures to see so large a paquet; tho' in a very pleasant party, I broke up very early to go home & read them which I did a great many times over before I could go to bed.
      I was astonished to hear of your having the Gout, I believe it was as Mrs. Burges says a little bit of Idleness, & your foot was asleep because you did not use it enough, however I rejoice that you think the air of Devonshire

agrees with you. I am happy for both of your sakes that you & Mrs. Burges like each other so much, I knew you would. But you will certainly rival me in her affection if you have learnt Spanish; & as for me I live with a set of people who I am sure do not know more than myself, & therefore I have not the spur of emulation to make me endeavor to acquire more knowledge, & as the human mind does not stand still, I fear you will find me more ignorant when I return than when I set out.

I think I shall find the Batteaux a very pleasant method of travelling; we are told also that we may row all along the coast of Lake Ontario instead of going in a Vessel, which will be pleasanter a great deal.

I have not been out of the Town since the snow has been gone, some Gentlemen have offered me Horses, but I have not rode so long that I feel quite a Coward & till necessity obliges me I think I shall not ride. There are excellent Horses in the Upper Country.

I assure I think this Winter has been a very bad prelude to going into the Upper Country if I am to find it a solitary scene as people say. I should have been fitter a great deal for solitude & enjoyed it more, coming from Black Down than after spending six months in the midst of Balls, concerts, assemblies & Card parties every night.

Detroit is a very gay place, but then I shall not be there in the Winter, which is the time amusements are most wanted.

Did Mrs. Burges shew you the Fuzileer I sent her? They are the prettiest looking people in a Ball room you ever saw, all young & dance better than any people I ever saw. I wish I could send you two or three to a Honiton Assembly or rather bring you into my Ball room now & then. There are not two pretty women in this Town. I am going to begin an apron to work in the Batteaux. I am so happy that the little Boy has got over the small pox before he sets out. I intended to have sent a better pair of Maucassons to Caroline, but they have not sent them yet to me, so I am forced to send a pair Sophia has worn, but I hope Caroline will not find that out, I have brushed them up, but the Indians do not come to Town so often as they used to do in Winter which has disappointed me; those I bespoke were to be much prettier colours, I think them pretty for little children in the House but I should be afraid if older ones wore them, their feet might be too large ever to wear the Duchess of Yorks Shoe or any tolerable sized one.

The drawing of a Jamaica view I copied from a most beautiful one, it is a very laborious & difficult one, but a very improving one; as you did not see the original perhaps you will not think mine amiss, but I am sensible of a thousand faults in the tinting. I remain

Your affect. Friend,
E. Simcoe

With eager wishes for more letters. I should have written you a better letter had I not been writing a great number, & therefore hardly know what I have written to any, but recollecting that I have set down a great many facts & circumstances I forget to whom they were addressed & perhaps you have not had yr share.

Sun. 29th We walked twice this day to Cape Diamond. In the Morning we saw a Merchant Vessel sail for England, the Recovery, in which I sent letters by Mrs. Toozey to you & other friends. Walking on Cape Diamond after a rainy day, I saw amongst the distant hills to the North a Cloud rise in a Conic form in a light sky until it united with black clouds above. We thought it might be a water spout. Last week the Thermometer fell 30 degrees in

3 hours & 54 in eleven hours. A beautiful Moth was sent to me. It remained all day in a torpid state & flew away at night.

Mr. Fisher of the Artillery exchanges duty with Mr. Wolfe in order to go to Niagara to take Views of the falls. I saw Musquitoes this Evening while walking on the lines. They are like Gnats. Last week I walked to Powell Place & Woodfield. The woods are beautiful & we went near to Sellery, that pretty vale Emily Montague describes, indeed her account of Quebec appears to me very near the truth.

A Boat going to the Isle of Orleans was overset a few days ago. 14 passengers among whom was Monsr. Hubert the Cure were drowned. Accidents often happen on this River by carrying too much sail. When the Wind is against the tide it is very dangerous, the Currents are excessively strong.

2nd of June Mr. Osgoode, Chief Justice of U. Canada, Mr. Russell, the Receiver-General & Mr. White, the Attorney-General arrived from England. Mr. Russell had his Sister with him.

Miss Rolle sent me a doll in the Duchess of York's Court dress. My cloathes for the 4th of June not being arrived I made myself a Turban like the doll's.

June 4th A splendid Ball at the Chateau, but the heat was so great that I was very near fainting after having danced Money Musk & the Jupon Rouge.

June 5th This afternoon we drove to Montmorency & drank tea there. I walked a little way up the River which dashes over a very Rocky bed among the woods which being now in leaf made the accompaniments of the fall much finer than when I was last here.

3

JOURNEY TO NIAGARA
June 8 to July 25, 1792

June 8th 1792 A 6 this Morning we left Quebec walked through the Port Louis Gate & descended the Hill to the Ance-de-Mer where we embarked in a large Batteau with an Awning, accompanied by Lts. Grey & Talbot. Another Batteau carried the Children & a third the servants & Baggage. In 3 hours we reached Pt. au Tremble landing a mile below the Maison de Poste. A small tent being pitched we breakfasted & afterwards went to see the Church which is a neat one & contains a Picture of St. Cecilia given by Gen'l Murray which is highly esteemed. We took an early dinner of which an eel caught here formed a part & as we had just finished our repast al fresco, the Bishop of Caps, who resides in this village came to wait on Coll. Simcoe. He is a man more esteemed for his learning than his Religion, being once accused of having Voltaire's works in his library, he replied, "Les meilleurs medecins tiennent les poisons en leur boutique." He apologized for not inviting us to his house as it was repairing.

We waited till near 6 for the tide when we embarked, & passed some beautiful high banks covered with wood. At Jacques Cartier 10 leagues from Quebec are Mills, on a River which flows into the St. Lawrance from between two very high Hills much enriched by wood. It is an exceeding strong pass & a very picturesque scene.

The Evening was delightfully calm. My admiration of the setting sun on the unruffled surface of this wide river was interrupted by meeting a Boat which brought English Letters forwarded from Montreal & the satisfaction of reading some of yours [Mrs. Hunt's] engaged my attention as long as it was light enough to read.

It was ten o'clock when we arrived at Cap Santé. The Man who kept the Maison de Poste was so ill that we could not be admitted there, so we walked towards a Cottage where the habitans were going to bed, but with all possible French politesse the Woman removed her furniture & Children & presently accommodated us with two empty Rooms with a thousand Compliments & Regrets that "des gens come nous" should be so ill lodged. The apartment was indifferent enough but as we travel with a boudet (which is a folding camp chair as large as a Mattrass), the Triton's cot, Blankets, & a Musquito Net Tent to hang over the bed, we soon furnished a room comfortable enough for People whom a long day's voyage had given sufficient inclination to sleep. The Gentlemen slept in a Batteau. It was too late to get our Provisions from the Boat & we supped on the Bread, Eggs & Milk the Cottage afforded.

June 9th   We rose at 6 this Morning & walked on the Hill which rises abruptly behind this house. It is a fine turf with large Trees scattered over it & has a very park-like appearance. To the east the View is finely terminated by the Church which is covered with tin as is usual in this Country. It is surprising to me that it does not rust. It proves the habitual dryness of the air. The effects of the tin roofs & steeples are very brilliant.

Beyond Cap Sante the tide ceases. We embarked at 9 & passed the Rapids of Richelieu after which the Steeple of the Church of Dechambeau embosomed in wood becomes a fine object. Coll. Simcoe wished to examine the ground at Dechambeau with reference to it as a military Position. I went on shore there with him while the Gentlemen proceeded in the Boat. I waited at the Maison de Poste (for I was indisposed) while Coll. Simcoe walked to the Point, & in about an hour we set out in a Calash & drove 9 miles thro' a beautiful woody Country over very rough Roads to Grondines where we dined & slept at the house of Madame Amelins [Hamelin] the Seigneuresse of this Village whom we saw in the Evening sitting in the Church Yard amid a large audience of Paysans, Reading & commenting on some hand bills dispersed by a Quebec Merchant (McCord), a Candidate to represent this County at the next Election.

The tone and air decide of the Reader, the attention of the Auditors & the flemish appearance of their figures would have afforded an excellent Picture. The Canadian Women are better educated than the Men, who take care of their Horses & attend little to anything else, leaving the management of their Affairs to the women.

I here saw a kind of Mespulus [medlar] which bore fruit they called Poires sauvage & a fruit superbe. Magnifique & superbe are words the Canadians apply on all occasions. Nothing could less call for such an epithet than the present fruit. A pretty wild plant, somewhat like buckwheat, called herbe a la puce is said to blister the hands & faces of those who touch it, tho it is not equally poisonous to all persons. Here I met with an ugly insect of the Beetle kind, called frappe d'abord which fetches blood wherever it strikes.

Sunday 10th We left Grondines at 8. The current becoming very strong the Men were obliged to tirer a la cordelle, or drag the boat by ropes. On a narrow beach under high, woody banks we picked up pieces of chalk or clay which drew like crayon but the strokes were not so easily effaced. I saw Millions of yellow & Black Butterflies called New York swallow-tails on the sand. We dined in the Boat & passed St. Pierre de Bequet, a village & its Church on a very bold projecting Point nearly opposite to Battiscan. We disembarked this Evening at Cap Madelaine the most dirty, disagreeable receptacle for Musquitoes I ever saw, the inhabitants even catching wood pidgeons in a most disagreeable manner. I took no sketch of a place I never wish to recollect. Mr. Talbot gave a shilling to liberate some wood pidgeons I must otherwise have seen & heard fluttering most disagreeably. I was much obliged to him for this polite attention.

Mon 11th We rose at 4 & embarked & went a league to Trois Rivieres, a Town which takes its name from three Rivers which spring from one source & after having flowed some miles separately, unite & fall into the St. Lawrance ½ a mile below the Town. There is a small Convent here, & they work remarkably well on Bark. We payed a great price for a bad breakfast at an Inn kept by an Englishman for we were not so lucky as to go to the French Maison de Poste where we should have fared better & paid less. 3 leagues from hence we reached Pt. du Lac, the entrance of Lake St. Pierre which is about 15 leagues long. 3 leagues farther we stopped to dine in the Boat in Machiche Bay, a small cove where the heat was *intense* and the Musquitoes numerous. From hence we passed extremely flat shores & confined scenery. The Gentlemen were impatient of the heat, & perpetually worrying the Conductor of the Batteaus with questions how far we were from Cap de Loup, complaining of the inconvenience of the trajet. At length he would say nothing except "Mais pourtant il ne fait pas froid" which indeed we were all sensible of.

We went on shore early this Evening at Riviere de Loup,[1] a village & pretty bridge in a flat cultivated Country. We were but ill accommodated here & nothing amusing occurred but Mr. Talbot's ineffectual endeavors to paddle a Canoe across the River. The difficulties he met with in this first attempt, & the handkerchief tied round his head, a la Canadien, diverted me much.

Mr. Grey cut his finger & applied the turpentine from the cones of the Balm of Gilead fir, a remedy for wounds greatly esteemed. Collins the nurse girl's slow manner, characteristic of the U. States, diverted us. Being desired to make haste, she replied,

"Must I not put the sugar in the children's breakfast?" in the true American tone.

T. 12th We embarked at 4 and soon after we left Lake St. Pierre, stopped at Sorrel & took some refreshment at Mr. Doty's, a clergyman whose wife is from N. York, & the House was the cleanest & neatest I have seen.

The situation of Sorrel is so flat, that nothing relieves the prospect but the Masts of a few small Ships building here. We dined in the boat & the heat was excessive but the Evening calm & so very pleasant as almost to persuade me it is worth while to cross the Atlantic for the pleasure of voyaging on this delightful Lake-like River, the setting sun reflecting the deepest shades from the shores & throwing rich tints on the water. This repose is finely accompanied by the Songs of the Batteaux men, which accord in time to the regular stroke of the Oars & have the best effect imaginable. No wonder Spenser, Ariosto etc., dwelt on the delight of sailing in a Boat on Lakes, and make it approach to Islands of Delight. After a day of fatigue & where strong Currents require peculiar exertion they sing incessantly & give a more regular stroke with the oars, when accompanied by the tunes. This practice has been learned from Grand Voyageurs, or Canadians who are hired by the N. West Company to take Canoes to the Grand Portage beyond Lake Superior. Now & then an Indian Halloo breaks the often repeated notes & enlivens the Sound. We admired one of their songs Trois filles d'un Prince so much that we desired it to be often repeated.

Our attention was engaged by hearing firing from the shore. The Batteau men said "C'est pour parler a Mons le Gouverneur" but who paid us this respect we did not find out.

We reached the Maison de Poste at Dautray before Sun Set pitched the little Tent & admired the rich tints & deep reflections from the opposite Shore. We met with tolerably good Rooms here. Mr. Littlehales,[2] Coll. Simcoe's Secretary overtook us here

& brought with him Letters from you Mrs. Hunt which made me very happy. He travelled Post from Quebec where he arrived in the last vessel.

W. 13th   We set out at 4 in the Morning. In the afternoon we saw the Blue Mountains of Chambly & Beloeil Mountain near Lake Champlain which we noticed with pleasure not having before seen any distant view during our voyage.

We passed Warennes a large village & handsome Church. That of Cap Sante was built in imitation of it. At 8 we reached Pointe aux Trembles 10 leagues from Dautray. Here we went on shore intending to go by land the remaining 3 leagues to Montreal. We found Capt. Stevenson just arrived in Mr. Frobisher's Phaeton sent for me (as a hired Calash is a wretched conveyance on the excessive rough Roads around Montreal). Notwithstanding the merits of the Phaeton & the driver, I every moment expected to have been thrown out by the violent jerks in passing over the Ruts in this bad road.

At eleven o'clock we arrived at Montreal, & after a little delay occasioned by the lateness of the hour, we got into the Government House[3] & I was delighted with the size and loftiness of the Rooms, which are so much better than any I had been in at Quebec. On the Road we passed a group of Indians sitting around a fire near the River which in this dark night afforded a good subject for a picture.

17th   The joy I felt in finding myself in spacious apartments was checked the next day by finding the heat here more insufferable than I had ever felt. The Thermometer continued at 96 for two days & the heat was not ill-described by a centinal [sentinel] who exclaimed, "There is but a sheet of brown paper between this place and hell." In the Town are abundance of Merchants' Store houses, the doors & windows of which are iron, & many of the houses, as well as Churches, are covered with Tin. By these circumstances, I believe, the heat is increased. The Government House is built on Arches under which are very large Offices, which might be made very comfortable Summer apartments.

I was so oppressed by the heat, that it diminished the pleasure of driving on the Mountain of Montreal. A mile from the town it rises in the midst of a Plain like the Wrekin in Shropshire. The View from it is remarkably fine commanding a vast extent of River diversified by Islands. The Towns of Longueuille, L'Assomption, etc. are opposite & the distance terminated by the Blue Hills of Chambly & belle Oeil.

The Town of Montreal is large & the spires of the Churches covered with Tin, give a brilliancy to the Scene & look like Mosques. The Country around is cultivated & orchards cover nearly all the top of the Mountain. Capt. Stevenson carried us two miles beyond the fine prospect towards La Chine I think merely to show how bad the road was, & we returned about 9 o'clock to Mr. Frobisher's Villa on the side of the Mountain, & drank tea there.

In going from thence to Montreal we saw the air filled with fire flies which as the night was dark appeared beautiful, like falling stars. I dined at Mr. Frobisher's House in the Town where the Chairs were the same as I have seen sold in London for four guineas each.

I dined with La Baronne de Longueille at a pretty House she & Mr. Grant have built on her island of St. Helen's, half a league from Montreal. Tho' the distance is so short, the Current is so strong that the passage is rather alarming. The Island is 4 miles in circumference, and the views from many points very pretty. Montreal & Longueuil are good objects from it. La Baronne has the only hot house I have seen in Canada. Ice houses are very general here but seldom for the purpose of furnishing Ice for a dessert. They use the Ice to cool Liquors & butter & the Ice houses are used for Larders to kept Meat.

June 22nd   We went from Montreal to La Chine (10 miles of very rough road) in Mr. Frobisher's Carriage. The river from Montreal to La Chine is so shallow & full of Rocks & the Currents so strong that the Boats always go up unloaded, the Baggage being sent in waggons. Sir J. Johnson the agent for Indian affairs has a neat looking house in this Village.

We slept at a very indifferent House which as it bore the name of an Inn we did not bring our Beds or Provisions, & were the worse off as to lodging. I disliked the dirty appearance of the bed & slept on a blanket upon the table. Opposite this place on the other side of the River is Cagnewaghea[4] a village of Indians who are Catholics. They have a neat Church there.

23rd   We embarked at 6. Soon afterwards left Pt. Claire & Isle Perrot to the north, & saw the junction of the Ottawa or Grand River with the St. Lawrance, the former pouring its dirty coloured water into the transparent stream of the St. Lawrance.

We soon arrived at the Cascades, the commencement of the Rapids above La Chine. The term Rapid is meant to describe shallow water, strong Currents & a rocky bottom which causes the whole surface of the Water to appear foaming & white like breakers at Sea. The Batteaux Men keep as close in shore as possible, & by dint of exertion & labor they tow & pole the Boat up against the Current. We went on Shore at the Cascades & walked a mile thro' a Wood & saw the boats pass some tremendous Rapids near this place, where Gen'l. Amherst lost 80 men during the last war by coming down without conductors in the Boats. Saw a swordfish [probably a gar-pike] in a little stream near the Mill. After our re-embarking we came to a very strong Current at Point au Diable.

The Gentlemen walked to lighten the Boat. I was tired by the heat & laying my head on a Trunk in the boat, I slept till the Rapid was past. Two leagues from hence we met with one more formidable so that the baggage in the Boats was moved into

Waggons & we went in a Calash as far as the Cedars where there is a tolerable Inn at which we slept. M. de Longueuille has a seigneurie near this place.

24th   Seven miles from Les Cedres is Coteau du Lac where we passed through Locks. A few Troops are stationed in a House here. Opposite to it is an Island called Prison Island for some Rebels having been confined on it during the last War, some of whom escaped by swimming across the Rapids by which it is surrounded.

A few miles beyond this entered Lake St. Francis & saw a part of the Blue Ridge of the endless Mountains. 4 leagues from Coteau de Lac is Pt. au Bodet, the center of Lake St. Francis & the commencement of Upper Canada.

We arrived here about Sun Set & at a small Inn on the Pt. found the principal Inhabitants of the Township of Glengarry (Highlanders in their national dress). They came to meet the Governor who landed to speak to them. They preceded us in their Boat (a Piper with them) towards Glengarry House Mr. Mcdonell's,[5] where the Gentlemen went, but the wooden awning of our Boat being blown off by a violent & sudden squall arising, we were glad to make towards the shore as fast as possible at Pointe Mouille & thought ourselves lucky that the Boat had not been overset. We met with a miserable wretched dirty Room at a Highlander's, the only House within some miles.

25th   We breakfasted with Mr. MacDonell 4 leagues from Pt. Mouille; his new House (Glengarry) he has not finished, & resides in that which he first erected on his ground. A Catholick priest, his cozen, was there who has lived 6 years among the Indians at St. Regis. They have a Church & he performs Divine Service in the Iroquois Language of which he is a perfect Master & he says their attention to the Church service is very great & the Women sing Psalms remarkably well. After breakfast we proceeded a league to

Coll. Grey's, from whence the Governor went to the Isle of St. Regis to visit the Indians at their Village, where they received him with dancing in a fierce style, as if they wished to inspire the spectators with terror & respect for their ferocious appearance. We slept at Coll. Grey's.

T. 26th   Capt. Munro came here & brought a Horse of Mr. Duncan's for me to ride. As it would be very tedious to go up the Long Sault in the Boat we propose riding beyond that & another Rapid called les Galettes. We set off about 10 o'clock. In our way we passed through Cornwall a settlement 4 miles from Coll. Grey's. There are about 15 houses & some neat gardens. Rode eleven miles to Mr. McDonell's at the Long Sault, his farm being very near the Grand Rapid, which Rapid continues near a mile; the Whole of the River foaming like white breakers & the banks covered with thick woods is a very fine sight.

Mrs. Macdonell sang Erse songs very pleasingly, & her children & servants speak no language but Erse. I wish'd they had not thought it necessary respect to dine very late. There are Wolves & Bears in this part of the Country. They sometimes carry off Sheep, Calves or pigs, but do not attack Men.

Mr. Duncan's Horse carried me very well. It is certainly necessary to have a Horse of the Country to pass the Bridges we every where met with, whether across the creeks (very small rivers) or swamps a ¼ of a mile long. The bridges are composed of trunks of trees unhewn, of unequal sizes & laid loosely across pieces of timber placed length ways. Rotten trees sometimes give way & a horse's leg slips thro' & is in danger of being broken. The horse I am now riding had once a fall thro' an old bridge. He now goes very carefully. Coll. Grey tells me that the juice of horehound & plantain mixed & drank & also applied to the wound cures the bite of a Rattle Snake. A Negro in Carolina obtained his freedom in the last war for the discovery. We had black Bass for dinner. Great numbers are caught near the Rapids.

They are extremely good, near as large as Carp, as firm as a Dory & of a very good taste, but we dined too late to be pleasant. I suppose it was meant for Respect.

W. 27th   We rode 10 miles to a tolerable Inn, where a dinner was prepared, but we were engaged to dine & sleep at Capt. Munro's, 12 miles beyond this place. The first 8 miles we went in the Boat, but the remaining 4 we rode.

An Irish Captain gave us a basket of wild Strawberries which were as large & as well flavoured as the best Scarlet Strawberries in Gardens in England. We passed Capt. Duncan's House a mile before we came to the Rapid Plat close to which is Mr. Munro's. His wife is a Dutch Woman & the House was excessively neat & clean & one of his daughters very handsome. We went to Mr. Munro's Saw Mill where a Tree was cut into 15 Planks an inch thick in an hour.

28th   We set out on horseback this Morning; took some refreshment at Mr. T. Frazier's 6 miles from the Long Sault & then rode five miles to Mr. W. Frazier's where we dined. His house is just beyond Les Galettes the last Rapid on this side Lake Ontario.

I observed on my way hither that the Wheat appeared finer than any I had seen in England & totally free from Weeds. Mr. Frazier mentioned an Instance of the fertility of the soil. One of his fields having produced a great quantity of Wheat & that what fell out in reaping had the next year produced a very fine crop without the field having been plowed or sown. There are many Dutch & German farmers about here whose houses & grounds have a neater & better appearance than those of any other people. This afternoon we proceeded in the boat to Monsr. Lormier's, an agent for Indian Affairs, where we had good Venison but indifferent Lodging. Coll. Simcoe stopped on the way to look at Isle Royale.

29th   We embarked early & met the 26th Regt. in a Brigade of Boats. We stopped to speak to Capt. Talbot, who is in Prince Edward's family. He had been to see the Falls of Niagara & was returning with the 26th Regt.

We passed today some Rocks beautifully variegated with yellow & grey tints, I believe Clay was among it, & saw a number of fine hemlock Spruce Trees. They are an exceeding handsome tree like Yew but of a lighter foliage tho as dark a Color & grow to a more immense height than English people can suppose probable.

We came to so miserable a house where we were to lodge tonight within a league of Grenadier Island that we preferred pitching a Tent for ourselves letting the Children sleep in the Boat, & left the House for the Gentlemen. While the Tent was pitching I fished & caught a small Perch. Many people carry trolling lines in their Boat & catch abundance of black Bass & other fish all the way up the St. Lawrance. Capillaire [maidenhair fern] grows in great perfection throughout this Country. Much surprized to find the Blankets so wet in a Tent altho the weather had been dry.

S. 30th   After passing Grenadier Island we came to the Thousand Isles. The different sizes & shapes of these innumerable Isles has a very pretty appearance. Some of them are many miles in extent, many of them only large enough to contain 4 or 5 trees Pine or Oak growing on a grey Rock which looks pretty variegated by the different Mosses with which the crevices are filled.

We passed the river Gananowui [Gananoque] and ½ a mile beyond it came to Carey's House which was so dirty a House that we again pitched the Tent, notwithstanding it rained incessantly the whole Evening & the greater part of the Night kept us quite dry & I slept vastly well. I was surprized to find how wet the bed clothes were in the Tent when I rose, & yet I caught no cold tho these nights were the first in which I slept in a Tent.

In spite of the rain Coll. Simcoe went to the Mill on the Gananowui River near its mouth where a harbour might be made for Shipping. This River has communication a great way back with the river Rideau & by some Lakes to the Ottawa River. These & other advantages make this one of the most Eligible Situations in this part of the Province for the Establishment of a Town, but Sir J. Johnson obtained a Grant of land hereabouts which prevents the probability of any such improvements being made by Government.

Sunday July 1st   We rose very early this Morning in order to take a view of the Mill at Gananowui before we proceeded on our way to Kingston. The scenery about the Mill was so pretty that I was well repaid for the trouble of going. Then we returned to our Large Boat & proceeded. After passing Grande Isle & Isle Cauchois we drew near Kingston which we were aware of before we saw the Houses as we discerned the white waves of Lake Ontario beyond looking like a Sea for the wind blew extremely fresh.

Kingston is 6 leagues from Gananowui, a small Town of about fifty wooden Houses & Merchants' Store Houses. Only one House is built of stone, it belongs to a Merchant. There is a small Garrison here & a harbour for Ships. They fired a salute on our arrival & we went to the House appointed for the Commanding Officer at some distance from the Barracks. It is small but very airy, & so much cooler than the great House at Montreal that I was very well satisfied with the change. The Queen's Rangers are encamped a ¼ of a mile beyond our House & the bell Tents have a pretty appearance. The situation of this place is entirely flat, & incapable of being rendered defensible, therefore were its situation more central it would still be unfit for the Seat of Government.

M. July 2nd   We went across the Bay this Morning to see the Ship Yard. There are two Gun Boats lately built on a very bad construction. Coll. Simcoe calls them the Bear & the Buffalo as they are so unscientifically built & intends they shall aid in carrying Provisions to Niagara. The present establishment of Vessels on this Lake consists of the Onondaga & Mississaga top-sailed schooners of [about 80] tons & the Caldwell which is a Sloop. They transport all the Troops & Provisions from hence for the Garrison of Niagara, Fort Erie & Detroit. They land them at Niagara from whence those for the higher Ports are forwarded 9 miles across a Portage by Land to Fort Chippeway, 3 miles above the Falls of Niagara from whence they are embarked in boats & carried 18 miles to Ft. Erie, from whence Vessels take them to Detroit at the extremity of Lake Erie which is 300 miles in length.

Coll. Simcoe went on board the Onondaga & says we shall find tolerable accommodation in her when we go to Niagara tho he is much disposed to row round Lake Ontario in a Boat, but everybody about us oppose the scheme, as tedious & dangerous. Probably those who are to be of the party do not like the trouble of such a voyage & I suppose Coll. Simcoe will go at last in a Vessel rather than oppose these Sybarites.[6] Some ladies came to see me, & in the Evening I walked.

T. 3rd   There are Mississaga Indians here they are an unwarlike, idle, drunken, dirty tribe. I observe how extremes meet. These uncivilized People saunter up & down the Town all the day, with the apparent Nonchalance, want of occupation & indifference that seems to possess Bond street Beaux.

7th   I walked this Evening in a wood lately set on fire, but some unextinguished fires being left by some persons who had encamped there; which in dry weather often communicates to the Trees. Perhaps you have no idea of the pleasure of walking in a burning wood, but I found it so great that I think I shall have some woods set on fire for my Evening walks. The smoke arising from it keeps the Musquitoes at a distance & where the fire has caught the hollow trunk of a lofty Tree the flame issuing from the top has a fine effect. In some trees where but a small flame appears it looks like stars as the Evening grows dark, & the flare & smoke interspersed in different Masses of dark woods has a very picturesque appearance a little like Tasso's enchanted wood.

8th   The Gov. went to Church & took the Oaths preparatory to acting as Governor.

10th   The Council met. I walked this Evening. Some Indians arrived from a distance. They fired a salute with Musquets which was returned with Cannon.

11th   The Indians came to dance before the Gov. highly painted & in their War Costume with little Cloathing. They were near enough to the House for me to hear their singing which sounded like a repetition in different dismal tones of he', he', he' & at intervals a Savage Whoop. They had a skin stretched on sticks imitating a drum which they beat with sticks. Having drank more than usual they continued singing the greatest part of the night. They never quarrel with White People unless insulted by them, but are very quarrelsome amongst themselves, therefore when the Women see them drunk they take away their knives & hide them until they become sober.

This Evening I walked thro' a pretty part of the Wood & gathered Capillaire ... I was driven home by the bite of a Musquito thro a leather glove. My arm inflamed so much that after supper I fainted with the pain while playing at chess with Capt. Littlehales.

F. 13th   Mrs. Macauley the Garrison Surgeon's Wife drank tea with me. She is a naval officer's daughter & a very agreeable woman.

Scadding caught a beautiful small grass green snake which was quite harmless. After keeping it a day or two he let it go. The way of clearing land in this Country is cutting down all the small

103

wood, pile it & set it on fire. The Heavier Timber is cut thro' the bark 5 feet above the ground. This kills the trees which in time the wind blows down. The stumps decay in the ground in the course of years but appear very ugly for a long time tho the very large leafless white Trees have a singular & sometimes picturesque effect among the living trees. The settler first builds a log hut covered with bark, & after two or three years raises a neat House by the side of it. This progress of Industry is pleasant to observe.

Sunday 15th July   I went to Church twice. The Clergyman Mr. Stewart [Stuart] is from the U. States. He preached good Sermons with an air of serious earnestness in the cause which made them very impressive.

M. 16th   We sailed ½ a league this Evening in a pretty boat of Mr. Clark's, attended by music to Garden Island.

W. 18th   We sailed towards the Mills.[7]

19th   The Gov. went today to see Carleton Island & returned at 6 with wild Raspberries which were excessively fine. That Island abounds with them & strawberries & Plums & the air is esteemed so healthy that the people go there to get rid of the ague, a complaint which is very prevalent in this Province. The *flowering* Raspberry grows wild here & bears a very insipid flat fruit. Mr. Fisher of the Engineers is here on his way to Quebec from Niagara. He shewed us some beautiful Sketches he has taken of the Falls of Niagara.

S. 21st   There are no rides about Kingston or any pleasant Walks that we have met with. Sailing is therefore our only amusement. Today we were prevented by rain from going to the Mills. It is in the Interest of the People here to have this place considered as the Seat of Gov. Therefore they all dissuade the Gov. from going to Niagara & represent the want of Provisions, Houses etc. at that place, as well as the certainty of having the Ague. However he has determined to Sail for Niagara tomorrow.

Monday 23rd July   At 8 this morning we went on board the Onondaga — Commodore Beaton. We sailed with a light wind. A calm soon succeeded & we anchored 7 miles from Kingston. The men who navigate the Ships on this Lake have little nautical knowledge & never keep a log book. This afternoon we were near aground. The Lake is beautifully transparent, we saw the bottom very plainly.

T. 24th   A wet day & a foul wind. I played at Chess or at Cards all the day. Our Devonshire steward was surprized to find in the Ship's Steward an acquaintance Charles Trump who had left Kentisbeare 16 years ago for stealing fowl.

W. 25th   A clear cold day, made little way, a head wind. I saw the spray of the Falls of Niagara rising like a cloud. It is 40 miles distant.

4

A YEAR AT NIAGARA
July 26, 1792, to July 28, 1793

T. 26th   At 9 this morning we anchored at Navy Hall,[1] opposite the Garrison of Niagara which commands the mouth of the river. Navy Hall is a House built by the Naval Commanders on this Lake for their reception when here. It is now undergoing a thorough repair for our occupation but is still so unfinished that the Gov. ordered 3 Marquees to be pitched for us on the Hill above the House which is very dry ground & rises beautifully, in parts covered with oak bushes.

A fine Turf leads on to the Woods through which runs a very good Road leading to the Falls. The side of our Hill is terminated by a very steep Bank covered with wood a hundred feet in height in some places; at the bottom of which runs the Niagara River. Our Marquees command a beautiful view of the River & the Garrison on the opposite side, which from its being situated on the Point has a fine effect & the poorness of the Building is not remarked at this distance from whence a fine picture might be made.

The Queen's Rangers are encamped within ½ a mile behind us. In clear weather the North Shore of Lake Ontario may be discerned. The Trees which abound here are Oak, Chestnut, Ash, Maple, Hickory, black Walnut.

Sunday, 29th   There is no Church here but a Room has been built for a Masons' Lodge where Divine Service is performed on Sunday.

M. 30th At 8 this Morning we set off in Calashes to go to the Falls 16 miles from hence. We stopped & breakfasted at Mr. Hamilton's[2] a merchant who lives 6 miles from here at the landing (Queenstown), where the Cargoes going to Detroit are landed & sent by land 9 miles to Ft. Chippewa.

We had a delightful drive thro woods on the bank of the River which is excessively high the whole way. As I approached the Landing, we were struck by the similarity between these Hills & Banks & those of the Wye about Symond's Gate & the lime Rock near Whitchurch in Herefordshire, which differs very little except in the superior width & clearness of the Niagara River.

Mr. Hamilton has a very good Stone House the back Rooms overlooking on the River. A gallery the length of the House is a delightful covered walk both below & above in all weather. After an excellent breakfast we ascended an exceeding steep road to the top of the Mountain which commands a fine view of the Country, as far as the Garrison of Niagara & across the lake. From hence the road is entirely flat to the Falls of which I did not hear the sound until within a mile of them. They are heard at Navy Hall before Rain when the wind is Easterly tho the falls are to the S.W. of Niagara. The fall is said to be but 170 feet in height. The River previously rushes in the most rapid manner on a declivity for 3 miles & those rapids are a very fine sight. The fall itself is the grandest sight imaginable from the immense width of waters & the circular form of the grand fall; to the left of which is an Island between it & the Montmorency Fall (so called from being near the size of the fall of that name near Quebec). A few Rocks separate this from Ft. Schlosser Fall[3] which passing over a straight ledge of rock has not the beauty of the circular form or its green color, the whole center of the circular fall being of the brightest green & below it is frequently seen a Rainbow.

I descended an exceeding steep hill to get to the table Rock from whence the view of the falls is tremendously fine. Men sometimes descend the Rocks below this projecting point, but it is attended with great danger & perhaps little picturesque advantage. The prodigious Spray which arises from the foam at the bottom of the fall adds grandeur to the scene which is wonderfully fine & after the eye becomes more familiar to the objects I think the pleasure will be greater in dwelling upon them. After taking some refreshment on the table Rock we went 3 miles to the Chippewa Fort admiring the Rapids all the way. The Chippewa River which falls here into the St. Lawrance is a dull muddy River running thro' a flat swampy country.

People cross from Chippewa to Ft. Schlosser, but great caution is necessary the Current is so extremely strong & if they did not make exactly the mouth of the Chippewa the force of the water below it would inevitably carry them down the falls without redress. Eight soldiers who were intoxicated met with this accident in crossing the River some years since. Their bodies were taken up entire some distance below the Falls. An Indian was asleep in his canoe near Ft. Schlosser. The Canoe was tied to a tree; some person cut the rope, he did not wake untill the Canoe had got into the strong Current. He found all his endeavours to paddle ineffectual & was seen to lay himself down resigning himself to his fate, & was soon carried down the fall.

In the Evening we returned to Mr. Hamilton's & slept there. I suffered exquisite pain all the day from a Musquito bite which the extreme heat increased & at night my sleeve was obliged to be cut open. I did not see any Rattle Snakes tho many Ladies are afraid to go to the table rock as it is said there are many of these Snakes near it. There are Crayfish in very small pools of water. Mr. MacDonnell said that pounded crayfish applied to the wound was a cure for the bite of a Rattle Snake.

T. 31st Returned to dine in our Marquee. Information is received from Prince Edward that he will be here the 20th of August which will prevent our going to Detroit immediately, as the Gov. intended. Here are numbers of winged Grasshoppers. They are hard scaly & ugly as Rhinoceros, & the color of dead leaves. The high grounds above Navy Hall are so covered with them that the whole field appears in motion.

W. 1st of August   We dined with Major & Mrs. Smith. He is in the 5th Regt. & Commands the Garrison. Lt. Smith, his Son, is married to a beautiful Irish woman. A great many Officers of the 5th are married. Tho the buildings look so well from the other side, I found the quarters very indifferent.

Mrs. Smith has two tame raccoons. They resemble a Fox, are an exceeding fat animal with a bushy tail. It is remarkable that they have a joint in the nose. When they eat they use their fore feet as monkeys do. I also saw a flying squirrel which I did not admire. Its tail was like a Rat & the eyes very large. I thought the ground squirrel much prettier. The black Squirrel is large & quite black. It is as good to eat as a young Rabbit.

F. 3rd   The Gov. set out this Evening to sleep at the Landing intending to go tomorrow to Ft. Erie 30 miles. Mr. Talbot drove me in the Caleche to the Landing & we returned to Supper at Navy Hall. We saw a fine Bald Eagle on the Wing.

4th   The Gov. returned to dinner quite unexpectedly having heard that the Vessels he meant to have seen had sailed from Ft. Erie to Detroit. Mrs. Macaulay drank tea with me. The weather is so excessively hot that I am quite oppressed by it & unable to employ myself. I am sorry I have not a Thermometer to ascertain the degree of heat. We have a very large bower composed of Oak boughs in which we dine it being greatly cooler than a Tent. We like this place much better than Kingston. Mrs. Hamilton & her sister Miss Askin dined with me. They are french women from Detroit.

The Queen's Rangers are encamped at the Landing & are employed in building Hutts near the River, to live in next winter.

It is a very picturesque place. The Gov. crossed the water from thence & ascended a very steep road to see the remains of the french Fort [at Lewiston].

From thence there is a fine view towards the head of Lake Ontario 50 miles distant. Near this fort are tumuli, bones have been dug up & it is supposed to have been an Indian burying Place.

I received some Shaddocks [an orange-like fruit] from the W. Indies which I thought an excellent fruit.

17th of August   I desired to drive out last Evening tho every body foretold an approaching Thunder Storm, which indeed came on with great violence when we were half way to the Landing. I feared that the Lightening would make the Horse run away but he only started at every flash of lightning. The recollection that it was my own determination brought us into danger was very unpleasant. However we got back safe, & in time to save the Marquees from being blown down. Mr. Grey's & Mr. Talbot's were overset, but the Gov. preserved ours by having the Cords held untill the violence of the Storm was over. The Tents were so near the River that we were afraid they would be blown into it.

We were so cold & wet we were glad to drink tea. It was quite dark & too windy to allow of our burning candles & when the forked flashes of lightning enlightened the air I was able to drink tea. I wrapped myself up in 2 or 3 Great Coats & intended if the Tent was blown down to take shelter under the great dinner table. The Rain & Wind did not cease for two hours, & we had no means of drying our Clothes & were obliged to sleep in a wet Tent. However we have not caught cold.

I received a very pretty set of Nankeen China from England today & in an hour after it was unpacked in the temporary kitchen (an arbour of Oak boughs) took fire & in the hurry of moving the China it was almost all broken. Luckily the weather was calm or the Tents might have taken fire. We are in daily expectation of the Prince. The Canvas Houses are not arrived or Navy Hall finished

& the dilemma has been whether to give Him the Marquees for his residence, or the damp House. It is decided to take the latter ourselves, so here we came in a cold, blowing dismal night.

I sat by myself in a miserable damp Room looking on the Lake where it blew quite a Gale the Bear Gun boat tossing about terribly & not a chearful thought passing in my mind, when I had the happiness of receiving a Letter from you which raised my spirits, tho for some hours after that pleasure, I feel more dejected than at any other time from the recollection of Absence from my friends.

The Bear is arrived from Irondiquet Bay & the Genesee River & brought two families from Carolina to settle in this Province. They have had a most terrible Passage being obliged to stay under the Hatchway almost all the time.

18th   We crossed the River & from a green bank had a very pretty view of Navy Hall.

20th   Cold weather, we walked.

21st   Very cold, we walked by the side of the Lake which is quite like a Sea beach only the marine smell is wanting.

Sept. 18th   The Prince came here the 20th of August. He went to the Ft. at Niagara & when a Salute was fired the Gov. was standing very near the Cannon & from that moment was seized with so violent a Pain in his head that he was unable to see the Prince after that day, & kept his Room a fortnight. He had a gouty pain in his hand before & it is supposed the Shock of the Cannon firing so immediately above him fixed the disorder in his head. He is now recovered & has a pain in his foot, which perhaps would more effectually relieve his head if it was more violent.

Lord Garlies & Capt. Markham stayed here a week but the Gov. was not well enough to see them more than once.

I send you May apple seeds. I think it the prettiest Plant I have seen, the leaves extremely large of a bright green the flower consists of 5 white petals of the texture of orange flowers but 3 times larger, 10 yellow chives round a large seed vessel which becomes a fruit of the colour & near the size of a magnum bonum Plumb, the seeds resembling a melon. The flower is on a short foot stalk one or two sitting between the leaves. They grow near the roots of old Trees in good land. The fruit is ripe in August. Manatoua means the Evil Spirit or Devil in the Iroquois language, Niche is friend & sago How-do-you do? These are the Indian words I have learnt.

Nov. 4th We have had a great many whitefish. They are caught here from October till April. In summer they go into deeper water; they are most exquisitely good & we all think them better than any other fresh or salt water fish, they are so rich that sauce is seldom eaten with them, but it is a richness that never tires it is of so delicate a kind. They are usually boiled, or set before the fire in a pan with a few Spoonfuls of water & an anchovy which is a very good way of dressing them. The sturgeon is about six feet long. Those that are caught here are infinitely better than those which go to the Sea. Cooks who know how to dress parts of them cutting away all that is oily & strong, make excellent dishes from Sturgeon such as mock turtle soup, Veal Cutlets & it is very good roasted with bread crumbs. The 5th Regt. have caught 100 Sturgeon & 600 whitefish in a day in Nets.

A great many settlers come daily from the United States some even from Carolina 2000 miles. 5 or 6 hundred mile is no more considered by an American than moving to the next Parish is by an Englishman. Capt. Duncan has sent me the Horse I rode to Mr. Frazier's.

Mr. Talbot went with Coll. Butler to distribute presents to the Indians at Buffalo Creek. He bought a very pretty Fawn Skin of one of them for me & I made it into a Tippet. He also brought me a cake of dried hurtleberries made by the Indians which was like Irwin's patent Currant Lozenges but taste of smoke.

The Indians make very long speeches at their Councils. One of them named Cowkiller spoke for 5 hours in a late debate between them & the people of the U. States.

I have seen some translation of speeches full of well expressed fine sentiments, & marking their reliance on the Great Spirit. They appear to have great energy & simplicity in their speeches.

The Ships sail for Kingston this week & remain there closed up by the ice in that Harbour till April. The Gov. will now have less to write & I hope fewer headaches. The Winter express indeed will afford an opportunity of sending some dispatches. It arrives here from Quebec late in Jany. & after going to Detroit returns here, it was established for the use of the Merchants & travels on Snow Shoes coming by way of the Fort Oswego. Capt. Stevenson is gone to England & Mr. Littlehales to Philadelphia to see Mr. Hammond.

I have met with a beautiful blue flower [fringed gentian] near the River. It is like a Jancinella. The edges of the Petal is finely sawed. The Cardinal flower which grows in the wettest & most shady places is a beautiful color. I am told the Indians use the roots medicinally.

I send you some Seeds of the Cotonier or wild Asparagus. It may be eaten when very young, afterwards it becomes poisonous. The silky Cotton in the seed vessel is very pretty & makes excellent pillows & beds. I hope you will grow enough to stuff a Muff. I do not know how to describe the flower it is so unlike anything I ever saw.

26th of Nov. We have had a very little Snow which is melted, the weather is again as the Autumn has continued very mild & pleasant. Mr. Bouchette has surveyed Toronto Harbour. It is 35 miles distant from hence across the Lake.

28th Nov.　Went to the Ft. this Morning. Mrs. Macaulay drank tea with me & I had a party at Whist in the Evening. The partition was put in the Canvas House today by which means I have a bedroom in it as well as a sitting room. These Houses are very comfortable about 30 feet long. The grates did not answer for burning wood & I have had a Stove placed instead tho as yet a fire has not been wanted. The weather is so mild that we have walked in the Garden from 8 till 9 in the Moon light these two last Evenings.

3rd of Dec.　The Gov. went to the Landing & I went to the Ft. to see Capt. Darling's stuffed birds. The most beautiful of them he called a Meadow Lark the size of a blackbird the colours the richest yellow shaded to Orange intermixed with black, the Recollect a light brown with a tuft on its head & the tips of the wings scarlet like Sealing Wax upon them, a blackbird with scarlet on the wings they abound here in swamps, a scarlet bird called a King bird the size of a small thrush, a Bird like a Canary bird but the colours much brighter, a Grand Duc Owl. Among the animals there was a Skunk like a Pole Cat with black & white marks.

9th　Capt. Brant[4] dined here. He has a countenance expressive of art or cunning. He wore an English Coat with a handsome Crimson Silk blanket lined with black & trimmed with gold fringe & wore a Fur Cap, round his neck he had a string of plaited sweet hay. It is a kind of grass which never loses its pleasant scent. The Indians are very fond of it. Its smell is like the Tonquin bean.

10th　The Gov. set out to walk to Burlington Bay at the head of Lake Ontario about 50 miles from hence.

15th　Mrs. Macaulay gave me an account of a Subscription Ball she was at which is to be held in this Town of Niagara (not at the fort) every fortnight during the winter. There were 14 couples a great display of gauze, feathers & velvet, the Room lighted by Wax Candles & there was a supper as well as Tea.

16th   I sat up all night by way of a descommunal this [or thing] to read Don Guevara[5] & the history of Prince Ctesiphon & some pages of Don Quixote, went to bed in my cloathes at 6, rose at nine, dressed, breakfasted at 10.

17th   The Gov. returned at 5 today from his walk to Burlington Bay. The shores of the Lake are for a great distance as high as at the Falls of Niagara, & several small rivers falling from that height make very picturesque scenes. He was delighted with the beauty of the Country & industry of the Inhabitants. He lodged every night in Houses where he was accommodated with a clean Room & a good fire.

23rd   I left Trojan my Hound in my Room while I went to dinner & he tore to pieces my best Map of Canada & the United States which I had taken great pains to draw. I must paste it together again but its appearance is spoiled. The Gov. made some very pretty Verses on the occasion.

29th   Coll. Simcoe walked to the Landing & Ft. Schlosser. The weather so mild we breakfasted with the door open into the Garden.

31st   A large Party at Dinner. Mrs. Hamilton came to see me. We play at Whist every Evening. Coll. Simcoe is so occupied during the day with business that it is a relaxation. I have not lost one Rubber since the 28th of Nov. We usually play 4 every Evening.

Mr. Chief Justice Osgoode[6] is now in his own House, which is so near that he always come in an Evening to make up our party. Till within this fortnight he resided in our House not having been able to meet with any that suited him & Coll. Simcoe finds him a very agreeable companion.

January 1793[7]   Mr. Littlehales returned from Philadelphia. He gave the following Journal of his travelling to New York. "Crossed the water at Queenston (the Landing) ascended the Mountain which is a part of the Alleghany. 6 miles beyond the Landing passed the Tuscarora village & 40 miles farther the Tonawanda village. The Tonawanda River is navigable for Batteau nearly to its source from thence thro a thick Wood full of swamps & Creeks 20 miles to Butter Milk falls so named from the richness of the Land to the Genesee River 95 miles from Niagara, thence to Lake Cayuga ferry 2 miles, 150 miles from Niagara, to Onondaga Lake 190 miles from Niagara." Mr. Littlehales travelled late, between Onondaga & Coneswaga Lake lost himself in the Woods & was 30 hours without provisions. Whitestown near Ft. Stanwix on the Mohawk River 250 miles from Niagara has 6000 inhabitants. 7 years ago it was a desert. From Whitestown to Schenectady 80 miles, fine meadows called German flats chiefly inhabited by Germans. Schenectady is a regular built considerable Town containing 3000 Dutch. It is 330 miles from Niagara. New York is finely situated. Mr. Littlehales stayed there but two days & proceeded to Philadelphia 600 miles from Niagara. He left it on the 5th of January & on the 9th reached Northumberland 140 miles passing by Reading over the Broad & Mahony Mountains. Sunbury is opposite Northumberland on the forks of the Susquehanna. Each Town has a thousand Inhabitants. Mr. Littlehales forded the Tioga 7 times, crossed the Conesto & Cohocto Rivers then went 60 mile over extremely steep Ridges of the Alleghany Mountains to Williamsburgh in the Genesee & arrived at Niagara on the 20th which by this Route is but 400 miles from Philadelphia.

Feb. 4th 1793   The Gov. set off from hence in a sleigh with 6 officers & 20 soldiers for the Mohawk Village on the Grand River where Capt. Brant & 20 Indians are to join him & guide him by the La Tranche River to Detroit, no European having gone that track & the Indians are to carry Provisions.

The Gov. wore a fur Cap tippet & Gloves & maucassins but no Great Coat. His servant carried two Blankets & linen. The other Gentlemen carried their Blankets in a pack on their Back.

8th   I draw maps, write read & work, so much that the days do not seem long tho I am alone. I am so persuaded that the Journey will be of service to the Gov.'s health that I rejoice he has undertaken it. This Evening I received some Letters from England brought from Montreal by Indians who hung the Packet so near their fire that the edges of the Letters are burnt & the dates illegible. I received a letter from the Gov. who had proceeded 40 miles & had had pleasant journey but it now Rains very much which I fear will spoil the Roads.

12th   I heard of the Gov.'s safe arrival at the Mohawk Village the 3rd day after he left this place. He was much pleased with seeing their Church & hearing the Women sing Psalms. The Indian women have remarkable sweet voices.

Sunday 17th   I heard that the Gov. was well & within 4 days of Detroit. I went to dine with some Ladies of the Queen's Rangers at the Landing. The Gov. has had a Hut built for himself & we have hung up the Tapestry in it which came from Stowe [seat of the Marquis of Buckingham in England] which makes the room very comfortable. I slept there.

M. 18th   Mrs. Hamilton drank tea with me. Mrs. McGill the Commissary's wife & Miss Crookshank her sister are pleasant women from N. York. I gave a dance this Evening. There were about 10 couple.

T. 19th   The Bugle horns sound delightfully here, they echo among the Rocks so finely. I called on Mrs. Hamilton in my way to Navy Hall & brought Miss Butler home with me.

W. 20th   I dined at the Chief Justice's who had a large party to meet me. I played seven rubbers at Whist.

21st   I received a letter from the Gov. dated Upper Delaware village. He had a pleasant journey passed a fine open Country without swamps. The La Tranche at 150 miles above its mouth is as wide as the Thames is at Reading.

25th   I had company at dinner & Cards in the Evening.

W. 27th   The coldest day we have had this winter. The Ther. stood at 55 at the C. Justice's tho the stove was almost red hot.

Navy Hall, Feby. 1793

My Dear Mrs. Hunt:

Expecting an express soon from Quebec, I prepare my letters beforehand, that they may be ready. I have the pleasure to inform you my little Katherine goes on vastly well, eats, sleeps & grows fat, so I hope she will not feel the want of a Wet nurse, which was what I could not procure for her. Will you do me the favour to join with Mrs. Montagu in answering for the little stranger. I shall be happy further to cement our friendship by this mark of it. I have already had her privately baptized. I long for the arrival of the express, as it is some time since I have heard from England. The accounts I have heard from *every* correspondent of the *great* improvement of the little girls under your tuition is a very great happiness to me, the greatest that can be next to being an eye-witness of it. The whole winter has been like an exceeding fine dry autumn in England; the climate is delightful & the country plentiful, & a pleasant society within a certain circle; in short, we have nothing to complain of but not seeing the children & the absence of some Friends.

Coll. Simcoe is gone to Detroit, *on foot* the greatest part of the way, a journey of about 600 miles, but as I am convinced the exercise & air will do his health & spirits great good I rejoice in his absence, though it will be a month or six weeks; he has five officers as companions, a dozen soldiers & twenty Indians with him as guides. As it is a service of no danger, & I think will afford him amusement, I am quite easy about it, & have so much writing, drawing, arranging papers & working to do that the days pass very quick; besides, I have now & then Card parties here & at the Chief Justice's, for I am become a great Whist player.

Francis is the most engaging pretty child you ever saw of his age; he is at present very handsome. Pray give my love to Miss Hunt; tell her there are as many feathers, flowers and gauze dresses at our balls (which are every fortnight) as at a Honiton Assembly, & seldom less than eighteen couples. I have not attended them because I was, the greatest part of the winter, in daily expectation of being confined. I have taken the Canvas House we brought from England for my own apartment; it makes two very comfortable & remarkable warm private rooms; it is boarded outside to prevent snow lying on it. The comfort I derived from these apartments was extremely great when I lay in, because being in a manner seperate from the rest of the House it was so very quiet.

The greatest inconvenience of this country is want of servants, which are not to be got. The worst of people do you a favour if they merely wash dishes for twenty shillings a month. The Sergeant's Wife I took with me I am happy to keep in my house, for she is a very steady person, remarkably fond of the Children & attentive to them; & a good worker, & Joseph makes himself very useful.

Mr. Scadding seems very well satisfied with his sixty pounds a year as clerk, & sometimes has the amusement of shooting; he looks as rosy as ever though he leads so much more sedentary a life. Adieu, my dear Madam — Believe me, very sincerely yours

E. Simcoe

To Mrs. Hunt
Wolford Lodge
Honiton, Devonshire

Mar. 1st   A Lady dined with me & we played at Whist in the Evening with the C. Justice.

8th of March   Mrs. McGill dined with me. A snowstorm the whole day drifted by a high wind, the River so full of Ice that it appeared immovable for some hours.

S. 9th   A fine clear day the River full of Ice. Towards two o'clock it separated & floated down & a boat came over from the Garrison. It was curious to see the Men land on the weak bordage [edge of the ice] which they crossed by laying the Oars on it, over which they stepped to the Shore, one man fell in but was soon assisted out of the water.

Sunday 10th   The Gov. & Mr. [D. W.] Smith returned. He stayed 4 days at Detroit. It is exactly 5 weeks since he left this place. He is remarkably well & not fatigued. He went a part of the way in sleighs but walked the greater distance. The Journal does not contain may incidents. The Map which accompanies it shews the various Creeks they passed on fallen Trees which requires some care and dexterity to cross. His Excellency's leaving Detroit under a Salute from all His Majesty's ships lying there is mentioned, as also that "His Excellency ordered Prayers to be read in the woods on Sunday & forty people attended. His Excellency & suite eat Raccoons & Porcupines which were good the latter like Pork." The Porcupine's quills stuck into Jack Sharp's neck (a Newfoundland dog) & they were very difficult to extract & made him ill for many days.

The Gov. rose early on the march & walked till 5 o'clock. A party of the Indians went on an hour before to cut down wood for a fire & make Hutts of trees which they cover with bark so dexterously that no rain can penetrate, & this they do very expeditiously; when the Gov. came to the spot the Indians had fixed upon to Lodge for the night the Provision was cooked, after Supper the Officers sung God Save the King & went to sleep with their feet close to an immense fire which was kept up all night. The Gov. found his expectations perfectly realized as to the goodness of the Country on the banks of the La Tranche, & is confirmed in his opinion that the forks of the Thames is the most proper scite for the Capital of the Country, to be called New London on a fine dry plain without underwood but abounding in good Oak Trees. A spring of real Petroleum was discovered on the march by its offensive smell.

W. 13th   Coll. Simcoe has the Gout in his hand.

Navy Hall, March 13th, 1793
My Dear Mrs. Hunt:
        The contents of your last letters, informing me of Mrs. Grave's quitting Wolford was not any great surprise to me as I thought such an event not improbable. Be assured, my Dear Madam, that the confidence we repose in your care & attention to our children makes us perfectly

indifferent to any expence that must necessarily be incurred by your keeping house for them, & the benefit they will receive from the good & religious principles you will instill into their minds will be cheaply purchased, pray do not be uneasy at any trifling expences which you deem proper to be incurred. Coll. Simcoe desired Mr. Flood to get a second-hand Carriage for yours & their accommodation. We are very anxious that they should stay at Wolford. I should never be satisfied about their health were they at Bath, as I have a great prepossession against that place for children. I hope with a carriage (and be as liberal of fires as possible) that you and Miss Hunt will reconcile yourselves to Wolford, as we should not be happy to have the children removed & it is a great pleasure to me to have them brought up so near Miss Burges that they may get the habitude of seeing her often, of acquiring a great regard for a friend to whom I am so much attached & I think it much better as you have determined it, to be at Wolford than to encumber her house with so many children though the offer was extremely kind of her.

As for Mrs. Graves' desire of having Eliza on a visit, we cannot refuse it; but it is Coll. Simcoe's & my absolute desire that she does not stay above a month or six weeks in these annual visits, because we should be sorry the child's education should be stopped or that she should be longer seperated from her sisters, which reasons alone determined us to deprive ourselves of her company. Besides, I think the Child has too great a tendency to weak Lungs to make it at all proper for her to be longer there was there no other reason. The other Children, of course, Mrs. G. would not wish to be troubled with; if she did the same system should prevail as with regard to Eliza.

Pray give my love to Miss Hunt, tell her I should have answered her letter, but I send this by a pacquet as the quickest conveyance to you, & letters sent by Pacquets cost such sums of money that I will not write to her till I send to Mr. Burgess. They are rather longer going thro the Secretary of State's office, but without there is anything material to be speedily answered, it is the best way to write on account of the expense.

Give my kindest love to the Children, tell them the same reason & being greatly pressed for time (as this is an unexpected opportunity) hinders my writing to them, & thanking Charlotte for her very pretty ruffles which I value much & Harriett for her letter. Tell Eliza there are no Cassava trees here. The country is not hot enough but her father thanks her for thinking of it. Let them know that their father is just returned from Detroit, looks remarkably well in health, & is grown really fatter tho he has performed a journey of six hundred miles in exactly five weeks & walked a great part of the way. I will write them a further account by the first opportunity of sending to Mr. Burges.

I enter exactly into what Miss Hunt's & your feelings have been because I have known & experienced enough of those kind of proceedings.

I am sure Miss Hunt's instructions are much better than Mr. Pigot's few visits, in short, we are quite happy in every account I hear of your proceedings with Respect to the Children, & are only anxious that everything should go on comfortably to yourself & Miss Hunt. Mr. Flood will be of any assistance in his power. Believe me to be, my dear Mrs. Hunt, with great regard & confidence in your friendship.

Very sincerely yours,
E. Simcoe

Coll. Simcoe desires his best compliments. Eliza or Charlotte have not sent me any drawing lately. I hope they continue to like drawing; she writes vastly even on one line. I wish I was as good an arithmetician as you have taught her to be. I think you were quite right to discharge a Gardener that must be a useless expense. I am glad Melly is still with you; I hope she continues to merit your good opinion, for I always liked her much.

To Mrs. Hunt
  Wolford Lodge, near Honiton
    Devonshire, England

16th   Coll. Simcoe so much better as to walk on the Sands. The Ther. 72 in the shade. There are thousands of Ducks up this River daily. They are called Cawines. They have a fishy taste & are never eaten, their down appears to me exactly the same as that of the eider duck. I lately dreamt of being fired at by small shot in passing through a wood, & have since had quite a horror of the sound of Musquet or anything military.

I have been much amused by reading Watson on Chemistry, in which there is an account of the making an artificial Volcano that I think would please you, an experiment of putting Diamonds & Rubies in separate Vessels & exposing them to a violent fire — the Diamonds are dissipated & the Rubies unchanged in weight or colour.

April 1st   Rode to Queenstown where we intend to reside a fortnight. Mr. Grey & Talbot are going to New York.

T. 2nd   Very warm weather.

W. 3rd   The weather extremely warm but we find the Log Hutts cool from the thickness of the Timber with which they are built.

We do not keep house here, as there are not Offices belonging to our Rooms we did not bring many servants but dine at the Mess. Immediately after I have dined I rise from table one of the Officers attends me home & the Band plays on the parade before the House till 6 o'clock. The Music adds chearfulness to this retired spot & we feel much indebted to the Marquis of Buckingham for the number of Instruments he presented to the Regt. The Bugles sound at 5 every Morning & Coll. Simcoe goes out with the Troops & returns to breakfast at nine.

5th   Fahrenheit's Ther. 78 in the shade, 112 in the Sun today at Navy Hall. Trojan has been so ill in consequence of a blow he received on his head since we left Navy Hall, that the Servants supposed him to be mad & shot him, which we regret most excessively, not believing he could have been mad as he ran into the water a short time before he was killed.

I gave a Dance this Evening.

A soldier was pointed out to me by the name of Swanbergh a Swede who had distinguished himself in a battle where the King of Sweden was present, this incident & the admiration I know you feel for Swedes caused me to observe somewhat peculiarly fine in his Countenance; when on further enquiry it proved that the man shewn was not Swanbergh, but a worthless Thief — so much for my skill in physiognomy.

6th   I rode a pleasant Horse of Mr. Mayne's[8] to Navy Hall returned here in the Evening but not being expected found a cold wet Room & spent an uncomfortable Evening. St. Denis of the 5th caught yesterday at Niagara 500 White Fish & 40 Sturgeon, this is common, the sturgeon one nearly 6 ft. long.

Sunday 7th   We dined with Mrs. Hamilton & walked in the Evening where I observed some trees on fire the flames in part concealed appeared like Stars & had a beautiful effect.

M. 8th   A very warm day. I rode to the falls there are still heaps of Ice below them, but it had not a brilliant or fine appearance as I had expected to see.

9th   Mrs. Richardson breakfasted with me. Very wet weather. We played at Chess all the day.

10th   Very cold & some snow. We drove to Navy Hall & slept there.

T. 11th   A very fine day. Went to Queenstown, walked by the River half a mile to a beautiful spot among the rocks. The rapid clear water with a bright tinge of Green from the reflection of the high banks covered with trees had a fine effect & we determined that it would be a delightful spot to have a cold dinner at, & the music would sound well among the Rocks.

13th   Returned to dinner at Navy Hall. Jacob & Aron, Mohawks came express from Detroit in 8 days, they walked 56 miles this day.

15th   I dined at the Fort & caught cold by crossing the water this very cold day. In a newspaper from the States was a paragraph "His Serene Highness of Upper Canada gives great encouragement to Settlers."

The Caldwell sloop arrived at Kingston from hence on the 6th of April, the day before the Harbour had been so full of Ice that she could not have got in. An Indian who speaks English being asked at what hour he arrived, pointed to the West & said "when the Clock was there." It reminded me of a line in Spencer, "The clock in Jove's high House."

18th   A Newspaper is published here called the Upper Canada Gazette or American Oracle. As yet it is filled with Proclamations[9]

& Advertisements. The only Printer to be met with was a french man named Louis Roy & he cannot write good English.

Scadding went with a Surveyor to the first forks of the La Tranche, as a Farmer he gives the most favourable account of the Land.

Capt. Shaw is arrived with his wife & 7 children from Oswego where he met his family & spent the Winter with them. The South Shore of Lake Ontario being uninhabited, from Oswego they brought with them an Indian to build Hutts & shoot Partridges & Ducks. They came the whole way in a Boat. The only alarm they met with was from Trees falling near their Hut one night. The Children had made fires for diversion too near large trees without considering which way the wind might blow them down, & the Hut was in danger by their fall.

T. 23rd of April   et dia del negro Eponomon, I thought of you as by agreement. I rode to the whirlpool, a very grand Scene half way between Queenstown & the falls, where the current is so strong that Eddies are formed in which hewn timber trees carried down the Falls from a sawmill upright. Vast Rocks surround this bend of the River & they are covered with Pine & hemlock spruce, some cascades among the Rocks add to the wild appearance. These scenes have afforded me so much delight that I class this day with those in which I remember to have felt the greatest pleasure from fine objects, whether of Art or Nature, as at Blenheim, the Valley of Stones, Linmouth & Linton. I met with some pretty flowers & a beautiful Millipedes. I gave a Ball this Evening. Some small Tortoises cut up & dressed like Oysters in Scollop Shells were very good at Supper.

24th   I rode to the Whirlpool with Mr. Pilkington.[10] As we came back it was almost dark & the fires the Indians had made by the Water side for the purpose of spearing fish had a picturesque appearance among the rocks. The light attracts the fish & the

Indians are very expert in spearing them.

26th   A very wet night. It rained into the Huts but I found one corner of the Room dry & there I placed my bed. Capt. Shaw has given me a tea Chest in bird's eye Maple. It is a beautiful wood, the colour of satten wood. The Tea Chest was made at New Brunswick. Capt. Shaw mentions many instances of persons settled in New Brunswick who having marry'd women from the United States were persuaded by them to quit the Country as they would not live without the Apples & peaches they had been used to at New York. The Americans are particularly fond of fruit. The Indians bring us Cranberries in Spring & Autumn which are as large as Cherries & very good, the best grow under water. They also supply us with Chestnuts which they roast in a manner that makes them peculiarly good.

29th   Rose before breakfast. At Navy Hall the Onondaga arrived from Kingston in 22 hours. There is a large Stone House built by the French in the Fort at Niagara & from thence it is said to take its name as Niagara in the Indian language signifies great House. Pray take notice to call it Niágara.

2nd of May   Coll. Simcoe set off accompanied by 7 Officers to go to Toronto. He means to go round by the head of the Lake in a Batteau.

3rd   I borrowed Sir. J. Reynold's "Discourses,"[11] they amuse me very much.

5th   A very cold day.

9th   I am feverish & ill. I caught cold by sitting late with the Windows open after a very hot day & the dew falls here most heavily.

13th Coll. Simcoe returned from Toronto & speaks in praise of the harbour & a fine spot near it covered with large Oak which he intends to fix upon as a scite for a Town. I am going to send you some beautiful Butterflies.

14th [May] Three Commissioners[12] who were appointed by the United States at Sanduski are arrived here & intend to stay at our House untill they receive further Orders from Philadelphia. Mr. Randolph is a Virginian. Genl. Lincoln & Coll. Pickering are from New England. Coll. Simcoe calls the latter my cousin, his ancestors left England in Charles the 1st's Reign & this Gentleman really bears great resemblance to the picture Mrs. Gwillim has of Sir Gilbert Pickering.

If the proffered Mediation of England with respect to this Treaty at Sanduski had been accepted by the States & Washington had gone thither, Gov. Simcoe would have gone to meet him. I am not sorry that circumstance is avoided.

14th of June I am just returned to Navy Hall after spending a month with Mrs. Smith at the Fort. The cold I caught the 9th of May turned to dumb ague (that is but little of the cold fit & a continual fever). With this indisposition, I found myself extremely inconvenienced by the Commissioners' residence in our small House & I accepted Mrs. Smith's friendly invitation to visit her & her nursing & great attention to my health enabled me to recover so soon as I have done.

Commodore Grant who commands the Vessels on Lake Erie was staying at Major Smith's. The Queen's Rangers have left the Huts at Queenstown & encamped on the Mountain above. It is a fine dry healthy spot & the Tents look extremely pretty among the large Oaks which grow on the Mountain.

23rd Mr. Talbot went to Sanduski to deliver Papers to Coll. McKee.

26th The Indian Commissioners went to Fort Erie. Coll. Pickering gave me a receipt to make Chowder of Salmon, Sea biscuit & pork; it is to be stewed for twenty minutes.

27th We dined alone for the first time since we left Quebec. The Gov. having no business to attend to & the weather delightful we crossed the water & drank tea on a pretty green bank from which there is a good view of Navy Hall & we enjoyed this half holliday amazingly.

28th of June We rode to Queenstown & slept there. The Ther. was 86 today.

29th Breakfasted in the Camp & rode on to the falls 7 miles, dined there & went to Birch's Mills 2 miles above the falls. We returned to Tea in the Camp, but the heat was so excessive we were obliged to stop on the road & drink milk & water & eat fruit at Mrs. Tyce's. The Thermometer has been at 96 today. We slept in the Hut but I determined in future to sleep on the Mountain. I saw a stuffed Rattlesnake which was killed near Queenstown in the act of swallowing a black Squirrel. The snake measured 5 feet six inches long & had seven Rattles.

Sunday 30th Returned to Navy Hall in a Boat the Commissioners left here which is a very good one with an Awning & Green Curtains. The heat excessively great.

July 2nd Jacob Lewis and Aron Hill came here. The latter was well dressed & looked very handsome. Lewis's wife was with him, a very pretty woman the only handsome woman I have seen among the Indians. We treated them with Cherries. The Indians are particularly fond of fruit. We have 30 large May Duke Cherry trees behind the House & 3 standard Peach trees which supplied us last autumn for Tarts & Deserts during 6 weeks besides the numbers the young Men ate. My share was trifling compared to theirs & I eat 30 in a day. They were very small but high flavoured. When tired of eating them raw Mr. Talbot roasted them & they were very good.

5th of July 1793   Francis has been very ill, & the extreme heat of this place is thought to be prejudicial to him. It is therefore determined that I shall take him to the Camp on the Mountain. I shall have an Establishment of Two marquees a Tent & two sentrys. The Gov. will come to see us whenever he has leisure, my dinner to be sent every day from Navy Hall. This day I embarked at one o'clock on board the Gun boat with Francis & Sophia & Mr. Mayne attended me. I left the Thermometer at 90 but found it pleasant on the water. It requires a strong steady wind to carry vessels to the Landing as the Current runs 4 notts an hour against them. The Gun Boat not having top sails catches but little wind between the high banks. It blew fresh when we embarked but soon became calm. Mr. Bouchette for the honour of his Vessel declared we were going on, but it was not apparent to Mr. Mayne or myself that we made the least way, we had the boat let down & proceeded the remaining three miles in it. I was much fatigued in ascending the Mountain, we reached the Camp about 5 o'clock. I dined alone. The Gov. came to supper. The Musquito Net was not brought & I passed a most wretched night. Mr. Talbot returned from the Miami. The Indians have sent a deputation to the Commissioners, to desire to converse with them at Niagara before they proceed to the Miami as Wayne's army has advanced nearer to them than they expected.

6th   The Gov. returned to Navy Hall, as did the Commissioners & some Indian Chiefs.

Sunday 7th   The Gov. came to Supper. The Indians have demanded whether the Commissioners have full powers to fix a boundary, they are to reply tomorrow. The Mississaga arrived with 270 Indians from St. Regis. They belong to the Tribe called the 7 Nations of Canada. They speak french are much civilized & have a good deal of the manners of french men.

M. 8th   Another Indian Council today at Navy Hall, at which the Commissioners declared they had full powers to fix a boundary.

T. 9th   It was determined in the Indian Council today that the Commissioners & Indian Deputies shall go to Sandusky to treat.[13] The 7 Nations having no Conductor or Officer with them Mr. Talbot will accompany them to Sandusky. The Houses of Assembly dissolved today.

My Marquee commands the most beautiful view of the River & Lake seen between the finest Oak trees among which there is always a breeze of wind. The Music Tent is at such a distance as to sound very pleasantly. Mrs. Hamilton & Mrs. Richardson were with me in my Arbour when we heard so violent a Clap of thunder as made us all stoop our heads, the lightning followed instantly. We ran into the tent & stayed untill a violent torrent of rain had abated. On coming out I observed an Oak tree which stood close to the Arbour was much blasted by the lightning. Mrs. Hamilton took Francis home with her lest he should catch cold from the Damp of the Tents after this violent rain. I drank tea & slept at Mrs. Hamilton's.

11th   I walked to the Camp. The Gov. went to Navy Hall. I drank tea with Mrs. Hamilton & saw the 7 Nations pass.

12th   Mr. Talbot dined with me in his way to Fort Erie.

15th   A wet day which is very dismal in a Tent but to see the light again & feel the air dry is such a pleasure that none can judge of but those who have felt the reverse.

16th We dined in the Hut & Mr. Mayne drove me to Navy Hall in the afternoon in a Gig we have had made in which he drove two Horses tandem, it is so light that we went to Navy Hall which is 7 miles in 3/4 of an hour & returned to the Landing by 8 o'clock. The Road is good but for the stumps of trees on each side which it requires attention to avoid, but my Charioteer left Westminster last year so you may conclude him to be a steady Person. He is a protegé of Ld. Amherst's. He supplies Mr. Talbot's place when he is absent.

18th The weather being very hot we went again to the Camp. In the Evening we rode to Mrs. Tyce's, a pleasant situation like some in Epping Forest, it is 3 miles from the Camp.

19th Went to Navy Hall, caught cold by going out this Evening without a fur tippet which the great dew renders necessary after the very hot days.

20th Capt. Shaw & 100 men set off in Batteaux for Toronto. I drank tea at the Fort.

21st Extremely hot weather. Road to the Camp this Evening & found it cooler & less damp than at Navy Hall. The Mountain is covered with a sweet purple flower the roots of which infused in brandy make a wholesome Cordial. It is called Oswego bitter. Mr. Russell says it is a wild balm of Gilead & that an oil may be extracted from it. The leaves dried are good in peas soup or forced meat. By some mistake my dinner did not arrive from Navy Hall one day last week, but I had some of the excellent New York biscuits which I eat & said nothing about my dinner, feeling a pleasure in being able to be independent.

22nd We crossed the water to the Ferry House opposite Queenstown & breakfasted in the Arbour covered by wild Vines

& beautifully situated on the bank of the River. We rode up the Hill to the spot where the french had a Fort. We saw a very extensive view toward the head of the Lake. On our return we found the Arbour so cool & pleasant that the Gov. sent for his writing Box & we stayed here the whole day. After dinner I ascended the Hill again & made a sketch. We supped in the Camp. The Caldwell sailed with Capt. Smith for Toronto.

23rd   Excessively hot weather. The Gov. went to Navy Hall. Francis is much better but weak. I see him almost every day but did not chuse to pay Mrs. Hamilton so long a visit tho I feel greatly obliged to her for keeping the child. I have just heard that the Onondaga is arrived at Navy Hall to take us to Toronto. Whether we shall remain there & the Regiment build huts for their winter Residence is not yet decided.

25th   Went this Evening to Navy Hall.

27th of July   I went to Church, drank tea at the Fort. My Marvel of Pine is in great beauty.

28th   An experiment of firing shells from Cannon was made at the Fort by the Gov's orders.

5

LIFE AT YORK
July 29, 1793, to May 11, 1794

29th of July   We were prepared to sail for Toronto this morning but the wind changed suddenly. We dined with the Chief Justice & were recalled from a walk at 9 o'clock this Evening as the wind had become fair. We embarked on board the Mississaga the band playing in the Ship. It was dark so I went to bed & slept until 8 o'clock the next Morning when I found myself in the Harbour of Toronto. We had gone under an easy sail all night for as no person on board had ever been at Toronto[1] Mr Bouchette was afraid to enter the Harbour till day light when St. John Rousseau an Indian trader who lives near came in a boat to Pilot us.

30th Tuesday   The Queens Rangers are Encamped opposite to the Ship. After dinner we went on Shore to fix on a spot whereon to place the Canvas Houses & we chose a rising ground[2] divided by a Creek from the Camp which is ordered to be cleared immediately. The Soldiers have cut down a great deal of wood to enable them to pitch their Tents. We went in a Boat 2 miles to the bottom of the Bay & walked through a grove of fine Oaks where the Town is intended to be built. A low spit of Land covered with wood forms the Bay & breaks the Horizon of the Lake which greatly improves the view which indeed is very pleasing. The water in the Bay is beautifully clear & transparent.

Sunday August 4th 1793   We rode on the Peninsula[3] so I called the spit of sand for it is united to the mainland by a very narrow neck of ground. We crossed the Bay opposite the Camp, & rode by the Lake side to the end of the peninsula.

We met with some good natural meadows & several Ponds. The trees are mostly of the Poplar kind covered with wild Vines & there are some fir. On the ground were everlasting Peas creeping in abundance of a purple colour. I was told they are good to eat when boiled & some pretty white flowers like lillies of the Valley. We continued our Ride beyond the Peninsula on the sands of the North Shore of Lake Ontario till we were impeded by Large fallen Trees on the Beach. We then walked some distance till we met with Mr. Grant's (the surveyor's) Boat. It was not much larger than a Canoe but we ventured into it & after rowing a mile we came within sight of what is named in the map the high lands of Toronto.[4] The Shore is extremely bold & has the appearance of Chalk Cliffs but I believe they are only white Sand. They appeared so well that we talked of building a summer Residence there & calling it Scarborough.

The diversity of Scene I met with this Morning made the ride extremely pleasant. The wooded part of the peninsula was like a Shrubbery. The Sands towards the Lake reminded me of the Sands at Weymouth & the sight of the high Lands presented a totally different Country to anything near the Bay, tho I was not more than 4 miles from it. I was very near riding into what appeared a quick Sand, which with a little Rain & wind we met with for half an hour as we rowed from the shore to the Mississaga were the only unpleasant incidents that occurred this day. After dinner we left the Mississaga & slept tonight in the Canvas House.

5th of August   The Children came on Shore, this afternoon we walked two miles [about 1 mile] to the old French Fort[5] but there were no remains of any building there. It rained very hard & I was completely wet as if I had walked through a River, for being in a shower in the woods is quite different from being exposed to it in an open Country, every Tree acted as a Shower Bath, as the path was just wide enough to admit of one person. We passed some Creeks & unhewn Trees thrown across, a matter of some difficulty to those unaccustomed to them. I should think it might be done with less danger of falling with Moccasins on the feet.

6th Having been wet through these last two days I declined going with the Gov. to see a mill[6] on St. John's Creek 6 miles towards the head of the Lake. The Gov. brought me some very good Cakes. The Miller's Wife is from the United States where the women excell in making Cakes & bread.

7th I rode on the Peninsula from 1 till four. I saw Loons swimming on the Lake they make a noise like a Man hollowing in a tone of distress. One of these Birds was sent me dead at Niagara, it was as large as a Swan, black with a few white marks on it. At a distance they appear like small fishing boats. The air on these Sands is peculiarly clear & fine. The Indians esteem this place so healthy that they come & stay here when they are ill.

9th Some Indians of the Gibbeway [Ojibwa] Tribe came from near Lake Huron. They are extremely handsome & have a superior air to any I have seen, they have been little among Europeans therefore less accustomed to drink Rum. Some wore Black Silk handkerchiefs covered with silver Brooches tied tight round the head, others silver bands, silver arm bands & their shirts ornamented with broaches, scarlet leggings or pantaloons, & black, blue, or scarlet broadcloth Blankets.

These Indians brought the Gov. a Beaver Blanket to make his bed as they expressed themselves, apologized for not having done it sooner & invited him to visit their Country.

10th of August I went again to my favourite sands, the Bay is a mile across. The Gov. thinks from the Manner in which the sandbanks are formed, they are capable of being fortified so as to be impregnable, he therefore calls it Gibraltar Point[7] though the Land is low.

Sunday 11th   Lt. Smith of the 5th Regiment (who is here as Acting Deputy Surveyor General) read Prayers to the Queens Rangers assembled under some Trees near the Parade. This Evening we went to see a Creek which is to be called the River Don. It falls in to the Bay near the Peninsula. After we entered we rowed some distance among Low lands covered with Rushes, abounding with wild ducks & swamp black birds with red wings. About a mile beyond the Bay the banks become high & wooded, as the River contracts its width.

Lt. Smith has drawn a fine map of the La Tranche River. From what has been surveyed it is proved that Charlevoix's Map describes the Country with great truth. If the line from the Road to the R. La Tranche was layed down according to its true bearings, on any Map but Charlevoix's it would strike L. Erie instead of the La Tranche.

13th   An Indian named Wable Casigo supplies us with Salmon which the Rivers & Creeks on this shore abound with. It is supposed they go to the Sea. The velocity with which Fish move makes it not impossible & the very red appearance & goodness of the Salmon confirms the supposition, they are best in the month of June.

I brought a favourite white Cat with grey spots with me from Niagara. He is a native of Kingston. His sense & attachment are such that those who believe in transmigration would think his soul once animated a reasoning being. He was undaunted on board the Ship, sits composedly as Centinel at my door amid the beat of Drums & the crash of falling Trees & visits the Tents with as little fear as a dog would do.

There has been a fever at Niagara. This place is very healthy & I think it probable we shall spend the winter here. Mr. Talbot is still at Philadelphia, Mr. Grey at Quebec. He has broken his arm there. The Gov. has the gout in his foot very slightly He has just received a Letter from Prince Edward lamenting his not obtaining leave to go to England.

August 24th   The Gov. has received an official account of the Duke of York having distinguished himself in an action at Famars by which the French were dislodged & driven out of Holland. The Gov. ordered a Royal Salute to be fired in commemoration of this Event & took the same opportunity of naming this station York. There are a few 12 & 18 Pounders which were brought here from Oswegatchie [later Ogdensburg] & Carleton Island. The Mississaga & Onondaga fired also & the Regt.

There was a party of Gibbeway Indians here who appeared much pleased with the firing. One of them named Canise took Francis in his Arms & was much pleased to find the Child not afraid but delighted with the sound. It was a damp day & from the heavy atmosphere the Smoke from the Ships' Guns ran along the water with a singular appearance.

25th   The Abbé des Jardins & a Monsr. de la Corne arrived here. They are sent by some french Emigres to examine whether a suitable Establishment could be allotted for them in this Country. The Abbé appears a cunning clever man, whose manners are those of one accustomed to live in the best society at Paris. La Corne is a Canadian who has been some time resident in France. The Gov. receives them with great civility, has ordered a Marquee to be pitched for them. He has recommended it to them, to travel towards Burlington Bay at the head of the Lake where the Country is open & the climate very mild. The soil & local circumstances they may judge of when on the spot.

The following anecdote was related by the Marquis de Bouillé to a friend of Monsr. de la Corne's. When Louis 16 went to Varennes the Marquis de Bouillé who was stationed at some distance with a considerable force has ordered his son if the King was in any danger, to come to him immediately by a road which ran as from a to b. When the young man found the King threatened through eagerness to acquaint his father he took a shorter road, & by that means missed the Marquis who had proceeded some leagues towards Varennes on the circuitous Road. This delay caused the Marquis to arrive too late to rescue the King.

28th   I walked with the Gov. on Gibraltar Point this Evening.

29th   The Gun Boat arrived from Niagara. An Officer from Detroit came in her who says the Indian Commissioners returned to the States without making Peace with the Indians, as they refused to give up what the Indians had invariably made the terms of accommodation.

30th   The Mississaga came from Niagara in 4 hours. Mr. Russell came in her.

4th of September   I rode to St. John's Creek [Humber River]. There is a ridge of land extending near a mile, beyond St. John's House [St. Jean Rousseau], 300 feet high & not more than three feet wide, the bank towards the river is of smooth turf. There is a great deal of Hemlock Spruce on this river, the banks are dry & pleasant. I gathered a beautiful species of Polygala.

I found a green Caterpillar with tufts like fir on its back. I accidentally touched my face with them & it felt as if stung by a nettle, & the sensation continued painful for some time. It was extremely calm when we set out but on our return we were almost seasick the water was so rough. A little breeze on this Lake raises the waves in the most sudden manner.

6th of Sept.   I have read Alfred's Letters.[8] I never expected to be so much entertained by a Political book or to have comprehended so much of the Politics of Europe. Mr. Osgoode suspects it to be written by Mr. Burgess [Burges].

I went today to ride to Gibraltar Point.

W. 11th　We rowed 6 miles up the Donn to Coons, a farm under a hill covered with Pine. I saw very fine Butternut Trees. The nuts are better than Walnuts, gathered berries of Cockspur Thorns. I landed to see shingles made which is done by splitting large blocks of Pine into equal divisions. We found the River very shallow in many parts & obstructed by fallen Trees. One of them lay so high above the water that the boat passed under the Rowers stooping their heads. It looked picturesque & a bald Eagle sat on a blasted Pine on a very bold Pt. just above the fallen Tree. The Gov. talks of placing a Canvas House on this Point for a summer residence. Vencal the Swede rowed the Boat, a very intelligent man born at Unterburgh.

13th　Mr. Pilkington coasted the Lake & arrived here in two days about 100 mile.

S. 14th　We walked to the spot intended for the scite of the Town. Mr. Aitkin's Canoe was there we went into it & himself & his man paddled. We went at the rate of 4 notts an hour. I liked it very much being without the noise of Oars is a great gratification. I gathered purple berries from a Creeping plant, seeds of Lillies & spikenard. To see a Birch Canoe managed with that inexpressible ease & composure which is the characteristic of an Indian is the prettiest sight imaginable. A man usually paddles at one end of it & a woman at the other but in smooth water little exertion is wanting & they sit quietly as if to take the air. The Canoe appears to move as if by clockwork. I always wish to conduct a Canoe myself when I see them manage it with such dexterity & grace. A European usually looks awkward & in a bustle compared with the Indian's quiet skill in a Canoe.

23rd I rode on the Peninsula. My horse has spirit enough to wish to get before others. I rode a race with Mr. Talbot to keep myself warm. I gathered wild grapes, they are pleasant but not sweet.

Capt. Smith is gone to open a Road to be called Dundas Street from the head of the Lake to the R. La Tranche. He has 100 men with him. I hear they kill Rattlesnakes every day yet not a man has been bit tho they have been among them for 6 weeks. Capt. Smith sent two of the Snakes in a Barrel that I might see them, they are dark & ugly & made a whizzing sound in shaking their Rattles when I touched them with a stick.

We dined in a Marquee today. It had become too cold in the Arbour. The Canvas House we use as a bed Room but the other is going to be erected for a winter Dining Room. I have gathered most beautiful white berries with a black Eye from red stalks. I cannot find out its name.

W. 25th The Gov. set out with 4 Officers a dozen Soldiers & some Indians to visit Lake Huron.

29th I walked on the sand bank & gathered seeds of Toronto lilies.

October 2nd The Gov.'s Horses returned from the Micicquean Creek from whence he sent me some seeds. I received the Comte de Gramont[9] sent from England by Mr. G. Davison. The Ground Mice are innumerable & most troublesome here. We want the Edict published in Spain to excommunicate & banish them. I send you a bat remarkable for its size & a beautiful black & yellow bird.

October 25th 1793 York I send a Map to elucidate the Gov.'s journey which was attended with danger as well as with many pleasant circumstances. The western side of the Lake is drawn from Mr. Pilkington's sketches, the Eastern from former accounts.

Mr. Pilkington who was one of the party, says the Scenery was fit for pictures the whole way & from his drawings I should suppose so. They rode 30 miles to the Micicaquean Creek now called Holland's River then passed a terrible bog of liquid mud.

The Indians with some difficulty pushed the Canoe the Gov. was in through it. The Governor went to the habitation of Canise the Indian who held Francis in his arms during the firing when York was named. Canise & his eldest son were lately dead, their widows & children were lamenting them & formed a group like Sissigambis & her family. Young Canise gave the Gov. a Beaver Blanket & made speeches of excuse for not sooner having made his Bed. The Gov. went to see a very respectable Indian named Old Sail who lives on a branch of Holland's River. He advised him to return by the Eastern branch of it to avoid the Swamp. They proceeded about 30 miles across Lac le Clie [Lac aux Claies] now named Simcoe in which are many Islands which Coll. Simcoe named after his father's friends & those Gentlemen who accompanied him. The River from thence to Matchadotch Bay afforded the most picturesque scenery, from the number of falls & Rapids upon it. Some of them were avoided by carrying the Canoes on the Shores, others they risqued going down.

In passing a rapid an Indian in the Gov's Canoe fell over & the Canoe passed over him. He rose up on the other side & got in again without seeming discomposure.

In returning one of the Soldiers cut his foot hear Holland's River. Mr. [Alexander] McDonnell & another Gentleman staid with him as he was unable to travel. The Old Sail received them hospitably & shot Ducks for them. A small quantity of Provision being left with them & an Indian who carried a large Cargo quitting the Party, reduced the stock so much that the Gov. set out with only two days' provisions & the expectation of 5 days' march to bring them to York. The Indians lost their way & when they had Provisions for one day only, they knew not where they were. The Gov. had recourse to a Compass & at the close of the

143

day they came on a Surveyor's line & the next Morning saw Lake Ontario. Its first appearance, Coll. Simcoe says, was the most delightful sight at a time they were in danger of starving & about 3 miles from York they breakfasted on the remaining Provisions.

Had they remained in the woods another day it was feared Jack Sharp would have been sacrificed to their hunger. He is a very fine Newfoundland Dog who belonged to Mr. Shane near Niagara but has lived at Navy Hall from the time of our coming there & walked to Detroit with Coll. Simcoe. He has been troublesome enough on this excursion as his size was very unsuitable to a Canoe but he is a great favourite.

Col. Simcoe had the satisfaction of finding Matchadash Bay such as gave him reason to believe would be an excellent harbour for very large Ships. A bay near Prince William called Penegatashene [Penetanguishene] a fine harbour. The fever at New York & Philadelphia amounts almost to the Plague.

A road for walking is now opened three miles on each side of the Camp. I can therefore now take some exercise without going to the Peninsula. Mr. McDonell arrived with the Soldiers from Holland's River. He brought some Wild Ducks from Lake Simcoe which were better than any I have ever tasted, these Birds are so much better than any in England from their feeding on wild Rice or folle avoine as the french call it. Capt. Smith is returned from cutting the Road named Dundas Street. It is opened for 20 miles.

They met with quantities of wild Grapes & put some of the Juice in Barrels to make vinegar & Capt. Smith told me it turned out very tolerable Wine. They killed numbers of rattle snakes every day but nobody was bitten by them. Capt. Smith brought two in a barrel to show me as I have never seen any alive.

28th of October The weather has been very cold for some days & the frost very severe notwithstanding which we feel it quite mild in the Woods. Today we walked 2 miles to a pretty spot by the side of a Creek, where we had a fire made of many large Trees & wild Ducks roasted by it & we dined without feeling the least cold. Coll. Pickering's Dish, chowder, is also easily dressed in the Woods, being prepared in a Kettle before we left our house.

T. 29th   The Gov. having determined to take a Lot of 200 acres upon the River Don for Francis, & the law obliges persons having Lots of Land to build a House upon them within a year, we went today to fix upon the spot for building his House.[10] We went 6 miles by water & landed, climbed up an exceeding steep hill or rather a series of sugar-loafed Hills & approved of the highest spot from whence we looked down on the tops of Large Trees & seeing Eagles near I suppose they build here. There are large Pine plains around it which being without underwood I can ride or walk on, & we hope the height of the situation will secure us from Musquitos. We dined by a large fire on wild ducks & Chowder on the side of a hill opposite to that spot.

Our long walk made it late before we had dined so that although we set out immediately afterwards & walked fast it was nearly dark before we reached the Surveyor's Tent. From there we went home in a Boat as the stumps & Roots of trees in the Road were so troublesome to walk among in the dark. Mr. Littlehales & some Gentlemen lost their way in attempting to return to the Camp an hour after us. They slept in the Woods about a mile distant.

30th   We have received from Montreal a Birch Bark Canoe such as is used by the North West Company to transport their goods to the Grand Portage. It requires 12 men to Paddle is large enough to contain four or five Passengers to sit very commodiously in the center under an awning. An Indian Woman came today with Pitch which is made by the Indians from Fir Trees, to gum the Canoe if any part of it is worn off by bringing it hither. She held a piece of pitch in her hand & melted it by applying a piece of burning wood. Her figure was perfectly wild & witchlike & a little fire with her kettle on it by her side, in a stormy dark day the waves roaring on the beach near which she stood formed a scene very wildly picturesque.

Nov. 1st   I walked this Morning. At 8 this dark Evening we went in a Boat to see Salmon speared. Large torches of white birch bark being carried in the Boat the blaze of light attracts the fish which the Men are dextrous in spearing. The manner of destroying the fish is disagreeable, but seeing them swimming in Shoals around the boat is a very pretty sight.

The flights of wild Pidgeons in the Spring & Autumn is a surprising sight. They fly against the wind & so low that at Niagara the Men threw sticks at them from the Fort & killed numbers, the air is sometimes darkened by them. I think those we have met with here have been particularly good. Sometimes they fix a bullet to a string tied to a Pole & knock them down. Coll. Butler was observing that they build where there are plenty of Acorns but do not feed within 20 miles of the place, reserving that stock of Provisions till the young ones can leave their Nests & then scratch the Acorns up for them.

Pidgeons have been shot with rice in their Craws on the Mohawk River. Rice does not grow nearer than Carolina, there it is presumed (considering the supposed time of digestion) that they must have flown 200 miles a day.

Nov. 8th   We have had a week of incessant rain.

9th   I went today for the first time in the N. West Canoe. A Beaver Blanket & a carpet were put in to sit upon. We carried a small table to be used in embarking & disembarking for the Canoe cannot be brought very near the Shore lest the gravel or pebbles injure her, so the table was set in the water & a long Plank laid from it to the Shore to enable me to get in or out the Men carrying the Canoe empty into the water & out of it upon their shoulders. We have less than "boards between us & eternity" for the Canoe is formed of Birch bark fixed on to thin ribs of very light wood with the Gum or Pitch the Indians make from fir Trees, & of which they always carry some with them lest an accident rub off any, or the heat of the Sun melt it.

We dined in a Meadow on the Peninsula where I amused myself with setting fire to a kind of long dry grass which burns very quickly & the flame & smoke ran along the ground very quickly & with a pretty effect. I was delighted with the swift & easy motion of the Canoe & with its appearance.

14th I went again in the Canoe untill we came in sight of the High Lands but it was so very cold I was very glad to walk part of the way back. We dined on the Peninsula. I passed a spot on the Peninsula where it was supposed an Indian had been buried lately. A small pile of wood was raised, a bow & arrow lay on it, & a Dog skin hung near it. Some Indians sacrifice Dogs, other Tribes eat them when extremely ill.

19th At this season of the year there is usually a fortnight of foggy weather, the air is perfectly dry & hot & smells & feels like smoke, it is called the Indian summer. I have never heard these smoky foggs well accounted for.[11]

20th We dined in the Woods & eat part of a Raccoon, it was very fat & tasted like Lamb if eaten with Mint sauce.

21st A Owl was sent to me shot at Niagara, it measured 5 feet from wing to wing when they were extended.

22nd Mr. Littlehales went on horseback to Niagara.

29th An Indian came here who by way of being in mourning for a relation was painted black round his face.

Dec. 2nd   The Great Sail, his Wife & 10 children came here, they grouped themselves like Van Dyke's family pictures. They brought us a Deer. Francis handed plates of Apples to them. He shakes hands with the Indians in a very friendly manner, tho he is very shy & ungracious to all his own Countrymen. A Mississaga called the Man of the Snakes was here also. The Mississagas dress very indifferently.

8th Dec.   The Onondaga was left under the care of a young lieutenant & ran aground. It is feared she cannot be got off untill the spring & then perhaps not without injury.

The Nicias defeated the Syracusans, Plutarch relates that they adorned themselves & their Horses & cropped those of the captives; was not this the origin of cropping Horses.

9th   The Gov. went to view the Onondaga in such rough Weather that the Waves came into the Boat & made everybody very wet.

12th   Mr. Grey has just received orders to join Sir. C. Grey in the West Indies. He is to go by way of New York. The Gov. & Mr. Talbot set out with him this Morning to accompany him as far as Niagara. Fine calm weather.

M. 16th   An exceeding rough day. At 8 tonight the Gov. & Mr. Talbot returned. They left Niagara at one o'clock yesterday, rowed till 4 in the Morning slept a few hours at Jones' at the head of the Lake & proceeded on the way hither. They arrived at Niagara on Friday in such rough weather that there was great difficulty in turning Mississaga Point.

19th   I walked to the Donn. There are great hopes of getting the Onondaga afloat.

21st   A hard frost. The Bay is half frozen over. The Man of Snakes came here.

Sunday 22nd   The Bay is quite frozen over. Mr. Talbot skaited to the other side. I walked today.

23rd   Very cold weather.

24th   Thunder and lightning last night, extreme hard frost this Morning.

26th   Wright & Herring returned from Niagara in a Boat. It is found practicable to walk & ride thither throughout the winter therefore we are not in as Isolé a situation here as it was expected we should find it. The news received of Adm. Gardner's having taken two 44-gun Ships off Sandy Hook & some privateers near Hallifax.

F. 27th   The weather so cold that some water spilt near the Stove froze immediately.

30th   I walked to the old Ft, returned by the Creek. I caught cold.

York 6th of Jany. 1794   The skin of a Cross Fox marked yellow black & white with a dark Cross on the back was brought here & sold for 4 dollars, sometimes they are sold for two dollars.

I sketched a likeness of the Great Sail, who came here today. The Indians call the stars we name Ursa Major a Fisher (or martin) with a broken tail. I received from Detroit a Stone carved by an Indian into a head & when it is known that they have no tools but the commonest kind of small knife it is surprizing to see it is so well done.

I sketched a Connewaghna [Caughnawaga] Indian today whose figure was quite antique. I have often observed (but never had more reason to do so than today) that when the Indians speak their air & action is more like that of Greek or Roman Orators than of Modern Nations. They have a great deal of impressive action, & look like the figures painted by the Old Masters.

14th   There is a great deal of Snow on the River Don which is so well frozen that we walked some miles upon it today, but in returning I found it so cold near the Lake that I was benumbed & almost despaired of ever reaching my own house & when I came near it the Hill was frightfully slippery. Near the river we saw the track of Wolves & the head & Hoofs of a Deer. The workmen who reside in a small Hut near the place, heard the Wolves during the night & in the Morning found the remains of the Deer. The Indians do not kill Wolves, they seldom take trouble that does not answer to them, & the Wolves are not good to eat & their skins are of little value.

Jan. 18th   The Queen's Birthday. The weather so mild we breakfasted with the Window open. An experiment was made of firing Pebbles from Cannon. A Salute of 21 guns & a Dance in the Evening in honour of the day. The Ladies much dressed.

Sunday 19th   The weather so pleasant we rode to the bottom of the Bay crossed the Don which is frozen & rode on the Peninsula, returned across the Marsh which is covered with ice & went as far as the Settlements which are near 7 miles from the Camp. There appeared some comfortable Log Houses inhabited by Germans & some by Pennsylvanians. Some of the Creeks were not frozen enough to bear the Gov.'s horse but mine passed very well. He excells in getting over difficult places, & in leaping over Logs which I like very much.

25th   Two soldiers went to Niagara. These Expresses are to go at regular periods by way of a Post.

26th   We went to the Donn to see Mr. Talbot skait. Capt. Shaw's

Children set the Marshy ground below the Bay on fire the long grass on it burns with great rapidity this dry weather. It was a fine sight & a study for flame & smoke from our House. At night the flames diminished & appeared like lamps in a dark night in the Crescent at Bath.

27th I walked below the Bay & Set the other side of the Marsh on fire for amusement. The Indians have cut holes in the Ice over which they spread a Blanket on poles & they sit under the shed moving a wooden Fish hung to a line in the water by way of attracting the living fish, which they spear with great dexterity when they approach. The Gov. wished me to see the process, we had to walk half a mile to the place. There was no snow on the ice & we were without cloth Shoes. The Gov. pushed a large limb of a tree before him which kept him steady & with the assistance of Mr. Talbot I reached the spot where they were catching Maskalonge (a superior kind of Pike) and Pickerell. I was almost frozen from looking on, though the apprehension of falling kept me warm while I walked.

31st One of the Horses drawing hay across the Bay fell into an airhole & was drowned. Scadding's[12] cottage burned down.

I am in great spirits today as the Gov. talks of going to Detroit in March & spending a month there very gaily, but the greatest amusement will be the journey. We shall ride to the Grand River from thence to the La Tranche where Canoes will be built in which we shall go down to Detroit in a few days, & we shall take Lake Erie on our return. This scheme particularly pleased me, as it will prevent our going to Detroit in July which I had dreaded on account of the extreme heat of that season.

Sunday 9th of Feby. The weather damp mild & dirty. When will the end of March arrive! I am quite impatient to set out for Detroit.

13th We rode to Town. I galloped on the Sands several times. I saw a Chippeway Woman carrying a linnen Bundle tied up like a Doll.[13] I was told it was customary for them to carry about this thing for several months after the death of their husbands. When an Indian intends to express his determination to get through any difficulty he says Garistakaw & after that always pursues the object.

21st Mr. Bouchette has got the Onondaga off the Shoal & she is not injured by the Ice. Mr. Littlehales came from Niagara.

1st of March The News received of the death of the Queen of France.[14] Orders given out for Mourning in which everybody appeared this Evening & the dance was postponed.

March 3rd The weather severely cold.

4th Do. Though I wore 3 fur tippets I was so cold I could hardly hold my Cards this Evening. This is the first time we have felt the want of a Ceiling which we have not had made in our drawing Room because the Room was rather low.

5th Very cold. I divided the Room by hanging across it a large Carpet which made it warmer. There has so little Snow fallen this winter that it was scarcely practicable to track the Deer, in consequence of which the Indians have been almost starved. A great many of their Women & Children come to our windows every day for bread which we cannot refuse them, tho having but a certain quantity of flour until the Spring supply arrives, it is inconvenient to give them what they require.

There have been apprehensions that the french Republicans at New York would attack Lower Canada from Albany this winter, but a mutiny on board some of their Ships carried them to France. If the Americans were to attack this Province I should go to

Quebec. I have just received your Letters in answer to which I can only say "Que diable avait elle a faire dans cette galere?"[15] What nonsense about the books! Did people but consider their happiness the first point of their Creed would be not to consider things as serious which are of no consequence.

14th   As I was riding across the Bay I felt the Horse sink under me & supposing there was a hole in the Ice I threw myself off; the Horse lay down to roll in the Snow. As I was falling I struck him with my whip & I believe that prevented his rolling over me. I was not hurt, but much afraid he should repeat the trick.

I dreamt some time since that the Gov., Mr. Talbot & I were passing a wood, possessed by an Enemy who fired ball at us as fast as possible. I was so frightened, that I have never since liked to hear a musquet fired & I am quite nervous when I hear of the probability of this Country being attacked.

In a Magazine we met with a very pretty hymn sung by Sicilian Mariners. It sounds charming played by the Band on the Water. The Master of the Band is a German who boasts of having performed before the King of Prussia in the Great Church at Strasbourgh.

15th   An express is Arrived from Lord Dorchester who orders Gov. Simcoe as soon as the navigation of the Lakes is open to go on the R. Miami[16] & establish a fort in a Country claimed by the Americans some distance below Detroit. The Gov. thinks the Order may be put in execution so much earlier if he goes down the La Tranche to Detroit, that he intends setting out tomorrow for the Grand River. This order of Ld. Dorchester puts an end to my scheme of going to Detroit which is an exceeding great Disappointment to me.

16th Sunday   I walked halfway to the Town with Mr. Talbot. The day was very windy, returned before Evening prayers. Mr.

Pilkington walked from Niagara. I copied some sketches he made going to Lake Huron. He says the Ther. was 5 degrees below 0 the 5th of this month at Niagara.

Are you not shocked at the siege of Valenciennes or any real action that has lately occurred, being represented on the stage in London. If English minds become hardened by seeing such sights as amusements, they will in time be as well able to become their friends' Executioners as the French have been.

17th A dance tonight.

18th The Governor & Mr. Talbot set out at half past 7 for Detroit.

19th This is the Month for making Maple Sugar, a hot Sun & frosty nights cause the Sap to flow most. Slits are cut in the bark of the Trees & wooded troughs set under the Tree into which the Sap — a clear sweet water — runs. It is collected from a number of Trees & boiled in large Kettles till it becomes of a hard consistence. Moderate boiling will make powder sugar but when boiled long it forms very hard Cakes which are better. I saw a number of Trees slit today as I rode with Mr. McGill to his farm.

In a month's time when the best Sap is exhausted, an inferior kind runs of which Vinegar is made. Cutting the Trees does not kill them for the same Trees bear it for many years following. Dr. Nooth at Quebec shewed me some Maple Sugar which he had refined, & it became as White as W. India sugar. The sap of Birch trees will make Vinegar.

21st The weather extremely warm. Mrs. Richardson spent the day with me.

22nd of March Abundance of Geese & Ducks seen which denotes the approach of Spring.

Sunday 23rd   A very hot day.

25th   I had a party at Cards this Evening. Some white fish were sent me today from Niagara & dressed for supper, they were the best I ever tasted.

27th   A strong easterly wind. All the Ice went out of the Harbour in two large sheets, each above half a mile long.

28th   Mr. Gamble returned from the Grand River where he had been to attend Brant. He brought a letter from the Gov. who went from the head of the Lake to Niagara sending Mr. Talbot to the Grand River to order the Canoes to be prepared. The Gov. expected they would be in readiness for him to leave Brant's on the 26th. The Ice would not allow them to move sooner. Mrs. Richardson spent the day with me.

29th   Rain & damp weather.

Sunday 30th   I walked on the beach.

T. 1st of April   I rode to the Town, a delightful Evening.

W. 2nd   I rode.

14th   Do. I saw a fine Eagle.

15th   Scadding came in a Boat from Niagara where the River is still full of Ice. I received some excellent White Fish from thence. A Boat arrived from the Bay of Quinte with Pork.

W. 16th   Walked towards the Old French Fort.

F. 18th of April   The Caldwell arrived from Kingston. She left it

155

the 16th. The Harbour was open on the 10th of this Month.

Friday May 2nd   Governor Simcoe arrived at 6 this Evening from Niagara. He rode from the Grand River to the La Tranche where he embarked on the 29th of March in Canoes & that day reached the scite intended for New London. The 30th he slept at the Delaware Village, the 31st at the Moravian Village, the 1st of April at a Trader's, the 2nd arrived at Detroit; two days the snow fell incessantly so that they were wet through in the Canoe which repelled a slight attack of the Gout the Governor was seized with. He saw wild turkeys & Eagles & shot a deer which the Wolves drove down to the River. The Gov. stayed 4 days at Detroit, & then went to Capt. Elliott's at the River au Raisin from thence rode 30 miles to the Miami & stayed at Coll. McKie's a little distance from thence.

On the way they passed an Indian Fort & swam the Horses over some Creeks. At Coll. McKie's there were very good wild Turkeys. On his return the Gov. saw Turtle Island & was detained some days among the Bass Islands in Lake Erie by contrary Winds. They went on some of the Islands & it being St. George's Day gave one of the Islands that name. The Gov. killed 7 Rattle snakes with a small stick on one of the Islands & Mr. Pilkington shot a Sturgeon. The Gov. arrived at Fort Erie the 25th of April.

Friday May 9th   At 7 this Morning we set off in a Boat with the Children & Mr. Talbot intending to reach the head of the Lake tonight, but a very stiff breeze rising ahead about 4 o'clock we put on shore 12 miles short of it. The Tents were pitched & fires made. The Gov. & I walked some distance on the beach & Mr. Talbot amused himself in barking Elm Trees as the Indians do & covering his Tent with it, for it proved a very Wet Night. We supped under Umbrellas. The Children & Junk [a nurse] slept on the Office Boxes in the Tent.

S. 10th We rose at day light, breakfasted & set off, but the weather was so misty that I saw less of the Country towards the Head of the Lake than I had expected & was prevented going into Burlington Bay. After some hours of wet weather it blew very fresh & cleared up. A wave washed into the Boat of which no notice was taken but Collins [a nurse] laid her Cloak on the other side. People sometimes cross from the 16 mile Creek to the forty but the Gov. does not like meeting those breezes which rise suddenly on this Lake.

We coasted to the 40 (40 miles from Niagara) & passed it at 3 o'clock. The mouth of this Creek forms a very fine Scene, a very bold spur of the Alleghany appears beautiful in the distance. It is about 3 miles off. Some Cottages are prettily placed on the banks of the River, & a saw Mill affords a quantity of boards which piled up in a wood makes a varied foreground. It was almost 6 before we reached the 20 mile Pond the Mouth of another Creek.

A small Inlet from the Lake carries you into this pond which is two mile long. The banks are very high of a fine Verdure & the summits covered with Wood which was now reflected with the deepest Shades in the Water & had a most beautiful appearance, which was soon heightened by the rising moon giving more force to the Shades. Two Houses of Coll. Butler's were distinguished at a distance.

We had not eat since 8 this morning. I was therefore desirous to get something for the Children & while some salmon we bought of an Indian as we passed Burlington Bay was preparing for our Supper, we walked half a mile with the Children to a farm House which we found inhabited by some Pennsylvanians whom Gov. Simcoe had assisted last Year at Niagara, we had here excellent Bread & Milk & Butter. We then returned to the Tents & Francis lay down on his Great Coat on the grass & went to sleep till his Tent was ready for him. We supped by Star light amid this fine scenery of Wood & Water, the bright fires of the Soldiers below the hill, contrasted with a dark sky now & then brightened by a gleam of Moon light had a beautiful effect.

Sunday 11th   We left this beautiful spot about 8 o'clock. The entrance to the 17 [i.e. 18], 16, 15 & 12 Mile Creeks appeared pretty as we passed them. It blew so fresh we were afraid of losing the Awning from the Boat. It was too Showery for me to venture in the Canoe. It was a pretty sight to see how swiftly she glided through the water. We arrived at Niagara at 12, & before two I wished to return to York, the heat here was so great & looking on land seemed to add to the heat & was quite disagreeable after having been accustomed to look on the Bay at York, & the River here though ½ a mile wide appears narrow after leaving that expanse of water.

6

LIFE AT NIAGARA
May 13 to September 12, 1794

13th May   I went to see Major Smith's House he has built on this side of the River. It is a very good one. The Town here is enlarged & called Newark.

14th   Mr. Pilkington goes tomorrow to see & give orders for fortifying the new Post at the Miami. He gave me some Sketches taken on Lake Erie.

15th   Some Ladies dined here from the Garrison. After they went I drove out in the open Carriage towards the Landing. The apprehension of War with U. States engages my attention very disagreeably, at the same time I reflect that I should not have less Anxiety in any other part of the world. Had we remained in England probably the Governor would now be going on the European continent where Campaign follows Campaign without a prospect of peace & here, if a War takes place the result must be speedily decisive.

16th   Drove this evening (after dining at the Receiver General's) towards the 2 mile Creek, the road horribly bad.

17th   So cold an E. wind that I had a fire, a large party at dinner. The new Merchant Vessel called the Gov. Simcoe[1] arrived. She sails remarkably well.

Sunday 18th   Very cold.

M. 19th   The wind changed & the weather warm.

T. 20th   I am always glad to have large Parties at Dinner for when I sit alone I do nothing but think of the threatened War in this Country. After the Ladies leave me Mr. Talbot drives me in the Gig towards the landing, the weather being usually too warm to walk, & the Gov. employs two or three hours on writing in an Evening. This Evening a Cow was laying in the Road & Mr. Talbot did not turn out of the way expecting she would, & before he was aware of it, one wheel went over her back, but as she lay quite still the Carriage did not overset.

21st   A large Party at dinner.

22nd   The Gov. & I dined alone. We fished near the Wharf.

24th   We rode in the Evening & were prevented going to the Garrison in the Evening by a great fog.

Sunday 25th of May   I persuaded the Gov. to ride this Evening. We had not rode a mile before there came so violent a shower that we were wet through in 3 minutes & the claps of thunder were so loud as to make the Horses start. After changing our cloaths we sat down to Tea & agreed with Mr. Talbot that the Rain had been the pleasantest mode of taking a shower bath, & the extreme violence with which it fell rendered us less liable to catch cold than we should have been under a gentle Shower.

W. 28th   All the Ladies from the Garrison & Newark drank tea here previous to the Ball which is to be given on the 4th of June.

29th   The Mississaga, the Caldwell, & the Gun Boats arrived bringing some of the Members of the House of Assembly from the Lower Townships, the speaker, etc. etc. dined with us.

York May 1794
My Dear Mrs. Hunt,

It is with pain I take up my pen to inform you of the loss we have sustained & the melancholy event of our losing poor little Katherine, one of the strongest healthiest children you ever saw, every person admired her as an extraordinary fine handsome child. She had been feverish two or three days cutting teeth, which not being an unusual case with children I was not much alarmed; on good Friday she was playing in my room in the morning, in the afternoon was seized with fits, I sat up the whole night the greatest part of which she continued to have spasms & before seven in the morning she was no more. Our own surgeon was absent & the one present had certainly much less ability. She was the sweetest tempered pretty child imaginable, just beginning to talk & walk, & the suddenness of the event you may be sure shocked me inexpressibly.

A few days afterward Francis was slightly indisposed but in the state of mind I was in, I fancied him dangerously ill, & sent express for our own Surgeon. This agitation turned my mind from the melancholy subject it before dwelt on, & I really think relieved my mind from the oppression I felt, more than any other thing could have done; tho the recollection of the loss of so promising a Child must long be a painful thing; to enhance the misery the Governor was at Detroit; he returned within a fortnight in good health but at his landing from Lake Erie was told of the loss of his Child & that I was not expected to live, on which latter alarm he rode 18 miles of bad road in two hours & was coming on instantly without settling his business at Niagara, but at Niagara he learnt that my illness was slight & merely proceeded from that melancholy event in the family, which affected him in a less degree than it would otherwise have done, if he had not been so frightened on my account; after staying a day at Niagara he came here & I am going immediately to return with him to Niagara for the meeting of the Houses Assembly will shortly be held there.

Francis is in perfect health, he has exactly Eliza's affectionate temper & the meekest little thing imaginable, tho a stout fine looking boy.

I hope on my arrival at Niagara to receive letters from you, we do not cross the Lake in the Vessels but row around it in a Boat. I think the change of scene will be a relief to us. I probably shall not send this till I get to Niagara from whence I will also write to Miss Hunt to inform you of our safe arrival, & hope there to find letters from you. The Governor unites with me in good wishes & I remain,

My dear Madam

Your sincere Friend

E. Simcoe

We hear nothing but reports of war with the States; in that case I & the Children go immediately to Quebec, that place will of course be besieged but it is thought better for me to be in a strong place were hostilities will be carried on *regularly* than here where constant depredations may be expected; I have a very good friend at Quebec Coll. Caldwell's Wife who has already gone thro the misery of one siege at Quebec in 75 & from her society I shall experience more comfort than from anything I foresee. She is a most worthy amiable woman.

Our kindest Love to all the dear Children
(rec'd August 7th 1794)

M. 2nd of June   The House of Assembly met today. We went to
the Garrison in the Evening & drank tea with Mrs. Smith. The
Mississaga, Caldwell & Gun Boats sailed. Mr. Brooking went in
the Mississaga.

T. 3rd   The Gov. goes to the Fort almost every day to see the
Works which the Engineers are repairing. I am glad to take this
opportunities of crossing the water (& glad he is induced to take
this little exercise) & walking on the Common behind the Fort,
as I consider the air so near the Lake & where the ground is high
to be much healthier than our side of the water. The Gov. stayed
so late with the Engineer this Evening that it was dark & Francis
fell asleep on the Common before he returned to us.

June 4th   The Ball was held in the Council Chamber.[2] The Gov.
& I & Mr. Talbot went in to the Room after all the company
were assembled. There were 22 couple. I did not dance. The
Ladies were well dressed. We supped at 12 in Room as large as
the Ball Room & we came away at 2 o'clock. The whole was
extremely well managed as Mr. Talbot ordered it himself.

Th. 5th   I was tired by setting up late & went to take an early
dinner at the fort with Mrs. Smith. The Gov. had a large party of
Gentlemen to dinner. Mr. Talbot came for me in the Evening &
it was so cold we were obliged to wrap ourselves up in Great
Coats & Tippits.

F. 6th   The Gov. went to the Chippeway Ft. & returned at night
wet through. Mrs. D. Smith has added a Boy to her family today.

S. 7th   Francis's birthday was not kept yesterday as the Gov. was from home. Today the little Cannon Mr. McDonell gave him fired a salute of 21 guns, & though they are not 2 inches long made a loud Report & pleased him much. Being 3 years old he was dressed in a Rifle shirt & sash, which gave him somewhat the air of an Indian. He found a dead snake, & gave it as a present to one of the Gentlemen with us. I went to the Fort this morning & walked in the evening. Mr. Talbot went towards the Landing in his Canoe.

10th Some Seneca Indians came here, Francis went to see them dance & afterwards imitated their dancing & singing surprisingly well.

11th I rode in the Morning & went to the Fort in the Evening to walk on the Common.

13th Mrs. Smith & I & Commodore Grant went to the Landing in a Boat & dined with Mrs. Hamilton, we carried Francis with us. Mr. Talbot came to meet us in his Canoe in the Evening.

14th The Mississaga arrived from Kingston. Mr. Brooking came in her.

16th Company at dinner. The Onondaga sailed for Kingston. Capts. Fitzgerald & Cleddowe went in her by whom I wrote Letters.

17th Capt. & Mrs. Charlton went in the Mississaga.

19th I went in a Boat this Evening.

22 Sunday Capt. Talbot sailed in the Governor Simcoe. I dined at the Fort & rode on horseback after I came home.

M. 23 A large party of the Members of the Houses of Assembly dined here.

T. 24 Mrs. Mason & a party from the Ft. dined here. We went on the water in the Evening.

W. 25th A large party at dinner went on the water in the Evening. Mrs. Mason saw a rattle snake in her garden under some Raddish Leaves.

F. 26 [27] I dined at the Garrison.

S. 28th Mrs. Smith dined with me.

Sunday 28th [29th] A Rattle snake seen near the Wharf not 100 yards from our House & it is supposed that there is a nest of them there.

3rd of July Mr. Tukel arrived from England.

5th We dined at Major Smith's & the Child was christened.

M. 7th The House of Assembly dissolved.[3] Wayne has insinuated to the 6 Nations that the Western Nations poisoned those of their Chiefs who died at the Meeting at Sandusky last year.

W. 9 Went this Evening to the Fort. Mr. Darling stuffed a bird for me called a Recollect. The appearance of red wax on its brown wings & the tuft of feathers on its head make it very pretty. The Indians shoot small birds with such blunt arrows that their plumage is not injured.

13th Mr. C. Justice Osgoode sailed for Quebec. The Gov. dined at the Mess.

14th   A large party at dinner.

15th   Rowed in a boat towards the 4 Mile Creek. Mrs. Smith & Mrs. Mason went with me.

16th   The weather very hot. We went out in the Boat. While we were walking in the Garden this Evening about 50 Indians Men & Women landed from their Canoes & encamped outside the paling, brought on shore their luggage & made fires, they were met by a Party of Senecas who sat round their fire. All this passed with so little noise or bustle that we scarcely heard there were people near us. What a noise an encampment of 50 Englishmen have made! But "rien de trop" should be the Motto of these people. Those who draw best & make no stroke without producing a Master effect, may be compared to Indians who never appear to make one motion that does not effect the purpose they intend. We sent some bread & meat to this party. There is always an appearance of distinction among these Savages, the principal Chiefs are usually attended by apparently inferiors who walk behind them. I call them Aide de Camps. I observe none but the chiefs shake hands with the Governor.

17th   We dined in a Boat a half mile from hence under a steep Rock which affords shade & to which the Boat is fastened. Down the side of the Rock a fine spring pours rapidly, & as clear as chrystal.

The Gov. was walking on the hill this Evening, when his shoulder & finger were struck by a shot, fired by a Soldier belonging to the Guard Tent who fired at an Indian Dog which had taken away some Pork. A shot remained in the Gov's finger & was very painful. A Gentleman walking with him was struck & the Dog severely wounded which caused great concern to the Indian Women. An Indian was also struck by the shot. The Gov. immediately gave him the Soldier's Gun to appease him, & reprimanded the Soldier.

18th   Major & Mrs. Smith dined under the Rock with us.

19th   The weather still excessively hot tho some Rain fell.

Sunday 20th   A Cold East wind. I breakfasted at the Garrison.

S. 26th   As I much wished to visit the 40 Mile Creek the Gov. allotted two or 3 days for this party of pleasure. Mr. Mayne was chosen to accompany us, & Francis was of the Party. At 2 o'clock we embarked with a fresh East wind which fell almost immediately but had occasioned so much surf that we could not go on shore at 4 Mile Creek about 2 miles further we landed & dined. We passed Mr. McNab's at the 8 Mile Creek & beyond the 12 we encamped on a pt. without noticing that the field abounded with a Coarse weed which is such a harbour for Musquitos that the tent was filled with them, & we were glad to rise & breakfast at half past three.

Sunday 27th   The weather misty damp & disagreeable. Francis caught cold & was so ill that we went on shore at the 18 Mile Creek & stopped at Sail's house ½ an hour.
    We stopped at the 15 and I took a Sketch of the Mouth of that River. We dined on the Beach at the 20 & went across the Pond to one of Coll. Butler's Houses where we slept, after taking great pains to smoke the House & fix the Musquito nett well, for this place abounds so much with Musquitos that the Farmer does not sleep in his house from June till September but sleeps in his Barn to avoid them. This pond is full of wild rice or folle avoine as Charlevoix calls it. The N.E. wind has filled up the inlet so much that the Boat was obliged to be drawn over the sand.

M. 28th   We rose at 6, left Francis with a servant, & set off for the Forty Mile Creek. By the time they had drawn the Boat over the Sand into the Lake, a strong N.W. wind sprung up which was exactly ahead of us & prevented our getting to the 40 till 2 o'clock tho with a fair wind we should not have been two hours, the fog excessively thick & perfectly counteracted our scheme of seeing the Country. However we walked through a village & beyond Green's[4] Mill a little way up the Mountain far enough to see where the Stream dashes over dark Rocks surrounded by Hemlock Spruce & other picturesque Trees.

A mile further is a Mill & small waterfall & at a season when the water is higher the Scenery must be wonderfully fine, at present it is well worth seeing. I drank tea at Green's & unwillingly left this fine scenery of which I had so slight a view. We were no sooner in the Boat expecting a rapid passage to the 20 than the wind veered & came right ahead, so it was ten o'clock before we arrived at the Inlet. It was quite dark & we were another hour getting the boat over the sand & rowing to the House. (Mrs. Green advised me to give Francis Crow's foot boiled in Milk till it becomes Red & thick, which she said would cure the present complaint in his stomach.)

There are 100 People settled at the 40 & there has been but seven graves in five Years. The Gov. promises that I shall ride on the Mountain above the Forty this autumn.

T. 29th   Embarked at 9 rowed a little up the Creek among the wild Rice & then turned to the Lake, the wind exactly contrary & so very fresh that we were obliged to go on shore at the 17 where we dined & walked to Scram's farm where the Woman was making straw hats. I gathered Crow's foot. Mr. Mayne had a fit of ague — in short everything went au contraire during this Expedition. We arrived at Niagara before eleven. A fine clear Evening now we are returned from our tour.

1st of August   The weather insufferably hot. We walked to Mr. Smith's & supped there, which was very pleasant as the Rooms are so much larger than ours at Navy Hall. Mrs. Smith now resides on this side of the water for the change of air for a sick Child.

2nd The heat extreme. We dined in the boat under the Rock. A Thunder Storm drove us into the House.

3rd The Gov. went early this Morning to the Tuscarora Village[5] dined on the water & returned early. The Ther. 96.

4th The thermometer 96 but Mr. Vandeleur who is just arrived from Detroit calls it cool weather. The Ther was at 101 in Fort Lenou [Detroit]. The heat & Musquitos do not affect me in the violent manner they used to do.

7th Rode in the Evening. The hurtle berries of this Country are larger than in England quite black & if dried in the sun make as good puddings as Levant Currants, quite as sharp. The Indians live in the woods where they grow at this Season of the year, & boil quantities of them into cakes.

Genl. Washington was seen last year at the Theatre at Philadelphia, lights carried before him to the Stage Box where he sat in a front Row, Mrs. Washington & the Aide de Camps on the seats behind him, the Music playing God Save George Washington to the tune of God Save the King. The Gentleman who gave this account went to the Theatre this year, & discovered Genl. Washington in a back row of the front Boxes without attendants, the Vice-President & Mrs. Washington in the same Bench & no notice taken when he came into the Theatre. The next day a paragraph in the Papers asserting that if Washington did not take the Post at Presqu'ile he ought to be guillotined.

F. 8th The Onondaga sailed with Mr. Vandeleur on board. The Mississaga arrived with the Bishop of Quebec,[6] his brother Mr. Mountain, & his son who is the Bishop's Chaplain. Mr. Le Moine arrived in his decked Boat from Kingston across the Lake. She left Kingston on Wednesday.

Sunday 10th   I went to Church. The Bishop preached an excellent discourse, Romans I, 16v. "I am not ashamed of the Gospel of Christ, for it is the power of God unto Salvation to everyone that believeth, to the Jew first and also to the Greek."

T. 12th   An express from Detroit. It is now decided that I am to go to Quebec next month. The hostile appearance Mr. Wayne's conduct bears makes the continuance of Peace with the U. States very doubtful.

14th   The Gov. went with the Bishop to see the Falls of Niagara.

15th   The Bishop sailed for Kingston. I wrote to Mrs. Caldwell to take a House at Quebec for me. Should the French & Americans assault Quebec this winter, I shall find more comfort in Mrs. Caldwell's society than in that of most others, as such a scene would not be new to her. She was in the Town when besieged by Montgomery, 1775. Coll. Caldwell was one of the most active defenders of it.

16th   I went to the Garrison this Evening.

17th   An Express from Detroit.

M. 18th   The Gov. & myself have colds which is very unusual. Notwithstanding, we crossed the water & rode to the Landing. I had not rode on that side of the River before. We dined in the Boat opposite Mr. Hamilton's at whose House we drank tea & returned to Navy Hall in the Boat.

T. 19th   The Governor had the shot extracted from his finger. It was so near the joint that it is feared the finger will always be stiff, it was a large shot.

W. 20th A wet day. Mr. Hamilton dined with us, the Cannon sent to Ft. Erie.

T. 21st Mrs. Hamilton & Mrs. Richardson here.

24th Sunday Mr. Crooks' new Vessel named the York sailed for Kingston, & Mr. LeMoine's decked Boat accompanied her.

M. 25th Capt. Shank arrived with the detachment from York to go to the Miamis.

T. 26th I received the finest red water melons from York I ever saw.

27th More detachments from York for the Miamis.

28th Mr. Sheafe returned from Oswego with News that Ld. Howe had taken 7 sail of French ships.

29th An Express from Detroit announces that Wayne has retired from the Miami Fort after having summoned it to surrender. He came within shot of it & found it stronger than he expected & that there was Cannon. The Match was lighted to have fired if he had not retired. Major Campbell who commanded shewed great discretion & propriety of conduct. If the Gov. had waited till the opening of the navigation of the Lakes to have gone to the Miamis as Ld. Dorchester proposed, the Fort would not have been rendered defensible by this time to have intimidated Mr. Wayne, & War would have commenced with the U. States.

1st of September The Merchants gave a Dinner to commemorate Ld. Howe's Victory on the 1st of June. The Gov. & the Officers of the Garrison dined with them. Mrs. Smith & some Ladies dined with me.

4th   The Militia dined with the Gov. I dined with Mrs. Smith.

8th   Mr. McKenzie[7] who had made his way from the Grand Portage to the Pacific Ocean is just returned from thence & brought the Gov. a Sea Otter Skin as a proof of his having reached that Coast. He says the Savages spear them from the Rocks, as the Indians here do Sturgeon. These animals are amphibious but generally in the sea.

Mr. McKenzie went down the River of Peace near 2 degrees north of L. Superior & came to the Rocky Mountains on which rise some Rivers that fall into the Atlantic & others which empty themselves into the Pacific Ocean. He went down a River which falls into the latter, & rises not 700 yards from the River of Peace. He afterwards travelled 17 days by land. There are a kind of large sheep on the Rocky Mountains their horns the size of a Cow's. The Indians near the Coast live on fish which they are very dextrous in catching, they dry salmon in boxes in a kind of upper story in their Huts. They prepare the Roes beating them up with sorrel till it becomes a kind of caviar & when the salmon are dried boil & mix them with oil. These Savages never taste meat, & think if any was thrown into the River the fish would go away. One of Mr. McKenzie's men having thrown a bone of a deer in the water an Indian dived & fetched it out, nor would they suffer water to be ladled out in a kettle in which Meat had been boiled. Are these not veritable Ichthyophagy [fish-eaters]? Mr. McKenzie observed those Indians who Inhabited the Islands on the Coast to be more Savage than the others. The Otter Skins are sold at a great price by those who trade on the coast to the Chinese.

9th of September   Mrs. Smith & the Ladies of the Garrison drank tea with me. The Gov. sets off for Detroit tomorrow & I shall sail for Quebec the next day. If I hear (with official certainty) at Quebec, that Peace with the U. States is agreed on in England I may return here this autumn, but if that news does not arrive very speedily it will be too late for me to return.

Sept. 12th   The Gov. set off this Morning for Detroit. Mrs. Smith came to take leave of me. The Mississaga is to sail as soon as the wind is fair, that not being the case this afternoon I was dissuaded from going on board but having so often seen a wind lost by not embarking before it had risen I determined to go on board & wait for it, which I did at 6 o'clock. Capt. McGill accompanies me in order to see that the Batteaux are properly prepared & attended.

7

VISIT TO QUEBEC
September 13, 1794, to June 16, 1795

September 13th   On board the Mississaga. At 6 this Morning we weighed anchor. The Ft. & Newark looked very pretty under a rising Sun as we left Niagara River. The wind is fair & we keep the South Shore so I hope to discern the entrance of the Genesee River. At 12 the wind changed & we kept the North Shore. Orders were given for my accommodation that no person should have a Passage to Kingston in the Mississaga, but I relented in favour of Brant's sister who was ill & very desirous to go. She speaks English well & is a civil & very sensible old woman.

Sunday 14th   We have had a very rough night, a head wind & nothing but being on Deck the whole day prevented my being very sick. In the afternoon being in the center of the Lake I discerned both the N & S shores. I also discerned a high point on the S. Shore called the Thirty Mile Creek from Niagara in sight of the Duck Islands.

15th   A very rough night. At 8 this Morning we anchored in Kingston Harbour. Capt. McGill went on shore & engaged the only King's Batteau which was here, & hired one of the Merchant's for my Baggage. Capt. Porter (the Officer commanding here) came on board to know my commands & some Ladies called upon me. At 12 we set off in the Batteau which had a comfortable low awning of twisted osiers which was more convenient at this Season when the weather becomes cold than the high Wooden

Awnings. In less than half an hour it began to rain and continued the whole day. We went only 18 miles to Gananowui. Cary's House being shut up we went to Fairfield's close by the mill. Mr. Stone is building on the Gananowui. Capt. McGill slept in the Boat. Fairfield accommodated me with a Room. The baggage boat was not arrived at Gananowui & my boudet being in it, I was at a loss what to sleep on till I recollected some planks I had in the Boat. I laid one of these supported by a small box at each end & put a Carpet over it, on which I slept admirably. Collins had a small Room within mine for herself & the Children.

Fairfield built the little Vessel I saw lying in Kingston Harbour. She contains 120 Barrels & is gone for flour to the Bay of Quinte. Fairfield told me he had been 35 miles back in the Country towards the Ottawa River, the Gananowui runs within ½ a mile of a River that falls into the Ottawa. The Indians carry over that Portage. He saw many Lakes 8 or 10 miles long. He went to catch White Fish but having no means of taking them but spearing he killed only 23. They are very difficult fish to spear, & he had not nets. The land above his house is considerably higher than any in this part of the country & falls every way from this height. Here are abundance of Ground Squirrels, but the men do not take the trouble of skinning them when killed tho the fur is so beautiful. Mr. Stone is building a Saw Mill here opposite Sir J. Johnstone's. It will work 15 Saws at once.

16th This morning Mr. Stone sent me excellent cream & butter. We did not embark till ten. The Morning was so wet that the Canadians were unwilling to move. The Sun shone a little while but the afternoon proved wet & it was dark before I came to Mr. Cowan a Potash maker opposite Oswegatchie. Here I had a large Room with 6 windows in it.

W. 17th We embarked at 6. The Tea Kettle was boiled & I breakfasted in the Boat, showery weather. Passed the Rapid called

Les Goellettes, the waves dashing against the bottom of the Boat sounded as if she struck on Rocks, & there appearance more agitated that those we see in a Shipwreck on the Stage. A mile before we came to the Long Sault there was a violent Storm of thunder lightning & rain, & as we were about to descend the Rapid another violent storm arose which was a grand accompaniment to a terrific scene. This Rapid is very long but it did not appear to me so frightful as Les Goellettes tho' the Current is so strong for the space of some miles that we went 9 miles in the hour without sailing. One man steers, the rest row occasionally but the Canadians are so accustomed to the navigation that with empty Boats the Man who steers is often the only one awake.

I dined in the Boat, at 3 stopped to deliver a Letter at Glengarry House, Major McDonell's. At 4 a thunderstorm occasioned us to stop at the bout du Lac St. François where Mr. McGill was [for] staying the night, but I thought it too early, & sailing across the Lake a good way from shore a violent gale of wind arose when we were in a line with Pt. Mouille. It thundered rained & became perfectly dark, the boat tossed violently, the Children crying & Collins sighing. The wind blew so strong off shore that I feared being driven out into the Lake & lost or driven to the United States Shore. Capt. McGill thought there was some difficulty as he promised the Men Rum if they exerted themselves to get to the Shore, which at last did, & I waited half an hour, intending to sleep in the Boat rather than proceed in such weather 5 miles to the Pt. au Bodet. There was no house nearer. The weather then clearing up & growing calm I consented to proceed provided they kept close to the shore, which they did & about 10 we arrived at Pt. au Bodet. Mr. McDonell the adjt-Genl of Militia was arrived there & he gave up his Rooms in which there were large fires, very comfortable after the cold rough Evening I had been out in.

T. 18   Embarked at 6 & reached the Cedars (18 miles) at 10, from thence I went 6 miles in a Calash to the Cascades from whence I was two hours going in the boat to La Chine. I waited there 2 hours for a Calash & set out in it with Francis but the road was so rough & the Carriage so indifferent that I was obliged to stop & take Collins with me to hold the Child or we should have been shaken out. I was so fatigued with this ten miles to Montreal that I determined never to go in a Post Calash again. The Carriage was driven tandem the first horse tied to the other by a rope which did not in the least confine him. The horses generally went different ways & at a great rate.

I went to Mr. Grey's at Montreal but his House being under repair Mr. Frobisher another Merchant requested me to be at his House where I should be better accommodated & indeed it is elegantly fitted up. He sent his Carriage for me.

F. 19th   Mrs. Frobisher came from her Country House to dine with me. I saw the large Sheep's Horn Mr. McKenzie brought from the Rocky Mountains. Major Duke called to enquire whether I would have Men from the 26th to row my Batteau but I preferred the Canadians. Mr. Smith of the Fusileers brought me Letters from England.

20th   A very wet day so I staid at Mr. Frobisher's.

Sunday 21st   I left Montreal at 9 with a good many Buffalo skins in the Boat, as the weather grows very cold & every ten leagues I feel it more so, the weather very windy & disagreeable, an unpleasant squall near Varennes. We afterwards passed St. Sulpice & LaValtrie a pretty village among Oaks & reached D'Autray 13 leagues from Montreal by 6 o'clock. I walked the last ½ mile to warm myself. I had a good fire at the Post House & wrote till eleven. I was charged 6 shillings for Rooms, fire & milk. I carried Tea, Tongue & Fowl or Herrings which composed our supper.

M. 22nd Set out at 6, passed Berthier at 12 came to N. York missed the House we were directed to go to, stopped at another while the Men lighted their Pipes, previous to passing Lake St. Pierre, had a distant view of Maskinonge, Riviere du Loup & Machiche, at 7 arrived at 3 Rivers had a good fire at the Maison de poste & very cheap (a much better house than the Inn kept by an Englishman where instead of two dollars I might have paid Eight).

After drinking tea (or supper) & the Children are gone to bed I dress my hair (which I have not had time to do in the morning) change my Habit & lay down on a boudet before the fire, covered with a fur Blanket. I do not undress when I have not my own bed, which is the case at present. I came 21 leagues today & felt it very cold, but the Children mind it so little that Francis will not keep on his gloves.

23rd Left 3 Rivers after breakfast. In the afternoon the weather was particularly fine & the scenery between Grondines & Cap Santé was peculiarly beautiful, illuminated by the setting Sun. The Churches of Deschambault & Cap Santé are very picturesque objects among the Wood & the high grounds near the latter are of the finest verdure covered with large detached Trees, has a very fine appearance, indeed going down the St. Lawrance affords the most delightful scenery whether it be between Kingston & Montreal among the numberless Wooded Islands of all sizes, the woody, Rocky Shores bordering the Rapids & the transparent clear waters.

From Montreal to Quebec the country is more diversified by Houses & Villages & is very pretty, excepting a part of it passing Lake St. Peter which is flat & low but from Deschambault it again becomes fine. The opposition of a strong current makes the voyage up the River very tedious but the velocity with which the Boat passes down affords incessant variety of objects & nothing can be pleasanter. I cannot tho but regret leaving the Climate of our Upper Country, the warmth of which gives an Idea of comfort to the most uninhabited Scenes.

We came 19 Leagues today & arrived at 6 at Cap Santé & I found myself at the House where I had met with so much civility on my way from Quebec. The Woman recognized & welcomed me with her usual French politeness; by great industry she had saved Money to make the miserable Cottage it had formerly been fit for the reception of travellers. She said my calling there accidentally had made her think of so doing. Her husband is quite uncivilized but she had been educated at a Convent. An Orchard full of fine apples was in great beauty just ready to be gathered. I had much satisfaction at seeing the progressive state of improvement making here. I was made very happy in receiving a Letter tonight from Mrs. Caldwell, pressing me in the kindest manner to reside with her till my House at Quebec could be prepared for me.

24th The Tide prevented my leaving Cap Santé till 9 o'clock. Fine weather. Passed the Mills at Jacques Cartier landed at a romantic spot named Cap Rouge 3 leagues from Quebec. I walked a mile to the Maison de Poste dressed myself & went in a Calash 4 to Belmont where I met with the most friendly reception that was possible.

25th I received a great many visits from my acquaintances at Quebec who all appeared very glad to see me.

F. 26th Many more visitors. Coll. Caldwell & Miss Johnson dined at St. Foix but I could not prevail on Mrs. Caldwell to leave me & I could not accept Lady Dorchester's invitation as my cloaths were not arrived.

29th The Bishop's family & Coll. & Mrs. Despard dined here.

30th   Coll. Caldwell proposed my taking his House at Sans Bruit which I felt disposed to do. I went to see it today. The weather was very cold & some snow fell which gave me an unfavourable idea of Sans Bruit & I did not like the thoughts of so cold a place. I called on Mrs. Mountain & on Mrs. Despard at Woodfield. It is said that peace is settled between G. Britain & the United States, but as I have not heard it officially (or even in that case could I tell how Wayne may previously have acted at the Miami) I cannot venture to return with Mr. McGill to Niagara. He sets out today. Some snow fell.

1st of October   Coll. and Mrs. Caldwell went to their Mill. Miss Johnson & I drove to Quebec.

T. 2nd   I breakfasted with Mrs. Murray & went to see the House offered me in Palace Street which I liked very well. Coll. & Mrs. Caldwell returned to dinner. We drank tea at Mr. Taylor's.

7th   We dined at the Bishop's, a very large party there & Coll. & Mrs. Despard.

8th   Miss Johnson & I went to Quebec.

Sunday 13th [12th]   Coll. Beckwith & several friends dined here. Coll. Caldwell having found that I am the daughter of his old friend Coll. Gwillim with whom he staid some time in London after the death of Genl. Wolfe, is now doubly kind & interested about all my concerns.

13th [14th] of October   I took possession of my House in Palace Street. Dined at the Chateau.

16th [17th]   I have bought a covered Carriole but until the Snow falls I cannot use it. Coll. Caldwell sends a Calash for me to go to

Belmont as it does not seem worth while to buy one for so short a time as I suppose it will be possible to use it.

17th [18th]   Dined & slept at Belmont.

Sat. 18th [Sunday 19th]   Came home, 22 visitors this Morning.

W. 22nd   Dined & slept at Belmont.

23rd   Came here, a great many Visitors this Morning. The certainty of peace relieves me from so much uneasiness, that I scarcely seem to feel the banishment from the Upper Country as much as I expected to have done. Yet at times I have doubts whether an American Mob may act in opposition to their Executive Government.

I have been amused by a Play called the Carthusian Friar written by a Lady, an Emigrant. Coll. Caldwell calls almost every day to know whether I want anything, & is so attentive to all my business that whatever offers of Service other people make, they premise with saying "If Coll. Caldwell has not done it already." Coll Beckwith has been very civil. I had added a Horse, a Cow & a Cat & a Canadian driver to my Establishment. Patras drives admirably. I have heard from the Gov. but the letter was dated Ft. Erie, 6 days after he left Niagara.

27th   Dined at M. Bàby's. Baron de Rue, M. D'Anoilt & many others there. The Office ordered to be shut on Sunday.

31st   Dined at the Chateau.

Nov. 4th   I have heard that all as well at Detroit the 13th of October & Gov. Simcoe returned to Niagara. Instead of the usual frost & snow at this season we have damp mild weather which disagrees with everybody. I have a cold which keeps me at home.

The Wind is East & has prevented the Fusileers sailing for Halifax, they have been on board Ship a week. An East Wind at this season is most extraordinary.

6th The Eweretta & convoy sailed this Morning.

11th I attempted to go to Belmont in my Carriole but the roads were too bad. I drank tea at the Chateau.

12th Dined with Madame Bàby.

13th Spent the Evening at Mrs. Ogden's.

14th Dined at Mrs. Winslow's.

15th The weather so bad I put off going to Powel Place.

16th Some snow. Francis & I went to Belmont in the open Carriole.

18th Drove from Belmont to Powel Place, went to Quebec at 4, dined & went in the Evening to the Chateau. When I left it called at home for my Great Coat & went with Miss Murray in an open Carriole at 10 o'clock at night to Belmont, a little snow but very mild.

20th Letters have been received from Gov. Simcoe dated Niagara Oct. 30th.

25th A heavy fall of Snow & the Ther. 5 degrees below 0. I dined at Mr. Ainslie's. Baron de Rue there, he was promised letters of recommendation by Coll. Harping who died. The Dauphin is dead.

F. 28th   I dined at Mr. Dunn's. The Stoves so heated that the Ther. in the room must have been at 90. Ice & fruit was in great request.

29th   A violent snowstorm & very severe cold weather, but in Miss William's Rooms where I dined the thermometer must have been 86.

30th   I dined at Belmont, returned in the open Carriole.

2 Dec.   Dined at the Chateau, supped at Mr. Taylor's.

3rd   I dined at Belmont.

4th   I dined at the Chief Justice's, a pleasant french party there.

5   Went to breakfast at Belmont, drank tea with Madame Báby.

6th   Dined at Mr. T. Grant's. I have had Letters from Gov. Simcoe tho nearly a month after the time I ought to have rec'd them. Mr. Gray kept them at Montreal till he had an opportunity of sending them by a Gentleman, in order to save the postage of so large a packet. The Gov. proposes my meeting at Pt. au Boudet the boundary of this Province in Jany or Feby as soon as the Ice is good. As I had not thought of moving till the Water communication was open, this scheme is doubly delightful to me as being an unexpected pleasure, & I think I shall like travelling en Carriole very much. Mr. Mayne is to meet me at Montreal. I desired he may not come further.

Lady Dorchester was so obliging to insist on sending me one of her open Carrioles — mine being a covered one was disagreeable in a Morning — & this will greatly add to my amusement, indeed she & Lord Dorchester have been uniformly polite & obliging to me, she is one of those few who appear to act upon principle, & with a consistency which is not to be moved. I think her a sensible pleasant woman & I like the Parties at the Chateau excessively for there are 40 or 50 people in an Evening, & I think it is very amusing to walk about the Room & have something to say to everybody, without a long conversation with any.

9th   I drank tea at the Chateau.

10th   Went to Belmont & to Powel Place where I dined & slept.

12   Went to Belmont.

13th   Lord & Lady Dorchester called upon me. Mr. Smith writes me word from Niagara that the Gov. went to York on the 13th of Nov. & was to proceed immediately from thence to Kingston in a boat coasting by the Bay of Quinté.

16th   At the Chateau. I am also sure to meet Madame Báby there who is one of the most agreeable people at Quebec.

17th   At Mr. Craigie's. The last ship that sailed the Bridget is lost. The August packet is taken by the french & 3 officers of the 4th Regt. who were on their way hither in her. One of their wives desired to preserve a book of Drawings & the Captors immediately threw it into the Sea.

19th   I supped at Mr. Plenderleath's.

20 21 22 23 24   At home on account of Francis's illness which Dr. Nooth cannot define, whether it was Worms, Gravel or Plumb stones or what.

25   I heard an admirable sermon preached by the Abbé des Jardins at the french Church, & afterwards an Excellent one by our own Bishop.

26th   Mr. Coffin gave a dinner & Ball on the Marriage of Mr. Ryland, Lord Dorchester's secretary. He had been engaged to the Lady 10 years, but pecuniary circumstances would not allow them to marry before he left England last year with Ld. Dorchester, those difficulties being removed she had had dependance enough on him to come this winter under the conduct of his friend, Mr. Finlay. I was so fatigued with having sat up with Francis for some nights that I did not enjoy the Ball.

29th   Met. Ld. & Lady Dorchester at Mr. Grant's so I did not go to the Concert.

30th   Drove in my open Carriole to Belmont, returned after dinner & went to Mr. Ainslie's, won five rubbers at Whist having been braced & brightened by the cold drive this afternoon.

31st   Drove to Pt. Louis Gate & walked on the plains with Lady Dorchester, supped at Mrs. Ogden's.

Thursday Jany 1st 1795   I dined at the Chateau. There were about forty persons. In the Evening there was a Rout for introducing Strangers. These Routs used to be held frequently, but since Mr. Carleton's[1] death which is many months since there has not been any.

My having dined at the Chateau without having been formally introduced is a compliment not usually paid. There were 63 Ladies this Evening. I won a Rubber at Whist, there was but one Card table. The people are unaccountably formal when they come to the Chateau tho Lady D. proposes Cards & wishes them to be amused.

F. 2nd   At M. Báby's, the Ther. ten degrees above 0. I preferred coming home in the open Carriole.

6th   I went with Lady Dorchester in her Carriole beyond Woodfield. The Carriole was large & pleasant & a seat in front for the Children. Her drivers are Canadians & therefore will not wear Liveries. The Canadian Coats with Capots & Sashes look very picturesque. I drank tea at the Chateau & Miss Carleton danced.

W. 7th   I dined en famille at the Chateau carrying the Children. Supped at Mrs. Taylor's.

8th   I went to Belmont.

9th   I went to Powel Place in a snowstorm & returned to Belmont at night.

11th   Coll. Beckwith mentioned Gov. Simcoe's having the rank of Major-General [as of October 1794].

12th   Dined at Madame Baby's, went to the Concert. Ther. 10 degrees below zero.

13   Dined at the Chateau, a Rout in the Evening. Miss Carleton is very ill, & Lady Dorchester the picture of Misery.

14   I went to Belmont in the open Carriole, dined & returned in time to go to Mrs. Le Maistre's where I play'd at Cards & supped. Spent two or three days at Powel place.

T. 20th   A Ball at the Chateau as the 18th was Sunday. The Ladies much dressed Miss Williams the most so. Miss Carleton stayed a very short time in the Room having been so excessively ill for this last week.

22nd Mild weather & a S.E. wind, which occasions a great deal of illness, & also inconvenience for the Meat bought as usual in large quantities in the autumn will not keep.

S. 24th I walked on the Plains with Lady Dorchester & have learnt to wrap myself up enough to defy the cold, but the weight of cloaths is very fatiguing. Dined with Mrs. Taylor. Drank tea at the Chateau.

25th At Belmont.

26th Drank tea with Miss Mountain. Lord Dorchester sent his Dormeuse that I might see whether I should like that sort of Carriage to travel in to Upper Canada. It is like an open Carriole with a head made of Seal Skin & lined with Baize, a large Bear or Buffalo skin fixes in front which perfectly secures you from the wind & weather, & may be unhooked if the weather is fine or mild, a low seat & feather bed to keep one's feet warm. I drove a mile or two in it & like it much, & bespoke one to be made the same.

27th I dined at the Chateau. Francis is ill.

28th I dined at Mr. Longmore's. Francis is worse. A Letter from Gov. Simcoe.

29th Dined at the Chateau & carried the Children there.

30 Dined at Mr. Taylor's, supped at Mr. Coffin's.

31st Lady Dorchester came to see me. I dined at the Chateau & supped at Madame Báby's. Mr. Mayne is arrived at Montreal & the Gov. on his way to Coll. Grey's to meet me. Sent off my Baggage on a Traineau to Montreal.

Sunday Feby 1st   Dined at Mr. Taylor's. Drank tea at the Chateau.

M. 2nd   Dined at Mr. Taylor's. Went to Miss Williams'. It was her birthday & there was a ball. Danced with Capt. Archdall.

3rd   Dined at the Chateau.

4th   Drive to Powel Place drank tea with Mrs. Craigie, went with her to the Concert, returned, played 3 Rubbers at whist & supped.

5th   Lady Dorchester called to take leave of me. I slept at Belmont.

Feby. 6 1795   I left Belmont at 2 o'clock, the Children, Collins & a great deal of Baggage in a heavy Dormeuse or Carriole with a Head built after Ld. Dorchester's. I went 6 leagues to Pt. Aux Trembles. It was quite dark before I arrived there, a tolerable Poste house.

S. 7th   I set off at 7, the weather bright & pleasant tho the wind is E. At Jacques Cartier the ice was so rotten that I was obliged to go a league higher to cross the River with safety. When I came to Ste. Ann's the Sun shone so bright I thought I should have time to go two stages further but when I came to the next stage, Champlain, I was frightened at the ice cracking on that River, & when I stopped at the Post House, it was so perfectly dark that I could not reconcile myself to going farther.

This was a wretched House & the people said travellers never slept at it, but on my repeating a request for a Room they gave me up their sitting Room, which appeared so dismal that I could not Sleep tho I lay down on a Boudet. In the night a great dog crept in from under the Stove & people were talking continually. The Children went to bed. I would not allow them to stay to breakfast in a place I had wished to quit from the moment I entered it. The people looked as if they belonged to a souteraine [cave dwelling]. When I came to Cap Madeleine I had the expectation of passing very bad ice within a mile which intimidated me so much that I would not stay to breakfast. We went 2 leagues above the usual place of crossing & even there saw water on each side of the Carriage.

We were driven by so *very* old a man that they sent another to take care of him the most dangerous part of the Road. I wanted to detain him the whole stage but he would not stay to affront the old man who he said had driven above 60 years. He was very near overturning us before we came to the 3 Rivers. It was Sunday & the streets filled with People so I would not go out to Breakfast but kept Collins (who never liked losing a meal) without her breakfast till 5 in the afternoon when we arrived at a very comfortable Post House at Maskinonge where I had a very good dinner & stayed that night. We had travelled 20 leagues & a half.

Monday 9th The Post Master General at Quebec having sent orders to all the Post Houses on the road to keep Horses ready for me, & told the Courier to pay for them, I had not the least trouble of waiting or paying. I said Labadie (the courier) paye tout & they asked me no farther questions. The weather has been delightful today. I thought the expanse of miles of ice from Pt. Au Trembles to Montreal looked very formidable, but it was good ice & we arrived at Mr. Grey's at 5 o'clock having travelled 24 leagues & a half since we left Maskinonge at 5 this Morning. The post horses are very good, they drive tandem & change every 3 leagues.

10 I set off at 8 this Morning in my Dormeuse. Mr. Mayne followed in a Carriole & Servants in a third. When I was told we were to go with the same Horses to Pt. au Boudet, 63 miles, I thought we should have a very tedious journey, but it was far from being so, the Ice was excellent.

189

It was a delightful drive across the wide part of the St. Lawrance below its junction with the Ottawa to the Cedars where we rested the Horses for two hours, & they brought us to Pt. au Boudet by six o'clock. When we were on Lake St. Francis, my Driver left the Carriage & walked behind with the other drivers; every ½ mile he came & whipped the horses violently, & I saw no more of him till we had gone another half mile the Horses steadily pursuing a slight track on the Snow, but had there been air holes in the track they pursued as sometimes happens on the Ice, what would have become of us? It put me in mind of the Rein Deer who travel self-conducted. The Gov. came half way to Pt. au Boudet today to meet me & returned to Coll. James Grey's as I was not arrived.

11th of Feby. I set out by 7 & by eleven had the pleasure to see the Gov. quite well at Coll. Grey's where we stayed till Friday 13th. Mr. Mayne returned today to Montreal. The Gov. & I set out towards Kingston, stopped an hour at a good Inn where the Sessions are held — the last House in Stormount, went about 35 miles to Mr. Patterson's at the Rapide Plat where we slept — a damp room. The Roads to the west of Montreal are excellent because they drive the Horses abreast & make the Carrioles wider.

14th Came to dinner at Johnstown[2] opposite Oswegatchie 15 miles from the Rapide Plat. This place was laid out for a Town but there are but a few Houses built, one of them is intended for an Inn. The Gov. has been residing at it for a fortnight expecting me here. I intend to stay ten days. Major Littlehales is with him & they keep a very good house promising to give me Turkeys & Vension every day. There are two comfortable Rooms & what I most admire are the Stoves in them. The weather is severely cold & bright. We play at Whist in the Evening. The Journey has quite established Francis's health though he was so ill when we left Quebec.

19th   I had not been here two days when I felt the violent effects of a cold I caught by sleeping in a damp room at the Rapide Plat, it had particularly fallen into my eyes & affected them so much that I think I shall never recover it totally. I was obliged tonight to throw off most of the wrappings I had bound about my eyes & head & go to a Ball given by the Inhabitants of the Province to the Gov., people came forty miles to it in Carrioles. I was really so ill I could scarcely hear or see & possibly neglected the very persons I meant to be most civil to.

20th   Drove 7½ miles to dine at Mr. Jones's, returned by 9 o'clock.

21st   Dined at Mr. T. Frazier's.

22nd   Dined at Mr. W. Frazier's.

23rd 24th 25th 26th   A great deal of Snow fell these days & the Inhabitants endeavoured to persuade the Gov. not to set out till the Snow was beaten, but a Gentleman residing with us had business at Kingston & assured the Gov. it would be excellent travelling; so we set off at 8 & met two Mr. Jones's who were coming to request the Gov. not to undertake the Journey yet. When they found him determined to proceed, they said they would go also, to beat the way & to hasten our Journey, they took us into lighter Carriages or we never should have got on the Snow was so heavy. We stopped at another Jones's where there was the largest wood fire I ever saw, he also set out to beat the Road & so did several other people. One Gentleman came some miles below Oswegatchie for that purpose & with his assistance we went 19 miles to Mr. Jessup's House in the Woods where we slept, but the People who so civilly travelled with us had to go back again as there was no accommodation for them or their horses. It was 6 before we arrived. It was the coldest day remembered in Upper

191

Canada. Mr. Jones's finger was slightly frost bit, he was speaking of a *pretty pond* near one of his Mills. I asked him of what size. He said 300 acres. Mr. W. Frazier's son drove my Carriole.

27th   We left Mr. Jessup's at 9, drove 9 miles thro the woods & opened our Alfortras at a small Cottage, then proceeded 18 miles to Cary's beyond the Gananowui. We went 4 miles on the Ice before we came to that River at the mouth of which the Ice is very bad, so we drove as fast as possible as that is thought the safest way on rotten Ice. I was very much frightened for it was dark & I knew that if they did not keep exactly the right track (which could scarcely be seen) we were in the greatest danger. When we arrived at Cary's we heard that Mr. Forsyth lost both his Horses 3 days ago at the mouth of the Gananowui by keeping too far from the Shore, they saved the Carriole by cutting the traces but neither he nor his companions were dextrous enough to preserve the Horses. The people of the States are particularly expert in saving Horses from drowning, they travel with Ropes which they fasten round the Horses' neck if they fall into the Water, pulling it stops their breath & then they float & can be pulled out; then they take off the rope as quickly as possible & the horse travels on as well as before.

When Gov. Simcoe was driven by Swayzie to Detroit, he carried these Choke Ropes & had occasion to use them.

28th   Cary's an indifferent House but warm. We left Cary's at 9 drove near the Mills at Gananowui, stopped at a farm at Howland's ½ way to Kingston, where we arrived at 6 o'clock having travelled 20 miles thro Woods. I was amused by observing the various barks of Trees — the most deeply indented & light coloured White Ash, the rugged shag bark Hickory, the regular marked Iron wood, the perpendicular ribbed Cedar, the Bass wood, the varieties of black and White Oak, the Maple, Chestnut, etc. the strong lines of the Pine, particularly the Norway, which is of a rich yellow brown &

when cut approaches to a bright orange colour, among all this the smooth bark of the Beach looked as naked as a frog & had a very mean appearance amongst the rest of the Trees.

Sunday March 1st Kingston We are very comfortably lodged in the Barracks in Kingston. As there are few Officers here, we have the Mess Room to dine in & a Room over it for the Gov.'s office, & these as well as the Kitchen are detached from our other Three Rooms which is very comfortable. The drawing Room has not a stove in it which is a misfortune, but it is too late in the winter to be of much consequence & we have excellent wood fires. I went to Church today & heard an excellent Sermon by Mr. Stuart.

T. 3rd A thaw. Mr. Frazier who drove my Carriole set out yesterday to return home.

7th Dined at Mr. Stewart's [Stuart's].

8th An express from York.

9th We are desirous of seeing the Bay of Quinté, the ice is as smooth as possible & I am told very pleasant to drive upon, & possibly the change of air may abate the violent cough I still have. We therefore determined to set out today. We called at Mr. Booth's farm 11 miles distant, the next 11 miles brought us to Mr. Macdonell's where we dined & slept.

10th Set off at 11 & drove 14 miles on this delightful Ice to Mr. Fishers in Hay Bay. He was not at home. We proceeded a farther 15 miles to Mr. Cartwright's Mills on the Appanee [Napanee] River & slept at his House, a romantic spot.

W. 11th We are now half way up the Bay of Quinté. Had we set out a week sooner we might have gone 60 miles farther but a general thaw is so soon expected that we do not venture. We are now travelling on a Coat of upper Ice formed about a fortnight since & between that & the original ice is 2 feet of water. The rapidity with which a thaw comes on is incredible, from the Ice being excellent in 6 hours it is sometimes impassable.

We set out at 11 & drove 14 miles to Trumpour's Pt. so named from a Man of that Name who lives there. He was formerly in the 16th Dragoons & lives by selling Horses, his wife gave me some good Dutch cakes as I could not wait to eat the Chickens she was roasting in a kettle without water. This house commands a fine view. We passed a village of Mohawk Indians opposite the Appanee River.

From Trumpour's we went to Mr. Macdonell's & slept there. This Bay is about a mile across thickly inhabited on the North Side. The farms are reckoned the most productive in the Province. This Journey has been of great benefit to my health.

12th   Left Mr. Macdonell's called at Booth's & arrived back at Kingston at 3 o'clock.

15th Sunday   An Express by Land arrived from Niagara & went by York & the Bay of Quinté, for the Navigation is not yet open across the Lake. Mr. Mayne arrived from Montreal, he says the roads are now very good. Mr. Stewart preached one of the most impressive & best sermons I have ever heard, the text "Now is the accepted time, now is the day of Salvation."

18th   An Express went to Niagara. A person lately crossing Lake Champlain passed a large Hole in the Ice & an infant alive lying by the side of it. By tracks it appeared as if a Sleigh had fallen in & it was known that a heavy-laden Sleigh with families in it left the country on the opposite shore the day before, probably the Mother threw the Child out as the Sleigh went down. The Gentlemen carried the Infant to Montreal where a subscription was raised for her Maintenance — a good circumstance this for the commencement of a Heroine's life in a Novel.

F. 20th A severe frost. Mr. Mayne drove me on the harbour & Lt. Frazier of the 60th Regiment drove the Gov. A large party at Dinner.

S. 21st The Gov. so ill today he could not leave his room to dine with Mr. Brackenridge.

31st Capt. Parr came to take command of the Garrison, he relieves Capt. Porter.

April 24th The Gov. has been so ill since the 21st of March that I have not left his Room since that day. He has had such a cough that some nights he could not lie down but sat in a chair, total loss of appetite & such headaches that he could not bear any person but me to walk across the Room or speak loud. There was no medical advice but that of a Horse Doctor who pretended to be an apothecary. The Gov. out of consideration for the convenience of the staff Surgeon had allowed him to remain at Niagara & his not being made to attend his Duty has caused me a great deal of anxiety to see the Gov. so ill without proper attendance. Capt. Brant's sister prescribed a Root — I believe it is calamus — which really relieved his Cough in a very short time.

25th Walked out this Morning.

26th I went to Church. It rained. My Umbrella was forgotten & the wet through my sleeves gave me a cold, which perhaps I was the more susceptible of from not having been out of the house so long.

27th   I had a fit of the Ague. The first Boats went down to Montreal.

29th   I had a fit of the Ague.

1st of May   The first Boats arrived from Montreal today. The unusual mild weather occasioned Lake Champlain to freeze very late.[3] Mr. Frobisher's sleigh was lost in crossing it, it contained many bags of dollars & valuable things.

Sunday 3   The Ague again.

M. 4th   As I am going away so soon, I am obliged to invite the Ladies to dinner, but I am so ill & weak, I was obliged to sit in the Drawing Room while they went to dinner.

5th   The ague.

6th   Ladies dined here. I walked in the Evening.

7th   Very ill indeed.

8th   Ladies dined here.

11th   I drank tea with Mrs. Stewart & much fatigued by that drive — only a mile.

T. 12th   I went on board the Onondaga but the wind coming ahead we could not sail.

13th   Still on Board the Onondaga, a contrary wind & wet weather.

14th   I saw the Mohawk launched. She is the size of the Mississaga.

She came with such rapidity that it appeared as if she would have run over the Ship we were in which was at anchor ahead of her. I went on shore & walked on Pt. Frederick & the hill above it. Miss Bouchette dined on board with me. I have not had the ague since I have been in the ship.

F. 15th   We weighed anchor at 12. After sailing 5 miles a head wind & stiff gale arose, we returned to the Harbour. At 2 the wind changed & we sailed again, a wet afternoon.

16th   Unpleasant cold weather, little wind.

17th   About 5 p.m. we were off Gibraltar Pt. It blew extremely hard from the Shore, the Captain chose to turn the Pt without shifting a Sail, he was supposed to be not sober & the Gov. ordered the English Lt. to give orders & he brought us safely into York Harbour. We were certainly in great danger, for the Onondaga is so built that she would overset sooner than carry away anything. I was unusually frightened having dreamt *twice following* the other night that I was lost in the Onondaga. My servant came several times to tell me we were going to the bottom. I told her to shut the door & leave me quiet, for the motion of the Vessel made me sick.

18th   At 1 o'clock we went on Shore.

York 21st   A moor hen which lives in rushes was brought to me today & repeatedly pecked at the reeds represented in the Tapestry not touching any other part.

Sunday 24th   Some Ladies dined with me. Walked in the Evening. The weather damp & cold.

25th   I went with the Gov. to the Mill on the Humber & gathered a beautiful species of Polygala or Milk Wort. I was slightly attacked by the ague.

27th   The ague.

1st of June   I went in a Boat to Francis's Estate, Castle Frank. I drank tea at Playter's.[4]

4th   Company at dinner & a Ball in the Evening as usual.

6th   Francis gave a dinner on his birthday to the Soldiers' Children. The Shaws dined with him at an Upper Table.

9th   We sent the Children & Servants in the Onondaga & intend going ourselves tomorrow in the Canoe. Dined at Commissary McGill's.

10th   The weather so bad we could not move.

11th   The wind continues adverse to our quitting York. We had a Dance this Evening.

15th   We set out in the Canoe at 7, dined at the 16 & arrived at Jones's, 3 miles beyond Burlington Bay at 7 in the Evening. I was delighted with the Canoe, the motion so easy, so pleasant, so quiet, like what I should suppose being in a Palanquin. We sat on Cushions on the bottom of the Canoe. The Indians brought us Strawberries not quite ripe. Jones's sister put them in a saucepan with water & sugar & boiled them & I thought them very good with my Tea.

16th   We left Jones at 7, dined near the 20 & arrived at 8 o'clock at Navy Hall.

8

NIAGARA
June 22 to November 4, 1795

22nd   The Duke de Liancourt arrived strongly recommended by the Duke of Portland, Mr. Hammond etc therefore Genl. Simcoe is obliged to pay every attention to him. He is attended by Mr. Gilmard, an Englishman, a French naval officer named Petit-Thouars & a Marquis de Blacon. Their appearance is perfectly democratic & dirty.

24th   Monsr. Blacon returns immediately to the United States where I hear he keeps a shop. Monsr. Petit-Thouars & Gilmard are going to visit York.

29th   The Gov. took the Duke de Liancourt to see the 40 Mile Creek. I dislike them all.

2nd of July   The Gov. returned. Mrs. McGill came to stay a few days with me during the Commissary's absence.

Sunday 12th   The Ther. 95 in the Shade.

21st   Mrs. McGill returned to York.

24th   Coll. & Mrs. Campbell from Detroit dined with me.

1st of August   Excessive hot day. Coll. & Mrs. Campbell went in our boat to Queenstown, we rode & from thence they drove up the Mountain & we dined in the Arbour by the side of the River from which we were driven by a violent Shower. We drank tea at Mr. Hamilton's & came home in the Boat.

5th We went to the Landing with Mrs. McCaulay & dined by the Rock which Hennepin[1] mentions — a very pleasant day.

M. 10th The Houses of Assembly dissolved.

11th We rode to Judge Powell's dined at Mrs. Tyce's & obtained her consent to our staying a fortnight at her House. She is to give us two Rooms & we are to have a Tent pitched for the Servants. This situation is peculiarly dry & healthy on the Mountain 5 miles from the Fall of Niagara. There is a shed or gallery before the House & some oak trees close to it, therefore there is always shade & cool air here, when we are suffering from intense heat at Navy Hall. We rode home in the Evening.

W. 12 We sailed in the Boat to the Landing & arrived at Mrs. Tyce's to dinner. In the Evening we walked to the Whirl Pool.

13th The Gov. drove me in the Carriage for the first time; we went to the Falls & returned by Star light tho the Road has many stumps of trees on the sides of which I was a little afraid.

14th We breakfasted at 6 & called on Mrs. Hamilton at the Chippeway. On our return stopped at Canby's Mill. From thence the Rapids above the Fall appear very grand. Near this mill about a year ago a burning spring was discovered which if a Candle is held to it will continue flaming a great while.

I went to see it today, but it has not been cleared out for some time & the Cattle having trod in it & made it muddy it did not deserve the name of the burning Spring. We had our small Tent & some cold meat hung under the Carriage. We pitched the

Tent near the Falls & dined, after which being fatigued by the heat, I lay down in the Tent & slept lulled by the sound of the Falls which was going to sleep in the pleasantest way imaginable. After tea we had a very pleasant drive home.

15th The Gov. drove the Children to see the Whirl pool & I rode part of the way, we carried our Tent & provisions as yesterday & dined on a Pt. from whence the Whirl pool & the opposite Bank of the River on which is a Mill form altogether a very fine scene, the Mill appears like a part of the Perpendicular flat Rock on which it stands. In the Bay (or whirlpool) formed by two immensely high Pts of land are now a number of Logs collected by Canby at his Saw Mill above the Falls, the dam which confined them having given way in a flood the Logs came down the falls & were stopped here by the various strong Eddies in this agitated pool, where they whirl about & probably will continue so till the end of the world for they never appear to go beyond the circle of a certain distance & sometimes are set quite upright by the currents, it is a curious scene.

16th A most excessive hot day. The Gov. went to Navy Hall.

17th The weather extremely warm, the Gov. returned at eleven. This Evening we drove to a farm inhabited by Painter. It is just opposite the Fort Schlosser Fall. I was so delighted with the sight of the Falls from this spot just above what is called the Indian Ladder[2] which gives so different a view of them from what I saw at the Table Rock that I am determined to return here again. The road is tolerable for a Carriage. It was quite dark before we got home.

18th Drove into the wood & gathered May apples, dined with Mrs. Powell.

19th At home all day — a Thunder Storm.

20th A wet morning. The Gov. went to Navy Hall. A cold Evening. Mr. Pilkington called.

22nd The Gov. drove towards the falls in the Evening.

23rd In the Evening we rode to the Mill near the Whirlpool. I made a sketch in which a large living Birch Tree suspended by the roots with the head downwards hanging between a bold rifted rock near a Cascade if well drawn would have a most picturesque appearance.

The miller who lives here has a project of finding means to drag these logs on shore in which case it will answer him to build a Saw Mill here, for it is not unusual for floods to bring down a quantity of logs from Canby's mill & the timber is not at all injured by having passed the Great Fall.

M. 24th Mr. Pilkington having been desired to put one or two short Ladders to make the descent easy from Rock to rock by the side of the Indian ladder (which is a notched tree) we set out today determined to make our way to the bottom of the Rocks below the Falls.

We stopped near Painter's House to look at the Ft. Schlosser fall & then descended the hill which I found much easier than had been represented, & very little more difficult than the usual way to the Table Rock although it carried us so many feet below it. I rested half way & sketched the Rock & Ladder above me. The view from the margin of the water is infinitely finer than from the Table Rock. We were near a mile distant from it. The Gov. walked with a guide nearly underneath it, but as the path over the Rocks was bad & not one picturesque scene to be gained by it I did not attempt going but sat endeavouring to sketch the scene till my paper was quite wet by the spray from the Ft.

Schlosser fall. The quantity of Cypress & Cedar with which the sides of the Rocks are covered adds greatly to the beauty & richness of the scenery. We dined on the Rocks beneath the overhanging Cedars. A Man speared a large Sturgeon this afternoon near where we were walking.

As we ascended the hill again when near the top of it, I stopped to observe a most picturesque view of the Falls seen in parts thro the rough spreading branches of Hemlock Spruce trees which formed a noble foreground & the setting sun added richness to the scene.

I rested myself at Painter's House where they prepared besides Tea those Cakes baked in a few minutes on an Iron before the fire which the people of the States make so well, eggs & sweetmeats & bacon or salt fish they usually offer with Tea. I believe it is a more substantial Meal with them than their dinner which is slight.

I came home by moon light after a most pleasant day. Indeed all the time I have been at Mrs. Tyce's has been filled up with seeing the most delightful scenery & nothing to interrupt the pleasure of dwelling on the sights. The waggons arrived to carry the Gov.'s baggage to Ft. Erie. He is going as far as Long Point.

25th   The Gov. & I & Francis went in the Carriage to Fort Chippeway but finding the Baggage had not arrived could proceed no further, dined & slept at Capt. Hamilton's who commands here.

We walked this evening & I made some sketches, the Weather excessively hot, the Gov. very ill. We slept in a Room in the Block House where the Logs were some distance apart. Without this contrivance used as loop Holes in case of attack, as well as for admitting air, I think the heat would have been insufferable; as it was I left my bed & lay on the floor.

26th   Went out early in the Boat with Capt. Darling & Smith. The latter brought me a Thermometer I had been long wishing for &

the Gov. bought it of an Officer going to England, almost immediately it fell out of my hands & was broken to my great vexation. The Gov. set out on Horseback but finding himself very ill made signs from the Shore to the Boat to come ashore which we did half way between the Chippeway & Ft. Erie & at a very good farm House he stay'd the whole of the day till 6 in the Evening when we proceeded in the barge to Ft. Erie. We ordered dinner & made ourselves quite at home here supposing it an Inn, & afterwards found we were mistaken. It was not an Inn but the house of a very hospitable Farmer. The whole of the Shore we passed today is flat & uninteresting. About Ft. Erie the verdure is greater than I have seen in Canada & being unaccustomed to Green without being enriched by warm brown tints it gave me' such idea of damp & Cold that I immediately put on a fur tippet & thought it quite uncomfortable, tho there was no particular change in the weather but only in the tints. I saw some of the Vessels which are built on this Lake & rigged like Snows.[3] They are beter painted & have a more respectable appearance than those on Lake Ontario.

We slept in an indifferent House two miles beyond the Fort kept by very dirty people but it has the advantage of being very near the Lake.

27th   An excessive hot day. We pitched the Tent among some Trees near the Beach which is a very pleasant spot & the House is too dirty to stay in. I dined in my Tent, the Gov. at the Fort. The beach is covered with flat rocks among & upon which are Crayfish in very shallow pools of water. I amused myself with catching them. The Lake is narrow here & has not the sea like appearance of Ontario. The opposite shore is seen & some rising land beyond it, but the flat Horizon without fine-shaped or pointed Hills.

28th   The heat intense, if my Ther. had not been broke I might have ascertained it. I sat in my Tent, the flat rocks & shallow water extend a prodigious way into the Lake. One of the Servants went to the Lake to wash his cloaths. Francis followed him up to his knees in water & sat on a Rock by him, presently an Indian went to wash his cloaths & the group looked very picturesque. Francis came back completely wet to fetch a loaf of bread he desired to give to the Indian. Commodore Grant arrived today from Detroit in the Chippewa the largest of the King's Vessels on this Lake. There was an Indian council today. The Gov. had company at dinner. I dined in my Room.

29th Breakfasted in the Tent. The Gov. went to an Indian council. H returned to an early dinner, intending to go this Evening 9 miles to Pt. Ebino [Abino, Ridgeway] in his way to Long Pt. I accompanied him in the Carriage to Ft. Erie from whence I went in a Boat to the Chippeway. Mr. Bing having just arrived from Detroit went with me. I slept at Capt. Hamilton's at the Chippeway where we arrived about 9. Mr. Bing went on to Niagara.

Sunday 30th The weather was so hot, I gave up my intention of riding to Mrs. Tyce's, but having no Gentleman with me I was obliged to drive the Carriage myself which I had never done & the Roads excessively rough till after passing by the Falls. I tied Francis into the Carriage & drove him very safely tho he complained of being much bruised & shook. A violent Rain began just as I arrived at Mrs. Tyce's.

M. 31st A Moravian woman married to a Farmer near here brought me a loaf of bread so peculiarly good that I could not but enquire about it. She said that it was made with Rennet & Whey, without Yeast or Water & baked in wicker or Straw baskets which is the method taught at the Moravian School at Bethlehem in the States where she was educated. The bread was as light as possible & rich like cake. This Woman brought a wild Turkey here during my absence, another has been seen.

Mrs. Tyce has the finest melons imaginable. I prefer Water Melons & eat two or three every day. The Indian corn is now just in a proper state for boiling or roasting, it begins to turn yellow. Francis & I dine upon it. All the vegetable are particularly good & I eat little else. The Asiatics eat no meat in the summer & I dare say they are right, & the heat nearly approaches to that in the East. The People here in the summer live chiefly on vegetables & a little salt pork.

Now the wild pidgeons are coming of which there is such numbers that besides those they roast & eat at present they salt the wings & breasts of them in barrels, & at any time they are good to eat after being soaked. There is a pond before this House where hundreds of them drink at a time, it is singular that this Pond rises & falls as the River does tho it is such an immense height above it. The May apples are now a great luxury, I have had some preserved, & the hurtleberries are ripe. Baron La Hontan says the root of the May apple (or as the French call them citrons sauvages) are poisonous.

1st of September   I rode to the little Mill near the Whirlpool, while I sat sketching the Trees around were covered with Pidgeons.

W. 2nd   A very wet day, notwithstanding I rode in the Evening to drink tea with Mrs. Powell who was alone. She is a very sensible pleasant Woman. It was very wet & dark coming home. Elderflower leaves take off the pain of the gout or Rheumatism.

4th   Dined at Mrs. Powell's, met Mrs. Richardson.

5th   Capt. Hamilton called. No news from Ft. Erie yet. An Extract from a Magazine "All that we know of *sentiment* is, that it supplies the place of Wisdom & Virtue; & is a rule of life that every Man & woman keeps in some elegant recess of the mind where there is no virtue refined enough for its regard & no vice it will not admit of."

Sunday 6th   I walked to Mrs. Powel's this Evening.

M. 7th   I walked a mile this Evening to the Spring from whence this House is supplied with drinking Water. I gathered 2 kinds of Yellow flowers which are sweet after sunset. I believe it is Salep. Cat mint in tea is a good stomatic & sweet marjoram tea for the headach. Sweet briar (and boiling water poured over it) put into Jars or Milk pans or anything that is to be washed out purifies them sooner & better than anything else. Mrs. Tyce uses it constantly in her Dairy.

8th   Mrs. Smith dined with me. I walked in the Evening to Mrs. Powell's. I was feverish & felt great relief from a Saline draught taken in the effervescent state, a little salt of wormwood water & two teaspoonfuls of Lemon juice. I hear the people in the Lower Settlement [Queenston] are suffering severely by the Ague. There are a great many sassafras Trees in the woods near Navy Hall & they are very beautiful & sweet. There are also a great many Sumach by the River I gathered the bunches of flowers of the Sumach last year & poured boiling water upon them which tasted like lemonade, it has a very astringent harsh taste.

9th   I walked this Evening into a field which was clearing to see the immense large fires.

10th   I dined with Mrs. Powel, whose company is very pleasant to me.

11th   I walked two mile thro' the Woods below the Mountain to see a spring which has been lately discovered which is said to cure lameness, blindness & every disorder. The water tastes like Ink & looks very dark. It smells very sulphurous & so does the earth all around it extremely strong of Brimstone.

S. 12th The Gov. returned & is far from well. He was pleased with Long Pt.[4] which he called Charlotteville the Banks of the Lake 150 feet high, on the shores grew weeping willows covered with vines, he gathered some Grapes already sweet. He returned up the Grand River, from thence crossed a short Portage into the Welland which he descended to Ft. Chippeway. He went part of the Journey on horseback & was much annoyed by passing wasps' nests. The wasps stung the Horses terribly.

M. 14th We walked to the Mineral Spring.

15th The Gov. much worse, the heat excessive. I fell thro a trap door in my Room into a Cellar but was not very much bruised. Extract from a New York news paper —"a handful of cold mud will cure the sting of a Wasp or Bee in a few moments. If a limb bit by a Rattle Snake is put in cold mud for half an hour it will stop the operation of the poison & prevent swelling."

19th We walked to Mrs. Powel's.

22nd We walked with Francis to the School where he goes every day a mile from this house. He carries some bread & butter or Cheese for Dinner with him & returns in the Evening.

24th Rode to the Mill.[5] The Governor very ill. His disorder is billious & fever.

25th Very hot weather. Rode to Lukes' farm this Evening. Mrs. Tyce has a number of Standard Peach trees, some produce small fruit, others large quite green but very well flavoured, tho' they look unpromising.

27th A wet day & very cold.

1st of October   Mrs. Powel drank tea with me.

2nd   Left Mrs. Tyce's, went to Navy Hall, a very cold night.

3rd   A sultry day.

15th   A most violent Storm on Lake Erie. Mr. Tukel lost.

28th   The Indian Summer commenced.

Nov. 1st   A little snow fell.

4th   Fine weather, we breakfasted with Mrs. Hamilton.

9

YORK AND NIAGARA
November 13, 1795, to July 20, 1796

F. 13th of Nov. We left Navy Hall at 8 o'clock in the Governor Simcoe & arrived at York at 5, drank tea with Mrs. McGill. Mr. Lawrance[1] is come with us, he is lately from the States. The Hessian fly has destroyed much of the Crops in the Bay of Quinty.

1st of Dec. A Summer day.

8th Do. Mr. Lawrance says the tough skins from the inside of Pidgeons' gizzards hung up to dry & grated to a fine powder is an infallible cure for Indigestion.

18th Francis brings all the Wood I burn in my Stove from the Wood Yard. I think the exercise is of service to him. He has today a little sledge to draw it upon. Mr. Jones says 7 hundred Rattle Snakes were killed near Burlington Bay this Summer. They live in Caves & in very dry weather go down to the Lake to drink, they are sluggish & moving in numbers at a time probably would be easier destroyed than many other reptiles. The Man is quite recovered who was much bitten by one last August.

20th A boat coming to the head of the Lake with Letters lost her bottom near the River Credit, but the Men were saved being near the Shore.

22nd   I walked towards the Town, the snow not deep enough to drive a sleigh.

25th   A frost. Mrs. Shaw dined with me.

27th   A slight shock of an Earthquake was felt this Morning about 5 o'clock by the Gov. & almost every person in the Garrison but myself. The weather is calm & there is no appearance of the Lake having risen. An express from Kingston.

28th   Walked to the Town. A party began today to cut a road hence to the Pine Fort[2] near L. Simcoe. Mr. Jones the surveyor says the Indians killed over 500 deer in a month within a fence of 7 miles, they cut down trees & laid them in a circle of that extent, the Deer are afraid to pass this apparent fence & were easily shot.

F. Jany 1st 1796   The Gov. infinitely better, can walk 4 or 5 miles without fatigue owing to the cold season of the year. An express went to Kingston. Mrs. Macaulay came to see me & we had a Dance. There are 10 Ladies' here & as they dance reels we can make up a Ball.

18th   A Ball & firing as usual on this day [the Queen's birthday]. A very very cold night.

19th   I walked with Mrs. Macaulay, a Bear killed by the Man of the Snakes. I do not like the Meat, it is like Pork. Mr. McGill drinks tea made of Hemlock Pine, it is not pleasant but thought wholesome.

23rd   We walked on the Ice to the House which is building on Francis' 200 acre Lot of land. It is called Castle Frank built on the plan of a Grecian Temple, totally of wood the Logs squared & so grooved together that in case of decay any log may be taken out. The large Pine trees make Pillars for the Porticos which are at each end 16 feet high.

Some trees were cut & a large fire made near the House by which Venison was toasted on forks made on the Spot & we dined. I returned home in the Carriole. Several people were fishing on the River Don thro' holes cut in the Ice, the small Red Trout they catch are excellent. I gathered black haws, the roots of the tree boiled are a cure for complaints in the Stomach.

Sunday 24th   A very cold day. I walked to Major Smith's Lot, on which I gathered keys of the Sugar Maple & partridge berries. They are scarlet growing on a creeping plant like stone crop.

25th   Very cold weather, the Bay frozen quite across.

28th   Drove to Castle Frank & dined again in the wood on Toasted Venison. The ice is excellent. The berries of the Mountain Tea or winter green are now in great beauty, their bright scarlet berries peeping thro the Snow & the rich colour of their green leaves, they taste like orgeat [barley sugar] but are of a very warm nature, & raise the Spirits.

29th   Excessive cold weather. I walked to the Town, the Gov. drove round the Bay to Gibraltar Point.

2nd Feby   Mrs. Richardson went with me to C. Frank, it is not yet floored, the Carpenters are building a Hut for themselves. I gathered fox berries, they grow like small red currants on a delicate plant. The water elder berries are here called Cranberries & are less bitter than in England. We had an immense fire today & dined on Toasted Venison.

W. 3rd   We drove on the Ice to Skinner's Mill[3] a mile beyond

Castle Frank which looked beautiful from the River. The ice
became bad from the Rapidity of the River near the Mill. At the
Mouth of the Don, I fished from my Carriole, but the fish are not
to be caught as they were last winter several dozen in an hour; it
is said that the noise occasioned by our driving constantly over
this Ice frightens away the fish which seems probable, for they are
still in abundance in the Humber where we do not drive, 15
dozen were caught there a few days ago. The Gov. finds great
benefit by driving out this cold weather & likes my Dormeuse
very much. The Children set in the front of it.

4th We drove 3 miles to the Settlement below the Town & at
Mrs. Ashbridge's[4] saw Callebashes which having holes cut in
them serve as Bowls to ladle water having a natural handle. I
brought away some of the seeds which are to be sown in March
in rich ground. Might not the use of these Callibashes which are
in shape like skulls, have given rise to the story of the southern
Indians drinking out of the Skulls of their Enemies?

I saw Mr. Richardson's Infant laid in a Box which he held by
a Cord, & was skaiting upon the Bay, this gave the Child air &
exercise.

5th Mrs. McGill, Miss Crookshank & a large party drove with
me in Carrioles to dine on toasted Venison by a large fire on the
Beach below the Settlement. We sat under the Shelter of the root
of an immense Pine which had been blown up by the wind and
found it very pleasant & returned 6 miles in 32 minutes. Had a
Card party in the Evening.

6th The Ladies did not catch cold & were delighted with the
novelty of dining in the air in winter, so today we went to C.
Frank. Mrs. Macaulay joined the party. The Ice was not quite so
good & the Snow melted. It was so mild we could not wear
Great Coats.

Francis has a small sleigh, which the servants have taught a Goat to draw, he is the handsomest Goat I ever saw & looks very well in harness. It is a very pretty sight to see Francis drawn in this Car. They used [accustomed] the animal to draw the sleigh by making him draw it full of wood, at first he was very untractable.

8th　We set out on the Ice with three Carrioles but driving too near a large Crack in the Ice near the shore the Horses in the first Carriole broke in, but being quickly whipped, recovered their footing on the ice & drew the Carriole over the Crack. We got out of our Carriage & Mr. Givins thought he would drive better & pass safely; but the Horses plunged much deeper & could not extricate themselves, with difficulty the Harness was unloosed & they were set free without injury, the water not being above 5 feet deep.

We walked to Mr. Mcauley's Lot[5] & dined in that part of the Woods & in the Evening I walked home but the Carrioles went very safely across the Bay keeping farther from the Crack, & perhaps the night air made the ice harder. John Macaulay who is but four years old, cut through some large pieces of Wood with an axe which made Francis emulous to become an axeman also, he is going to begin tomorrow.

9th　A strong easterly wind, a vast quantity of Ice driven by it out of the Bay, ½ a mile of Ice that we drove over last night is totally gone. A Mohawk named Jacob & his wife came here. They are very handsome people & very well dressed. She works any pattern given her in beads remarkably well, they brought Francis a present of Cranberrys.

10th　A wet day. The Post arrived from Niagara.

11　Do.

12th   There is very little Ice left in the Bay, fine weather.

13th   Mr. Pilkington arrived from Niagara. The sudden thaw obliged him to wade across the Inlet at the head of the Lake.

14th   Snow & frost, a dance tonight.

16th   Fahrenheit ther. 9 degrees below the freezing pt. today which is as low as it has been any part of this winter at Niagara. A concert.

17th   The Ther. 15 degrees higher than it was yesterday.

18th   We walked to the Town & from thence drove on the ice to dine at C. Frank, the ice was good. Mr. Pilkington sketched the House. The Winter Express arrived from Quebec.

The Party who went to cut the Road from hence to Lake Simcoe called the Yonge Street are returned after an absence of 7 weeks. The distance is 33 Miles & 56 Chains, they brought 2 Trout from Lake Simcoe weighing about 12 pounds each, but they are not as good as the smaller Trout. There are plenty of Black Bass, Maskinonge & White Fish in that Lake. I heard an anecdote of Black Bass which if true renders it probable they remain in a torpid state during winter. An old Hollow Tree which lay on the margin of the Lake half under water being stopped at the Mouth & taken out 30 black Bass were taken out of it.

Mr. Lawrence who went with the party from motives of curiosity speaks well of the apparent quality of most of the Land, 20 miles from hence near Bond's farm he saw two small Lakes near each other from whence many fish were taken. He saw no wild animals. He met with some Indians who invited them to feast on Bear's Meat. Their appeared to use many ceremonies on this occasion which he did not understand. The Head is always presented to the Chief of the party & they make a rule that all that is dressed of Bear's Meat must be eaten at the feast. Mr. Lawrence brought me two small wooden bowls & spoons, they are made by the Indians from the knots of excrescences growing on Pine or other large Trees, they are stained red by the juice of the inner bark of the Hemlock Pine of which they make a decoction on purpose. The Children will use these bowls as basons at breakfast when travelling.

19th   Mr. Pilkington went in a Boat to the head of the Lake. We dined in the Woods on Major Shanks' farm Lot where an Arbour of Hemlock Pine was prepared, a band of Music stationed near. We dined on large Perch & Venison. Jacob the Mohawk was there. He danced Scotch Reels with more ease & grace than any person I ever saw, & had the air of a Prince. The picturesque way in which he wore & held a black blanket, gave it the air of a Spanish Cloak, his leggins were scarlet, on his Head & arms silver bands. I never saw so handsome a figure.

22nd   I went to C. Frank. The ice of the River very good.

T. 23rd   A Boat crossing the Bay to the Store houses on the Pt. was driven among the Ice by a strong E. wind & could not be extricated until 8 at night, when a Boat carried planks to lay where the Ice was rotten & assisted the Men on the Shore.

Last Sunday I rode to Mr. McGill's Lot above 3 miles from hence where I was surprized to see the land rise so suddenly, a narrow Pine Ridge was on a steep ascent, a quantity of good building stone near it. The weather very cold, it snowed fast.

25th   I went with a party of Ladies to C. Frank. The ice still good tho the weather warm & hazy like Indian Summer. The young Shaws dined with us.

26th Mild weather. We regret losing the clear cold air. A boat arrived from the head of the Lake in 4 hours.

1st of March A Card party tonight.

2nd The weather very cold. I gathered partridge berries.

3rd Frost & snow.

5th The Winter Express set off for Quebec. An Indian & a Canadian came from Matchadosh Bay in five days, & said they could have travelled the journey in four. We rode up the Yonge Street & across a pine ridge to C. Frank.

Sunday 6th Rode to C. Frank.

7th Very cold weather.

12 Mrs. Macauley came, a dance in the Evening.

13th Geese & blackbirds seen which denotes the approach of Spring.

14th Rain.

15th Thaw & rain.

18th A great deal of Snow.

19th A thin Ice covered the Bay.

27th Easter Day. The Ice went out of the Bay this Morning driven by a strong E. Wind, in the Evening the Wind changed to the W. & drove it back & as it beat against the shore in a floating surface of very small pieces it made an uncommon & fine sound, which I listened to a great while from the terrace before the House.

30th Wild Pidgeons arrived.

31st Walked to C. Frank & returned by Yonge Street from whence we rode. The road is as yet very bad, there are pools of water among roots of trees, & fallen logs in swampy spots, & these pools being half frozen render them still more disagreeable when the horses plunge into them.

2nd of April The York Packet sailed for Niagara & the Genesee.

3rd Some Indians brought Maple Sugar to sell in birch bark baskets. I gave three dollars for 30 pounds.

4 Capt. Mayne arrived from N. York in 18 days. Some Indians brought some excellent Wild Geese from L. Simcoe & several kinds of ducks which were very pretty as well as very good. The large black Duck is esteemed one of the best. The Abundance of wild rice off which they feed makes them so much better than Wild Ducks in England.

10th A little snow. A Man arrived from Kingston, he left it the 1st of April, the Bay was then entirely frozen. We walked to C. Frank & rode home. The air full of Pidgeons. I think they are fatter & better here than at Niagara.

16 Commissary McGill went to Kingston.

17th Mrs. McGill dined with me, we walked to Mrs. Macauley's in the Evening came home by 9 o'clock.

18th Francis has not been well. We therefore set off to C. Frank today to change the air intending to pass some days there. The house being yet in an unfinished State, we divided the large Room by Sail Cloth, pitched the Tent on the inner part where we slept on wooden Beds.

It is quite a Summer's day. Musquitos arrived at 3 o'clock. A large wooden Canoe was launched here today built by one of the Men who ought to have been busy in working at Castle Frank.

19th A Letter from Major Littlehales dated Niagara 17th of April mentions the River being full of Ice.

20th The Porticos here are delightful pleasant & the Room cool from its height & the thickness of the logs of which the House is built, the Mountain Tea berries in great perfection. Francis is much better & busy in planting Currant bushes & Peach Trees. There is an Insect which is not to be got rid of, it bores into the Timber, & is heard at night it is like a large maggot. I have seen them taken from under the bark of Trees to bait fishing hooks.

23 A strong E. Wind. Went to the Garrison in the Evening as we are soon going to Niagara.

29th The wind & weather unfavourable for the Canoe. Therefore we determined to sail in the Mohawk. The Governor was too ill to go on board before two o'clock. The wind blew very hard N.N.W. We reached Navy Hall in 3 hours ¾. It was so excessively cold I could not remain on deck & so rough that I was sick in the Cabin & wished I had gone in the Canoe.

30th Still very cold & snow. The Vessel lately built on L. Erie & named by Ld. Dorchester the Francis is arrived at Ft. Erie.

219

May 3rd   The Ottawa left Detroit the 27th of April & came to Ft. Erie in 36 hours. Commodore Grant says Peas were stuck [trained on sticks] at Detroit tho not sown here, but probably that snow storm which fell as the Ottawa left the Detroit River killed them. It does not answer here to sow seeds in the Gardens till May, for tho the weather may have been long good, when Ice comes down from the Upper Lakes late in April, it occasions the air to be so cold that Gardens near the River suffer very much. Major Dodson made those soldiers who would otherwise have kept a Cur, keep a sporting dog, by which means he was enabled to Hunt Hares & Deer last Winter at Kingston.

5th   Sultry weather.

8th   A very cold night, we always feel the N.E. wind severely being so much exposed to it. At York we are only open to the North. Snow fell last night. Mr. & Mrs. Hamilton dined here.

9th   A wet cold day.

12th   Received a Cap from Miss Bond from Philadelphia.

15th Whit-Sunday   Coll. Butler buried.

16th   The Houses of Assembly opened.

17th   Rode before breakfast. Felt agueish.

22nd   Went to the Garrison. Mr. Todd dined here. Miss Russell has preserved some winter Cherries which are very good.

24th   I rode with Mr. & Mrs. Jarvis to the Mountain to call on Mrs. Powell. I gathered Sasafras in bloom. I have been drinking the buds in Tea & it has removed the symptoms of Ague. Mrs.

Powell mentioned the Bordage continuing so long on the River at Detroit, that it was not unusual to see Caleches on dusty roads, Carioles on the Ice, & Ships sailing at the same time.

25th   Walked in the Woods. May apples, Ladies' Slippers in blossom & a beautiful shrub here called dog wood, it is more like · a Gum Cistus.

28th   A wet day, the Gov. ill.

1st of June   News received of the Treaty⁶ being ratified between G. Britain & the United States.

3rd   The Houses of Assembly prorogued. I went with some Ladies to hear the Gov.'s Speech on the dissolution. Miss Russell has a Collection of Plants dried by merely shutting them in books, I wish I had thought of doing so.

4th of June   Mr. Pilkington has erected a Temporary Room adjoining our House for the Ball room tonight. It is 60 feet long & the end ornamented by Colours. We danced 18 couple & sat down to supper 76.

5th   Mrs. Smith dined here. I rode in the Evening as far as Mr. Shane's.

6th   Francis 5 years old today. Mr. Pilkington drew his picture. The Gov. drove me to the Landing to take leave of Mrs. Hamilton, it was very cold returning. I drank tea at Mrs. Smith's & met Mrs. Montigny & Miss Hay from Detroit.

Tuesday 7th We left Navy Hall at 10 o'clock in the Canoe followed by a Boat. Dined at the 12 mile Creek. Some heavy showers in the afternoon induced us to put into the 20 where after being tolerably wet & climbing up a Hill covered with wet grass we found an empty House the Inhabitants gone to live where *Bradt* did last year. We had a fire made, dried our Cloaths & Beds, drank tea & slept well without Musquitos, but the smell of Musk Rat Skins which had been drying in the House was disagreeable. Some Strawberries ripe & the fields covered with blue lupines.

W. 8th We set off at 7 but the Men paddled idly as they did yesterday so that we did not reach the 40 (9 miles) till 12 o'clock. I was out of patience that the Canoe was so disgraced. We encamped on the Pt. where the boards are piled that are brought from the Saw Mill, the Plank afforded a Shed for the Tent. We walked to J. Green's, & as a Room was prepared for us we slept there, but dined at the Pt. ¾ of an acre near the river produced Green 800 Punkins last year, they have Melons in proportion. eat punkin pye which with Lemon Juice was very good. Punkins excellent food for Milch Cows. Francis dipped in the lake. Breakfasted at 7 & set out.

T. 9 I saw very grand Rocks in going towards the Mountain & passed 3 water falls, the first sombre & beautiful from the Water falling from various directions over dark Mossy Rocks. The 2nd was pretty from the fine scenery of tall Trees thro' which it shone — the 3rd just below an old Saw Mill, falls smoothly for some feet & is a bright copper colour having passed thro swamps, it then rushes into white foam over regular ledges of rocks spreading like a bell & the difference of colour is a fine contrast.

The course of this River is a series of falls over wild Rocks the perpendicular Banks on each side very high, covered from top to bottom with Hemlock Pine, Cedars, & all forest Trees of an immense height. By keeping near the bank the water is seen below. There are stones in this water that appear like petrified Shells, but Green was not at home, & I could not get any fetched to me. Returning we noticed a Scene of Rocks, the Lake below towards Burlington Bay, & ½ a mile to the East an extensive distant view towards the Genesee River overlooking the Country from hence to Niagara. I saw a Cream colored Hawk with black tipped wings & a scarlet tail.

We saw a Rift in the Rocks a narrow pass where Wolves descend from the Mountains to commit depredations on the Sheep below. The Woods are full of sarsaparilla. I gathered some wild flax at Green's. In his Garden he has quantities of Melons near the River, & last year cut 800 pumpkins from ¾ of an acre of land, they are esteemed excellent food for Cows making the butter particularly good. We dined today at our Encampment & slept at Green's.

10th   A very wet night. I rode today towards Anderson's, dined at one at the Encampment & sent the Children & servants to the Head of the Lake in the Canoe. Mrs. Green went as a guide to conduct us on horseback across the Mountain. Green has lately at the Governor's request & expense cut a road through the wood making it passable for me to ride. The Gov. thinks the Country will derive great benefit by opening a road on the top of the Mountain (where it is quite dry) from Niagara to the head of the Lake, instead of going a most terrible Road below full of swamps fallen trees etc. We crossed the Creek by the old Saw Mill at the head of the falls I mentioned yesterday, & found the whole of the way very dry & good, stopping frequently on the edge of the bank to look over the extensive wooded plain below us, which is bounded at 4 miles distance by Lake Ontario & the opposite North shore with Flamborough Head discernible.

The steep Cliffs of the Mountain on the top of which we were are rocky covered with wood, the view enlightened by fleeting gleams from a Setting Sun, the view to the west terminated by Burlington Bay.

The spot that most engaged our Attention was named by Green the Tavern because when cutting the road the Men generally met there to dine, & more wood being here cut down the view was less obstructed by the Trees, from hence we observed the Canoe with the Children in it. After we passed these 9 miles it grew dusky & Mrs. Green rather misled us, but at last we found a way tho a very steep one to descend the Mountain. A mile before we came to this descent we passed Stoney Creek a small stream that falls 97 feet in an amphitheatre of bare red Rocks which looked as if they ought to be covered by a falling Lake instead of so small a stream. At the foot of the Mountain we came to Adam Green's Mill.

It was 8 o'clock & we had 5 miles of that terrible kind of Road where the Horse's feet are entangled among logs amid water & swamps, to ride by Moon Light or rather in the dark for in the Woods the glimmering of the Moon is of little use but rather throws shadows which deceive the traveller tho to a picturesque Eye they are full of indistinct & solemn beauty, but little serviceable to Horses, who plunge to their knees in mud pools half full of loose logs.

By day light I much fear these roads & had particularly dreaded this but not being able to see or try to avoid the danger, & my nerves braced by this cold & dry night I went thro' it not only well, but with a degree of pleasure, admiring the unusual brightness of the stars, & the immense apparent height given to the Trees by the depth of Shade. I was so engaged by the Scene that I did not much advert to the cold which was very great in passing the swampy grounds.

After three miles we came into good galloping ground on fine turf by the side of the Lake till we came to the King's Head Inn[7] at the head of the Lake where Walbekanine & a number of his tribe (who are encamped a mile distant) were assembled to compliment the Gov. & fired Musquets in our Horses' faces their usual mark of respect which frightened me & my Horse very much, he started & I shrieked but the sound was lost in the Whoops of the Indians. They gave us the largest Land Tortoise I ever saw.

S. 11   This House [the King's Head Inn] was built by the Gov.
to facilitate the communications between Niagara & the La
Tranche where he intended the Seat of Government to be, & its
situation was not without reference to a military position.

   Another Inn was intended to be built at the Grand River.
There are 8 rooms in this House besides two low wings behind
it joined by a Colonade where are the Offices. It is a pretty plan.
I breakfasted in a Room to the S.E. which commands the view
of the Lake on the S. shore of which we discern the Pt. of the 40
Mile Creek, Jones Point & some other Houses. From the Rooms
to the N.W. we see Flamborough Head & Burlington Bay. The
Sand Cliffs on the N. Shore of Burlington Bay look like Red
Rocks. The Beach is like a park covered with large spreading
Oaks. At 8 o'clock we set out in a Boat to go to Beasley[8] at the
head of Burlington Bay about 8 miles. The River & Bay were full
of Canoes, the Indians were fishing, we bought some fine Salmon
of them. When we had near crossed the Bay Beasley house
became a very pretty object. We landed at it & walked up the hill
from whence is a beautiful view of the Lake with Wooded Points
breaking the line of Shore & Flamborough head in the background.
The hill is quite like a park, fine turf with large Oak trees dispersed
but no underwood.

   We walked two miles on this Park, which is quite natural, for
there are no settlements near it. Beasly the Indian trader [i.e.
settler], can scarcely be called such, trading being his whole
occupation, but the country appears more fitt for the reception
of Inhabitants than any part of the Province I have seen, being
already cleared.

   The Gov. finds the Country on the banks of the La Tranche
is like this but the plains infinitely more extensive. Further west
of this Terrace we saw Coote's Paradise so called from a Capt.
Coote who spent a great deal of time in shooting Ducks in this
marshy tract of land below the Hill we are upon. It abounds with
Wild Fowl & Tortoises, from hence it appears more like a river or

Lake than a marsh & Mordaunt's Pt. in the distance takes fine shape. I was so pleased with this place that the Gov. stayed & dined at Beasly's. A strong E. wind prevented our sailing back. We therefore arrived late & found a Salmon & a Tortoise ready dressed for our dinner.

Walked on the beach in the Evening. Beasly gathered me a weed somewhat like milk wort, a small white flower with a long Root which tastes hot & aromatic which he called Rattle Snake Plantain. I think it is what Charlevoix calls seneka. There are several different plants called Rattlesnake Weed from being supposed to cure the bite of that snake.

Sunday 12   Riding near Jones' House & Pond we saw 3 deer. I suppose going to the Pond. They stood still some time. We went to Adam Green's. He shewed us a spring of salt water which looked thick & blue as it fell into a tub from whence I tasted it. He & his daughter guided us to see the fall of Stoney Creek from the bottom.

We went through pathless Woods over Rocks, Logs & in fact the most difficult walk I ever took & if the girl had not preceded me I should have given it up. We came too near the fall to see it in a picturesque view. I crossed the River on stones. A man climbed a considerable height up part of the Red Amphitheatre to get me a piece of the Stones. He had no apparent footing it was so perpendicular. He formed a singular appearance.

This part of the Mountain is said to abound with Rattlesnakes, & why I did not meet them in these unfrequented places I know not. I gathered a great many plants, Green gave them all names, & I stopped at his House to write them down. Ginseng, a root which the Merchants tell me they send to England & in some years has sold at a guinea a pound, Sarsaparilla — Golden thread — the roots look like gold thread. When steeped in brandy they make a fine aromatic tincture & liquorice plant; consumption vine, a pretty Creeper. Green's daughter was cured of a consumption by drinking tea made of it. Poison vine in appearance much like the former but differs in the number of leaves, one has 5, the other 7. Madder, toothache plant, a beautiful species of fern, Sore Throat weed, Dragon's blood, Adam & Eve or ivy blade, very large, which heals Cuts or burns, droppings of beach, enchanter's nightshade, Dewberrys, Wild Turnip which cures a cough — it is like an Arum.

They prepared me some refreshment at this House, some excellent Cakes baked on the coals, Eggs, a boiled black squirrel, tea & Coffee made of Peas which was good, they said Chemists Coffee was better. The Sugar was made from black Walnut Trees which looks darker than that from the Maple, but I think it is sweeter.

Green's wife died a year ago & left ten Children who live here with their father in a House consisting of a Room, a Closet & a loft, but being N. Jersey people their House is delicately clean & neat, & not the appearance of being inhabited by 3 people every part is so neatly kept. I sent a Boy to gather a flower I forgot to bring from the Mountain & he met a rattle Snake. We rode back to the King's Head to dinner.

M. 13 The Wind being against our going to York we rode on the beach & had a sweet view of Burlington Bay. We passed the Indian Encampment. Their Hutt & Dogs among the fine Oak Trees they are under formed a picturesque appearance. Afterwards we sailed to the N. shore of Burlington Bay & pitched our Tent near a House where we had the Tea kettle boiled but we found the sand flies very troublesome. I found a pretty small tortoise but boiling it took the polish from the shell.

14th The Wind so high & contrary we could not attempt going to York. This place is so delightful I do not regret it.

15th Capt Brant called on horseback on his way to Niagara but left his Sons & Attendants here till the wind proves fair for them to proceed. The Boys are going to School at Niagara. They are fine children about 10 years old. They dined with us & gave Francis a Boat. Francis gave the Mohawks a Sheep for their dinner & afterwards they danced & played at Ball. A violent E. wind & terrific surf — a prodigious Sea this Evening. I stood for some time under an Umbrella to admire its grandeur, it proved a very wet night. Brant's sons slept in our House, & the Indians found shelter under a number of Planks, these are here to finish the House.

16th Rode to the inlet & embarked in the Boat for the continued E. wind had raised such a swell we thought the Canoe would not be pleasant. The wind was light, soon became calm & continued so until 12 o'clock when it rose violently from the W. which coming against the late swell formed a terrifying sea.

The motion was disagreeable & my fears awoke also, till we landed at 3 at the River Credit 12 miles from York. We were surprised to see how well the Canoe made her way thro' this heavy Sea. She rode like a Duck on the waves. After dinner we walked by the River of Credit. Numbers of Indians resort here at this Season to fish for Salmon & the Gov. wishing to go some way up it, which our Boat was too large to do, he made signs to some Indians to take us into their Canoe which they did, they were two men in her which with ourselves & Sophia completely filled the Canoe. They carried us about 3 miles when we came to the Rapids & went on shore.

The banks were high one side covered with pine & a pretty piece of open rocky country on the other. On our return to the Canoe a small snake was in it & the Indians took it out with that caution & abhorrence the Indians have to Snakes which they seem to dread more than the Europeans do. We returned to our Boats where not having any Provision left or money the Gov. made signs to them that they should be recompensed for their trouble if they came to York. There is abundance of Salmon caught in this River. About 5 the weather being calm we set out & arrived at York at 9.

17th June   Very warm day. Mrs. McGill & Macauley dined with me.

20th   Part of the Regt. [Queen's Rangers] embarked for Niagara.

25th   We intended to have gone to the Humber in the Canoe attended by music & spend a pleasant day there but Francis being ill with fever prevented it.

29th   Very ill & feverish having been alarmed about Francis.

30th   Sent the Children to C. Frank in a Boat. We rode there through these pleasant shady Pine Plains, now covered with sweet scented Fern. There is no underwood under the Pines so it is good riding.

July 1st   A large party from the Garrison to dinner. A boat with Music accompanied them, we heard it in the Evening untill they had passed the town, it sounded delightfully.

3   The Gov. went to the Garrison & returned to supper. Some heavy thunder showers fell this Evening & the Musquitos more troublesome than ever. It is scarcely possible to write or use my hands, which are always occupied in killing them or driving them away. This situation being high does not at all secure us from those nats.

4th   I descended the Hill & walked to Skinner's Mill thro the Meadows which looked like Meadows in England. Playter was hay making. Going down the Hill some Dragon's blood seed fell out as I passed which I collected.

6th   I passed Playter's picturesque bridge over the Donn, it is a butternut Tree fallen across the river the branches still growing in full leaf. Mrs. Playter being timorous, a pole was fastened thro the branches to hold by. Having attempted to pass it, I was determined to proceed but was frightened before I got half way.

7th The weather excessively hot & we find the underground Room very comfortable, the windows on one side are cut thro the side of the Hill.

The winter we were at Kingston, Deer were continually seen about here, but the noise made by the Carpenters at work upon the House last winter prevented them from coming. A fine Eagle shot at the Town.

10th Rode very pleasantly through the Pine plains, gathered tea berries. I saw Musquito Hawk's nests, at least the Eggs & young birds lying on pieces of bark on the ground. Query, whether the Musquito Hawk is not the Whipper will which makes such a noise every night. We had Company at dinner. I walked down the Hill in the Evening & gathered Dragon's blood, Lychnis de Canada, Trylliums, toothache plant, Liquorice, wild lillies etc.

11th A very wet day & the Musquitos so numerous that smoke would not drive them away, when it grows dark I take my candle & sit to read on my bed under the Musquito net which is the only protection from them.

12th We rode to the Town by the new Road opened by the Government farm & thro the Town, it is the shortest way in point of time. The Road is so much better than Yonge Street. Dined with Mrs. McGill, returned to C. Frank.

13th The Gov. rode to the Garrison this Morning. In the Evening we went in a Boat, caught a Sun fish.

14th Walked thro the Meadows towards Coon's saw millions of the yellow & black butterflies New York swallow tails & heaps of their Wings lying about. Gathered wild Gooseberries & when they were stewed found them excellent sauce for Salmon. In the afternoon the Gov. received his leave of absence, & information that the Pearl frigate Capt. Ballard is at Quebec & is to take him to England. She sails August the 10th.

15th Rode to the Garrison & slept there.

16th Hot & sultry weather.

18th Rode to dine at C. Frank, so heavy a shower of Rain that we were obliged to quit the lower Room the windows of which are not glazed — slept here.

19th Mrs. McGill & McCauley breakfasted here. I returned to the Garrison with them in Mr. Bouchette's Boat & rode back to dine at C. Frank. Mr. Pilkington came in the Evening. It was very damp & cold. I was glad to stand by the fire.

W. 20th Took leave of C. Frank, called at Playter's, dined with Mrs. McGill. Slept at the Garrison.

10

DEPARTURE
July 21 to October 16, 1796

21st of July Took leave of Mrs. McGill & Miss Crookshank. I was so much out of Spirits I was unable to dine with her. She [Mrs. McGill] sent me some dinner but I could not eat, cried all the day. The Gov. dined with Mr. McGill & at 3 o'clock we went on board the Onondaga under a salute from the Vessels. Little wind, soon became calm.

22nd Light wind & contrary.

23 We were opposite the 50 mile Creek from Niagara.

24th Opposite Presqu'isle in the Bay of Quinté.

25th A side wind towards Evening fair & fresh, at ½ past 11 at night we anchored in Kingston Harbour.

26th A cold day. The Governor breakfasted on Shore, at eleven we embarked in a Batteau, at 6 stopped at a rocky Island 6 miles below Gananowui, where we made a fire & boiled the tea kettle, there is a pretty bay here. I called the Island Isle au trippe from gathering trippe de Roche on the rocks. It is a kind of Liverwort which the Canadians going to the Grande Portage boil & eat on very hungry days but it is not wholesome.

We proceeded 3 miles to a beautiful rocky Island (as we thought but it proved to be the main shore) among the thousand

Isles. I called it Bass Island from the number of black Bass I saw swimming in shallow water near the shore. We supped at 10 the stars shining unusually bright. We placed the beds on the Trunks in one of the Batteaux which was covered with sail Cloth over the awning. We slept extremely well & so cool that we determined to keep the Batteau so fitted up for the rest of the Voyage rather than go into Houses now the Gov. is so unwell & suffers from the heat, besides the fresh breeze on the Water keeps away the Musquitos. We heard a wild kind of shriek several times in the night, we thought it was Loons which scream in that way. An American said he guessed it was the Painters (so they call Panthers) as the sound came from the shore of the United States where these animals abound.

27th   We breakfasted & set off at 7 — it rained. Passed Toniata Isles & the River of that name then the Isles au Baril on one of which we landed. The wind & sea so high we had difficulty in turning the Pt. from whence we had a pretty view of the other Islands. Dined here & gathered hurtleberries. We afterwards came to Capt. Jones; the prettiest Pt on the River, he has a fine farm & garden, & water melons tho so much to the N.E. Here we waited till the tea kettle was boiled, & then proceeding passed Commissary Jones' Saw Mill, E. Jones' Wind mill & Mr. Cowan's pot Ashery near Johnstone.

Stopped for the night at Pt. au Cardinal just below Les Goelettes which terrifying Rapid we passed in a minute. Here Mr. Hugh Munro is building a Mill. The Timbers are uncovered & it has the appearance of a Sketch of a Ruin in Italy. Some Merchants' Batteaux were drawing up round the Pt with the greatest labour, exertion & difficulty & the velocity with which a Boat appeared flying downwards with great Rapidity formed a Contrast well worth seeing. We supped at 10 on a fine piece of dry ground under a plumb tree & sheltered by some boards belonging to the Mill, a cold windy night. A stiff breeze astern kept off the Musquitos. I was only afraid the Cable of our Boat which was tied to a Tree, should by this fresh breeze get loose & leave us to drift down the Rapids.

28th   We breakfasted at 7. I made a sketch & embarked. Passed the Frazier's farms & Pt Iroquois where the Indians formerly fought a battle, Pt au Pins, a fit place for a fortification, Pt Acola, where Mr. Munro's Saw Mill stands near the Rapide Plat, Capt. Duncan's, Grosse Pt, Pte au Gobelet & then we came to the Long Sault which extends 9 miles.

We descended the Long Sault in an hour without sailing & seldom rowing, tho near particular currents they rowed with great exertion. The most agitated part is towards the end of the rapids where the river becomes wider, here I had an opportunity of seeing the Boats which followed us, they appeared to fly. I compared them to Race Horses trying to outrun each other. The velocity was extreme, sometimes the Whirlpool turned them round, at others the head of one & the stern of another Boat appeared buried under the Waves. I sketched the Boats. These Rapids appeared little formidable to me last year. I suppose my mind was then more engaged by the cause of my Voyage & the Governor's situation at the Miami, then I thought not of myself, now I had nothing to think of but the present danger & was terrified.

In the entrance of Lake St. Francis we went to a small Island south of our course, we had the tea kettle boiled & walked about for some time, their were many wild vines, Nut, Gooseberrys & Sumach Trees, one of the Latter we carried away to make Chessmen of, as the wood is said to be beautiful. The weather immoderately hot, & no wind since we left the Rapids. The clouds foretel Rain.

We stopped at Pt Morandiere which stretches a great way into the Lake, we were agreeably surprized to find it a stony dry piece of land, the swamps are to the north of it.

I was very hungry & impatient for supper, but much afraid from the dark appearance of the sky that I must have left the Ducks untasted, for I must have retired to the Boat immediately if the Rain began, or I never could have passed the slippery Rocks I had to cross after they were wet. However the sky cleared we supped & sat admiring the stars till after Eleven o'clock. A prodigious number of moths or flies here, which burnt themselves & lay in large heaps in the fire but I did not see Musquitos.

29th   Breakfasted at 6 set off with a fair wind, passed Pte au Bodet at 9, then Pt au foin, a pretty spot, passed the Rapids near the Coteau de Lac, passed Pt. Au Diable & stopped at Pt au biron on a Hill from whence the view towards the Coteau de Lac is very pretty.

There is a good Seigneurie House falling to Ruins. We saw Batteaux drawing round this Pt where the Current is particularly strong. They used great Exertion in poling & tirant a la cordelle [drawing with a line] & pushing the Boat being above their knees in water. We embarked after dinner, & notwithstanding the immoderate heat they insisted on taking off the awning to go down the rapids of the Cedars. The preparation seemed formidable but the ensuing trajet more so. People usually go from hence in Calashes four miles to the Cascades, but the Gov. wished to see all the Rapids & would not go on shore.

This Rapid is much more frightful than the Long Sault. I cannot describe how terrifying the Extent of furious dashing white waves appeared, & how the Boat plunged & rose among them, the waves sometimes washing into the boat. Our keeping rather too near the shore made it worse. There is a place called the Run near the Locks which is like going down the stream of an overshot Mill & I really thought we should never have risen out of it. The Men rowed with all their might & in passing it called out Vive le Roy. We passed a Rock which really seemed to fly from us. The Children called out "How fast it runs." We did not leave this agitated & agitating scene till we came in sight of Pt Claire & Isle Perrot, & had seen the junction of the transparent St. Lawrance with the dirty water of the Ottawa.

We slept tonight at Isle aux Soeurs. The Island consists of a table-shaped Hill of fine turf, from whence are three fine views. To the N. West looking over the immense width of the St. Lawrance which is like a Lake, is seen the Isle au Paix, Isle Perrot, Pt Claire — in the distance Lac des deux Montagnes the Country about the Rideaux & Ottawa Rivers & some distant blue highlands. To the N.E. a rich woody foreground with a pretty sandy Beach & the blue Mountain of Montreal in the distance.

To the South the Village & River of Chateauguay winding among woods & cultivated Country to a great distance, the Seigneury House & the River falling in to the St. Lawrance forms the near view. This Island & a House on it belongs to the Nuns who reside at Montreal, & here they take care of Insane persons. We pitched the Tent at the foot of the Hill & near the House.

30th A little rain. I walked to the Seigneurie House which looks like a Flemish building, examined a Raft lying in the Chateauguay River & thought its construction very curious.

At 9 we embarked & at 11 stopped La Chine to take a Pilot to conduct us to Montreal through the Rapids, which extend almost the whole way & are thought to be the most dangerous of any as the water is so shallow. The great width of the River adds terror to the scene which presents miles of foaming waves. We stopped a little while that we might not overtake or run foul of an immense Cajeux or Raft that was going down, however, she struck on a Rock & we passed her. It was a fine wild accompaniment to the Scene we were in. The distant view was fine, on one side the Mountain of Montreal & the Town extending below, the Island of St. Helen's & nearer to us that of St. Paul's with some Ruins of burnt Houses upon it. On the other side the Town of La Prairie with the blue Hills of Chambly & Beloeil in the distance.

The Gov. wished me to sketch, I believe he wished to take off my attention from the Rapids. I was more disposed to have cryed than to have talked, reason told me there was no danger because Canadians pass the Rapids safely so many times every year, but one has to resist all that can affright the senses of seeing or hearing so the Pilot to make himself appear brave was perpetually reminding us of the great danger which only his knowledge could save us from. We arrived at Mr. Grey's at Montreal.

Sunday 31st Went to church in Genl. Christie's Coach.

Francis's surprise at a Room on Wheels was great. He had never been in any but an open Carriage. This House of Mr. Grey's is very pleasant from Venetian blinds being fixed into all the Window frames which throws such a sombre light that all the Women who call'd here looked handsome, tho they were not so in broad daylight, et je me sentis valoir dix fois plus qu'un autretemps.

We drank tea at Mr. Frobisher's Country House. It commands a noble view towards La Prairie, St. Helen's, Chambly & beloeil the Town of Montreal & a Cultivated Country in the near view. Francis being accustomed to Centinels, asked (when he saw Mr. Frobisher's dogs' houses before the door) whether the people here kept dogs as Centinels. Mrs. Frobisher has an excellent Garden, there was strawberry spinach[1] which she shewed me as a pretty but very poisonous plant. I assured her I had often eaten it in Upper Canada. I have not caught cold in the whole of this Voyage which I attribute to living so totally in the air.

At Kingston my Trunk fell into the water in taking it from the Ship, so I have had none but damp clothes to wear since, & no opportunity of airing them as I have met with no fire but where the Men were cooking.

1st of August I dined at Mr. Frobisher's, immoderate hot weather & a little rain.

237

2nd Left·Montreal at 8, passed Long Pt, Pt aux Trembles, Varrennes, St. Sulpice with a strong fair wind, dined in the Boat near La Veltrie. Soon afterwards fell a heavy thunderstorm. They furnished the Boat at Montreal with so miserable an awning that it let the Water thro', & sent very unexperienced bateau Men who scarcely knew how to manage the boat. We were quite wet, but being near D'Autray went on Shore & determined to sleep there, having been there twice already I knew we should be well accommodated. A very cold night. The Maitre de Poste, La Fontaine & his Wife, very old people were perfectly Flemish figures. They supped in the Room next to ours. I observed they eat onion broth, fat Bacon & finished by drinking sour milk; after supper they played a game at Cards they called le grand Brisque, which they seemed to be much amused by.

W. 3 Left D'Autray at 8 wrapped up in that fleecy Hosiery [cloak] which has been the companion of all my travels. At 5 this Evening we came to Pt du Lac St. Pierre 3 miles from 3 Rivers where the Batteau Men wished to go, but the Gov. being determined not to lodge in a Town insisted on their going into this little Bay which doing unwillingly they struck us against rocks, it being very shoal as they had said. We found the beach very pleasant & walked from thence to a rising ground where are the remains of Barracks built by Sir F. Haldimand in 1789. Gathered very fine wild Raspberries. We were overtaken by a Thunder Shower that wetted me through but what was worse on our return found the Canvas & Awning of our Boat had not been properly fixed & that the beds were quite wet. There was no remedy so I sat by the fire & dryed my Habit, eat my supper & slept in my Cloaths on the damp Bed, without catching any cold.

4th Drew a plant of wild rice which was in blossom, gathered Cardinal flowers, a beautiful purple flower, sand cherries Poires sauvages & some Raspberries. We went out of the Bay without touching a Rock, stopped 5 minutes at 3 Rivers to speak to Mr. Mountain. At 5 this afternoon we went on shore at a most beautiful Pt, St. Pierre de Becquet. It is a very steep ascent from the Beach to the Village among wood & Rock. We went to the Cure's who very civilly shewed us his House & Garden, & the Church which is very Neat, from the Garden is an extensive view. The Mouths of the Rivers Batiscan & St. Anne are seen on the opposite Shore with distant Blue Hills. This is the finest point on the River & a good Military Position. Madame Báby has Lands here.

Descending the Hill we gathered nuts & wild fruits. Farther down the River the view of Richelieu, Deschambeau, Grondines in the distance with bright lights from the setting sun was very beautiful. We slept at Grondines in a Room belonging to Mr. McCord of Quebec. He represents this Village in the Parliament at Quebec. We could not sleep on the water as the tide obliged the Boat to be brought on Shore. A very cold night, we supp'd upon the Beach.

5th We set off at 7, was extremely delighted with the high Banks & beautiful scenery in passing Deschambeau, Richelieu & Cap Santé opposite to which is Pt Platon where we went on shore & admired the situation which is fit for a fine House, there is a good farm belonging to the Convent des Ursuline at Quebec.

We dined in the Boat opposite the pretty Village of St. Augustine & two leagues further went on shore at Cap Rouge. The Commissary at Montreal ought to be ashamed of sending us such Batteau Men. They frequently asked me how far we were from Quebec & many such questions. The only man at all accustomed to the trajet was dying of Ague & of no use. From the St. Lawrance we walked a mile (the tide being out) over wet ground like marsh interspersed with rock which brought us to a House where we got a caleche which carried us a mile to a kind of Post House where we dressed & set out in a caleche ascending a prodigious steep but winding Road among Red Rocks & Wood & four miles brought us to Belmont where we found our friends well & happy to see us. They have just finished an addition to their House which makes it very comfortable.

As a proof of how much the Gov. has suffered from the illness he had last Autumn (the fever lasted from August till November) he was excessively fatigued by the Exercise of driving 4 miles in the Calash.

6th   A wet morning. Mrs. & Miss Prescott[2] called on me. The Bishop's youngest child died last night, they sent a very polite message requesting us to use their House at Quebec & their Carriage. The Bishop's family are going immediately to 3 Rivers to visit his Brother.

7th   Went to Church at Quebec.

8th   Went to Quebec, called on Miss Mountain, dined at the Chateau, returned to Belmont in Mrs. Prescott's Carige. A heavy thunder shower when we were at dinner but the weather still sultry. The Country about Quebec is charming. The Gov. not having seen it in summer is surprized at its beauty, the distant Mountains appear more grand when the wooded Country below is discerned, interspersed with the Villages of Charlesbourg, Lorette & Montmorency.

The Pearl frigate is gone on a cruise but expected here on the 10th.

9th   The Gov. went with Coll. Caldwell to his Mills & returned much fatigued.

10th   Genl. & Mrs. Prescott dined here. I was very ill from the heat. I never felt the air so oppressive in U. Canada.

11th   Left our hospitable friends at Belmont & went this Evening to reside at the Bishop's House at Quebec where we are very comfortably lodged. Our obligation to the Bishop is great for there are no tolerable accommodations here for travellers, & no lodgings to be hired but what are very miserable, as Mrs. Prescott experienced before the Château was vacant.

12th   There is a fog like our Indian Summer with insufferable heat. In the Evening we walked upon Cape Diamond & to our favourite walk on the Terrace. There is a Cerise or Grappe in the Bishop's Garden as large as an Apple Tree. The fruit is the size of a large currant.

13th   We dined at the Chief Justice's [Osgoode's]. Met Mrs. Prescott.

14th   Went to Church. Sat in the Gov.'s seat. Called on Mrs. Dalton & saw her beautiful drawings. I read a poem called Caissa[3] in Jones' collection of Asiatic Poems.

15th   Walked to Cape Diamond before breakfast.

16th   News arrived of the Active being wrecked off the Isle of Anticosti. The Crew got safe on shore & Lord & Lady Dorchester were taken from hence to Gaspey in a Schooner which fortunately for them was passing Anticosti a day or two after they were wrecked. From Gaspey they were to go to Hallifax probably in the Pearl which detains her from being here.

17th   Dined at Belmont, Sultry Weather.

18th   The Ship Adriatic arrived from Hallifax. Dined at the Chateau, Ther. 88. We are under great anxiety least Lord Dorchester should take the Pearl to carry him to England from Hallifax.

19th   So ill I could not dine with Madame Baby.

20th   So ill I could not dine with Mrs. Dun.

21st   So ill I could not go to Church. Mrs. Prescott called.

22nd 23rd   Dined at home the heat insufferable. The only hours that are tolerable are from 8 till 10 at night when we walk upon the Ramparts.

24th   Drank tea with Mrs. Winslow, in the night the wind changed & it became very cold.

25th   The Bishop & Mrs. Mountain called on their return from Montreal where they have spent the last fortnight. I drank tea with Mrs. Smith. It was too cold to walk with pleasure in the Garden.

27th   Madame Báby obtained the Bishop's Order for our admission at the Convent of Ursulines. The Nuns were very civil & pleased at my recollecting those I had seen before.

29th   *M.* Dined at Woodfield. 2 ships of those destined to go under convoy of the Pearl sailed today, tired of waiting for her.

30th   Dined at the Chateau.

31st   Dined at Belmont.

1st of Sept.   We dined at Mr. Finlay's at Woodside. It is a very pretty situation, Quebec & Charlebourg are good objects from it but the weather was hazy. I walked thro pretty grounds in the afternoon.

2nd   A wet day.

3rd   Drank tea with Miss Mountain. The Pearl arrived from Halifax in 14 days.

4th   Coll. & Mrs. Caldwell dined with me.

5th   Dined at Woodfield. Walked in the Evening towards Sellery [Sillery] & saw a beautiful view of Cape Diamond, the Isle of Orleans etc. under a setting Sun.

6th   As I was getting into the Cariage to go to the Chateau the Street was full of smoke, which we supposed to be from a Chimney on fire. Soon after we arrived at Mrs. Prescott's the Gentlemen were informed that the fire which had begun in a barn of Hay was raging furiously in St. Louis Street & approaching the Bishop's House. Gen'l Simcoe immediately went there, & remained the whole afternoon giving directions to some of the Crew of the Pearl by whose exertions the Bishop's House & Houses adjoining were saved tho' they several times caught fire. Mrs. Prescott & I were looking out from the Upper windows when we saw a spark on the Recollect Church & in a few minutes the whole building was in a blaze.

The Churches & Houses being covered with shingles (wooden tiles) burnt rapidly & the shingles being light were also easily blown by the wind which was high & had it not changed probably the whole town would have been destroyed. The Ships in the River weighed anchor. Some papers were blown to Pt Levy on the opposite side of the River. Our Trunks being sent to the Chief Justice's I went there to change my cloaths for we were all in full dress as Mrs. Prescott was to have a Ball in the Evening. I was terrified in passing the Parade, the heat was so great from the Recollect Church, Engines kept playing on the Chateau which was in great danger. I afterwards took the Children into Palace Street & sat with Mrs. Roslyn of the 5th [Regiment] till 8 o'clock when Gen'l Simcoe came to fetch us to the Chief Justice's where we slept for tho the danger was at an end, the sight of everything still burning around the Bishop's House, made me wish not to sleep there.

7th   Drank tea with Mrs. Taylor & supped at the C. Justice's our baggage being sent on board the Pearl.

The Ruins of the Recollect Church brightened from within by fire not yet extinguished had an awful grand appearance as we walked home in a dark night, the effect of color was very rich.

I sent an Enquiry after the health of the Ursulines since their alarm, & the exertion they had made in carrying water to the Top of their House, which was endangered by the fire, I received a very polite note from the Superieure, & a basket of Plumbs from their Garden.

8th   Breakfasted at Woodfield returned to Quebec with Mrs. Caldwell & dined with Coll. Barnes.

Saturday 10th September 1796   At Eleven embarked on board the Pearl. The Cabbin is larger than that in the Triton but the Guns are very incommodious. I was busy arranging my Trunks & kept as few as possible with me, because I was informed if we met French ships, we must clear for Action & all the Baggage would be tossed below in Confusion. I met with one Trunk of the Bishop's Cloaths, but had an opportunity of a Boat passing to send it to Quebec.

I find nothing missing but a very pretty Indian basket, in which there were Shoes. Capt. Leveson Gower of the Active takes his passage to England with Capt. Ballard, & four of his lieutenants — Mr. Bond, Mr. Merriott, Mr. Worth, Mr. Deighton, Master of the Active. Capt. Gower lives in the Cabbin.

About 5 we struck ground. The sensation was unpleasant but we were instantly off. Capt. Gower thought of the Active. We anchored at night.

11th   Weighed anchor at 5. At 9 passed a Brig going to Quebec. Passed the Kammarakas & Pilgrim Islands.

M. 12   The wind fair but obliged to lay to, for the Merchant Men under our Convoy. There are ten. The Brook Watson & Earl of Marchmont are very bad sailors.

13   Fair wind & cold. We cannot carry sail enough to keep the Ship steady, on account of those bad sailing Merchantmen.

W. 14th   Wind S.E. Standing for the Bird Islands.

15th   A head sea hauled close to the Wind. I was unwell all day.

16th   A very wet Morning after a rough night & hauled close to the wind. It cleared up at 12. At 6 the Captain spoke with the Merchantmen & agreed to bear away for the Streights of Belle Isle about 50 leagues off. We are now in sight of George's Bay & a fine leading wind.

17th   A fine wind, passed Scaring Island at 12. Rather sick, I found myself better by eating orange Marmalade. A great swell tonight.

Sunday 18th   During the night I heard the Officer on watch tell Capt. Ballard there was a Sail in sight, & he ordered ammunition to be got ready. I got up & tho it was dark contrived to collect my things & lock them in the Trunk as I thought we might be suddenly called upon & the Cabbin cleared. I then went to sleep again. The next morning I heard that the Sail was a Brig from Quebec which had overshot her Port. Capt. Ballard said we had been in great danger during the night. It was very calm & a very heavy swell set us on the breakers which we were quite near, everybody was alarmed & went upon Deck & a sudden breeze springing up from the breakers, saved us from going upon them.

We had entered the Streights of Belle Isle & passed an Island of Ice. At 9 I saw an Island of Ice at a great distance it was near Green I.

At 12 we passed Portreau Bay. I looked at it through a glass & made a sketch of it. The Country appears to be Ledges of Rocks with a few scrubby Pine scarce able to grow on so harsh & dismal a soil. I discerned 2 waterfalls near the Coast. After passing Portreau Bay a fishing boat with Jersey men came along side to inform the Captain that 2 days ago three large Vessels supposed to be French went into Temple Bay about 40 miles distant. The Boat brought fish & while we lay to, some exceeding fine cod were caught. A slight breeze & excessive cold weather. This afternoon we sent the Trunks below & the Cabbin was partly cleared to prepare for meeting the French.

M. 19th   A head wind all night, towards morning a heavy Gale & great fog. We were driven back between Portreau Bay & Green I. At one it cleared, grew calm & the wind fair but a very great Swell.

20th   This morning at 8 we were opposite Temple Bay but it was too hazy to see any distance. A fair wind. At eleven we were abreast of Belle Isle, which is one entire dismal barren rock. At 12 two French Frigates & a Brig were seen. They soon took 6 of our Merchantmen who not having obeyed the Pearl's signals were a great way ahead of us. We cleared for action. Capt. Gower conducted me down two flights of steps into the bread room which just held me, the Children & my servant, there I spent 6 hours in perfect misery every moment expecting to hear the Guns fire, as we lay to for the Enemy. Never having been in real danger before, I had no Idea what it was to be so frightened. Some refreshment was sent to me but I could not eat. The Sailor who brought it said, "You had better take it now, for there is no knowing when you may be able to get any more." I presently was informed that the Progress in which Genl. & Mrs. England were was taken. At 6 o'clock Capt Malcolm of the Marines very obligingly offered me his Room, one flight of steps higher, which I found much cooler than the bread Room, tho only 6 feet long & 4 wide. I lay down with an excruciating headache which essence of Peppermint relieved.

W. 21st   At this Room, Cabbin or Cupboard is below Decks I heard people talking all the night & could not help listening even to the Cabbin boys. I heard half sentences & supposed the rest, & it seemed inevitable for us [not] to escape being taken. However the next day at 12 I was persuaded to go into the Gun Room (the Cabbin being cleared & bulk heads thrown down) & I found that a more cheerful place, & the Officers of the Active having no duty played at Backgammon or Cards with me all day long, for it was the only relief I found. Some Gentlemen were continually coming down from Deck & various were the opinions, some thought the French would come up with us, others did not. The French were following at 3 leagues distance. We are now a mile to the northward of Belle Isle between that & the Labrador Coast. Islands of Ice were passing all the day which made the air very cold. I wished to see them, but had not spirits to go upon Deck, & I was told we should probably see them for some days to come.

It is supposed the Ephron got away from the Enemy after she was taken but she has not joined us. A fine breeze towards Evening. The Pearl took the Brook Watson in tow twice & her Master let the hawser go. I was glad when we got rid of her. The Adriatic is with us, & the London was this Morning but Guns were heard tonight off the N. shore & it is feared she is aground. Mr. Deighton, the Master of the Active says he knew a ship which had her bottom knocked off by the Ice & yet she came safe into her Port. I played at Backgammon & cards till ½ after ten.

22nd   A fine day but very cold. We are still in the Gun Room where the Motion is so little felt that I like it much better than the Cabbin. I played at Backgammon & Cards which tranquilizes my mind but it will be a great while before I recover my fright. It is supposed the French Ships are commanded by Citizen Barny[4] a famous Rebel during the American War. He drinks nothing but water & as he lives hard we suppose he will fight hard. The N. York paper mentioned his cruising off this Coast.

23rd I slept more quietly last night as it is thought we are safe from the pursuit of the French. We breakfasted in the Cabbin. It seems a fortnight since we left it so much has the agitation of mind apparently lengthened the time. The Cabbin appears dull. It is excessively cold. We are in Lat. 53-54. We ran 150 miles since yesterday in the Lat. of Cape Charles. If the present wind continues driving us so much to the northward we shall soon be at Greenland. Mr. Hill went to the North Sea & was obliged to eat Salt Pork raw for if it was boiled it presently became a Cake of Ice. This man relates so many terryfying adventures that I scarcely feel safe to be in the same Ship, for it seems impossible he can perform any Voyage in a quiet way.

S. 24th A S. wind. At 3 o'clock hazy weather raw but rather less cold, Lat. 54-55. I copied the action of the 1st of June from Capt. Ballard's drawing taken on the spot.

Wind S. W. An exceeding heavy gale all night & this day put in the dead lights the weather so bad. Meat could not be roasted, but we had a Pork Pye, & tho I dislike Pork on Shore it is very good on board Ship & an excellent Salt Fish pudding. The Fish having been boiled the day before was now chopped up with potatoes parsnips herbs pepper salt & boiled in a Bag.

26th S. W. A sail in sight which proved to be the London. A fresh breeze still sending us North. I copied 9 plans for the Action of the 1st of June.

27th   A head wind, damp disagreeable weather.

28th   A dreadful night, a very heavy gale. We did not breakfast till 12 o'clock. The Forestay Sail split, a heavy sail all day Lat. 56-10 I continued drawing as long as they left a Table in the Room. The Ships were soon discovered to be India Men. In the Evening we passed another to whom we spoke. She was from Jamaica, had parted company from her Convoy in a dreadful Gale of wind 4 days since in which her top sails were split. We ran 9 knots an hour under bare poles.

Sunday 9th   We spoke to a West India Vessel called The Lioness & took her under Convoy. She parted company from 130 sail in the late gale. A fair wind today & we ran 8 knots an hour. I went on Deck tonight to see the lead heav'd & the Ship lay to. It was a terrific sight when she turned her side to the wind, the waves seemed as if they would overwhelm the Ship & the noise was frightful.

10th   Passed the I. of Scilly this Morning, 3 or 4 sail seen, we spoke to one under Danish Colours, the Land's End seen at one o'clock.

11th   We stood close for Berry Head intending to go on shore in Tor Bay but the wind freshened so much it was impossible to get on board the fishing boats which we saw at a little distance. Two hours sooner it might have been done, but we lay to 2 or 3 hours in the Morning to press men out of the Indiamen, & since that the wind has risen. Sophia wishes to be on Shore, but Francis never having been sick thinks it a pitty to quit the Ship he is so fond of, & leave Beau & Belle the Captain's dogs who are his constant play fellows. He is determined to be a sailor.

W. 12th   A fine day & fair wind, but we lay to so long for the

Convoy that we did not pass Dover till late. We anchored in the Downs[5] at 8 o'clock. It is difficult to go on shore here if the weather is not very calm notwithstanding the extreme skillfulness of the Deal Boatmen. We passed Beachy head where the Cliffs are white & Hastings a brick Town this Morning. In the afternoon the Diamond & Melampus Frigates passed us. It is a very fine sight to see those large Frigates cut thro the Waves with so much swiftness, & they are handsomer objects than a line of Battle Ships which are heavier, they were painted black & yellow with white figure heads. A pretty light small Vessel followed them supposed to be Russian built.

T. 13th   We anchored very near a large Indiaman. I was waked in the night by hearing a sailor call out that we should be aboard the Indiaman, & having heard of such accidents in the Downs, I did not like the alarm.

This Morning I was much pleased with seeing the number of Vessels in the Downs. The Ville de Paris got under weigh & passed close to us, but being under jury masts she looked extremely heavy & clumsy, & of immense size. I liked the Frigates better. A wet morning; we landed at one o'clock. Capt. Ballard, Gower & some Officers of the Pearl dined with us at the Inn at Deal.

We took a friendly leave of Men who having lived so much in their company for 7 weeks, I felt great interest, they both offered their best services for Francis. From my experience of people I am as anxious he should be a sailor as he is to be one. Francis came downstairs in the Inn backwards, as he used to descend the Ladder on board the Pearl. I felt it a great happiness to find the Rooms steady & not roll like the Ship.

14th   Genl. Grinfield came to breakfast with us & invited us to dine at Dover with Mrs. Grinfield which place we set out for after breakfast & drove 11 miles thro a bleak barren Country but when I came to the Hill at Dover I was amazingly struck with the grandeur of the scene the Grand appearance of the Castle on those very high Cliffs, part of the building in good & habitable preservation the Rest in Ruins, a grand scite & a building adapted to it. The bold Cliffs, the Town & Beach beneath, form a charming Picture, & the horizon of the Sea was terminated by the fleet which sailed yesterday the Ville de Paris towering above the rest, we sailed round her before we came on shore but a large Frigate such as the Diamond is a finer sight to my taste. The fresh E. wind has probably sent them back.

We walked round the works which are enlarging about the Castle. Capt. Bruyere of the Engineers went with us, he has been long in Canada to which country he was much attached therefore I was delighted to talk with him.

We noticed the Roman brick very visible in one of the Towers which is in Ruins. We distinguished the coast of France a part of which looks like beachy head. I was shown the Church of Calais & the entrance of Boulogne Harbour. Saw the Brass Cannon given to Queen Elizabeth by the Dutch, it is 24 feet long beautifully carved with figures of Britannia & the God of the Scheldt. We went through the Communication lately cut underground thro the Hill from the Castle to the Town, it is a handsome stone staircase of twelve hundred steps, at the bottom of every 2 or 300 feet it is lighted by a passage & window at the extremity of the Rock, we descended with a Lanthorn, it cost £700. I was much pleased with Capt. Bruyere, for he talked with delight of Canada. He married a sister of Mrs. Selby's of Montreal.

It was extremely cold walking on the Hill. We spent some hours very pleasantly with Mrs. Grinfield & at night set off for Canterbury. A very violent rain this Evening. Canterbury is 15 miles from Dover. We arrived in the dark very much fatigued.

15th   Damp raw weather. Went to see the Cathedral which I greatly admired, the style of Building is peculiarly grand & simple, & the ascent to the Choir by steps has a grand effect. There is a monument of Edward the black Prince in Brass in great preservation. The Armour, helmet & Gloves he wore at Cressy are hung over it.

A head of Dean Watson carved in stone, done in Italy is a fine piece of sculpture, & there are many pieces of stone work curiously executed, there is a great deal of painted glass, a good picture of a Pope but it has been shot thro during the Civil Wars in Cromwell's time.

Thomas Becket's tomb is plain. The Stone around is deeply worn, by having been knelt upon, as is said. There is a good monument of Henry 4th & his Queen. The Ship called the Great Harry with 4 masts built in Henry 8's reign is represented in Stone. This Cathedral has the advantage of Salisbury in not having been modernized.

The country from Canterbury to Dartford is woody & beautiful, some views of the Medway & Thames.

I thought very fine the Thames covered with Shipping from the upper road at Rochester the prospect is pleasant & within 3 miles of Dartford is a good view of the Thames.

The weather is damp raw & unpleasant. I could not but observe as we passed many good Houses that those Mansions appeared very comfortable habitations in which people might live very happily, but it could not be supposed they could ever be induced to go out of them in such a damp Climate for the fields looked so cold, so damp, so chearless, so uncomfortable from the want of our bright Canadian Sun that the effect was striking & the contrast very unfavourable to the English climate. We slept at Dartford.

16th   A beautiful Country from Dartford to London. 15 mile At Welling I passed a remarkable fine Cedar of Lebannon. Arrived at the hotel in Cork Street [London] at 10 o'clock.

NOTES

Foreword by Michael Gnarowski

1. Although the title of the 1911 edition reads *The Diary of Mrs. John Graves Simcoe, Wife of the First Lieutenant-Governor of the Province of Upper Canada, 1792–1796*, the diary entries begin on September 26, 1791, when the Simcoe party actually set sail for Canada.

2. The subtitle of this edition states that the book contains two hundred and thirty-eight illustrations, the addition being a frontispiece portrait with a facsimile signature of J. Ross Robertson.

3. There is a claim to nobility by the Gwillims, who could trace an ancient lineage and descent from the Royal House of Wales.

4. The bateau was a special kind of boat typical to French Canada. Isaac Weld, Jr., in his delightful *Travels Through the States of North America and the Provinces of Upper and Lower Canada During the Years 1795, 1796, and 1797* (1800), describes the bateau as "… a particular kind of boat, very generally used upon the large rivers and lakes in Canada. The bottom of it is perfectly flat, and each end is built very sharp, and exactly alike. The sides are about four feet high, and for the convenience of the rowers, four or five benches are laid across, sometimes more, according to the length of the bateau. It is a very heavy awkward vessel, either for rowing or sailing but it is preferred to a boat with a keel for two very obvious reasons; first, because it draws less water, at the same time that it carries a large burthen; and secondly, because it is much safer on lakes or wide rivers, where storms are frequent …" (Volume 1, Letter XXIII).

Introduction by Mary Quayle Innis

1. *Canadian Letters, Description of a Tour Thro' the Provinces of Lower and Upper Canada in the Course of the Years 1792 and '93* (Montreal, 1912), 8–9, 22.

2. The muffle was the moose's lip.

3. Prince Edward, later Duke of Kent, was the fourth son of George III and later the father of the future Queen Victoria. He commanded the 7th Royal Fusiliers in Canada from 1791 to 1794.

4. Simcoe Papers, microfilm A606, Public Archives of Canada.

5. *Correspondence of Lieutenant Governor John Graves Simcoe*, E.A. Cruikshank, ed. (5 Vols. Toronto, 1923–31), Vol. I, 205.

6. *Canadian Letters*, 43.

7. *Correspondence of Simcoe*, Vol. III, 142.

8. Elizabeth Russell Papers, Toronto Public Library.

9. *Ibid.*

10. William Jarvis Papers, Public Archives of Canada.

11. *Ibid.*

12. *Canadian Letters*, 45.

13. The emigré duc de la Rochefoucauld-Liancourt, who was travelling in the United States, decided to visit Upper Canada and arrived with letters of introduction to Governor Simcoe. He and his party visited the settlements and his account gives a lively picture of the country. La Rochefoucauld-Liancourt, Francois de, *Travels Through the United States of North America … 1795, 1796, and 1797* (2 Vols. London, 1799), Vol. I, 256.

14. Lincoln, Benjamin, "Journal of a Treaty Held in 1793, with the Indian Tribes North-West of the Ohio, by Commissioners of the United States," Massachusetts Historical Society, *Collections*, 3rd series, Vol. 5 (1836), 123–24.

15. Jarvis Papers.

16. Diary of John White in *Ontario History*, Vol. 47, 1955.

17. Elizabeth Russell Papers.

18. Jarvis Papers.

19. *Canadian Letters,* 55.

20. Shepherd-White Papers, Public Archives of Canada.

21. Jarvis Letters, Women's Canadian Historical Society of Toronto, *Transactions,* No. 23, 1922–23, 20.

22. *Canadian Letters,* 55.

23. Jarvis Papers.

24. *Canadian Letters,* 55.

25. Elizabeth Russell Papers.

26. Shepherd-White Papers.

27. Bouchette, Joseph, *The British Dominions in North America* (2 Vols. London, 1832), Vol. I, 89n.

28. *Correspondence of Simcoe,* Vol. I, 17.

29. Bouchette, *loc. cit.*

30. *Revolutionary Services and Civil Life of General William Hull; Prepared from His Manuscripts by His Daughter Mrs. Maria Campbell; Together*

with the History of the Campaign of 1812, and Surrender of the Post of Detroit by His Grandson, James Freeman Clarke (New York, 1848), 289–90.

31. Elizabeth Russell Papers.

32. Russell Papers, Public Archives of Ontario.

33. Jarvis Papers.

34. Quoted in H. Scadding, *Memoirs of Four Decades of York*, Upper Canada (Toronto, 1884), 2.

35. La Rochefoucauld-Liancourt, Vol. I, 241–42.

36. Simcoe Papers, microfilm A605.

37. *Ibid*.

Chapter 1: Journey to Canada

1. Mrs. Simcoe's Diary was addressed to Mrs. Hunt, who had been left in charge of the four little Simcoe girls at Wolford. It was sent to her in sections.

2. Charlevoix, François Xavier, *Histoire et Description Générale de la Nouvelle France* (Paris, 1744).

3. The name Genesee occurs frequently in the diary. The Genesee was the only large river flowing into Lake Ontario from the south and the area surrounding it in New York State was the scene of active immigration in Simcoe's time. The large tract was ceded by the Indians to the United States and part of it prepared for settlement by Charles Williamson, the agent for an English land company.

   Lord Dorchester and Governor Simcoe feared that the Genesee would detain settlers who might have continued to Upper Canada, and that settlements there would involve commercial rivalry and military danger. Governor Simcoe's letters during 1791–94 were filled with references to the violence of Mr. Williamson, the fear of Indian raids, rumours of fever at Genesee, rumours of rapid settlement there. Simcoe referred to "the overrated Genesee" and hoped that people would move from Genesee to Upper Canada, finding there richer land on easier terms and the benefits of British government.

4. Lahontan, Baron de, *Nouveaux Voyages de M. le Baron de Lahontan, Dans l'Amérique Septentrionale* (2. Vols. The Hague, 1703), Vol. I, 16.

Chapter 2: A Winter in Quebec

1. Sir Alured Clarke, lieutenant-governor of Lower Canada, 1791–96.

2. Thomas Talbot served as Governor Simcoe's confidential secretary till 1794 when he returned to his regiment in England. In 1803 he founded the Talbot Settlement in Upper Canada.

3. Mrs. Caldwell was the wife of Colonel Henry Caldwell, receiver general of Lower Canada and legislative councillor.

4. Sir Frederick Haldimand (1718–91) was governor of the Province of Quebec from 1778 to 1786.

5. Madame Baby, wife of Honourable François Baby, adjutant-general of militia and member of the Executive and Legislative Councils, was one of Mrs. Simcoe's closest friends in Canada.

6. Captain Aeneas Shaw, captain in the Queen's Rangers, settled in York in 1793. He was a member of the Legislative Council and later of the Executive Council of Upper Canada.

7. Madawaska was a French community in the most westerly part of New Brunswick, for a long time isolated from the rest of the province.

Chapter 3: Journey to Niagara

1. Rivière-du-Loup, in Maskinonge County, seventy-two miles west of Quebec, later called Louiseville.

2. Major E.B. Littlehales acted as military secretary to Governor Simcoe throughout his stay in Canada. He was the author of "Journal of an Exploring Excursion from Niagara to Detroit 1793," published in *Canadian Literary Magazine* in 1833.

3. Now the Château de Ramezay.

4. The Caughnawaga Natives were Iroquois converts to Christianity who were gathered by French missionaries in the seventeenth century at Caughnawaga in Laprairie County.

5. Colonel John Macdonell was captain in Butler's Rangers, and later first speaker of the Legislative Assembly of Upper Canada.

6. At this point five lines are omitted, about the flower described in the same words in the entry for September 18.

7. Kingston Mills was built in 1782–83 by Robert Clarke for the government.

Chapter 4: A Year at Niagara

1. Navy Hall was a group of four wooden buildings which had been used as winter quarters for sailors on the lake and to hold stores.

2. Honourable Robert Hamilton, a merchant at Niagara, was a member of the first Executive Council. He had in the words of the duc de la Rochefoucauld-Liancourt "a very fine house, built in the English style, he has also a farm, a distillery and tan-yard." His wife, Mrs. Simcoe's friend, was a daughter of Askin, the Detroit fur trader.

3. Fort Schlosser was on the American side of the river almost opposite Chippewa. It was an earthwork fort built by Colonel Schlosser in

1760. Chippewa and Schlosser were known as the Upper Landings and Queenston and Lewiston as the Lower Landings on the Canadian and American sides respectively.

4. Joseph Brant (Thayendanegea), leader of the Mohawks, brought a large number of them to Canada after the American Revolution and received a grant of land at Burlington. In 1791–92 he was negotiating for peace between the Native tribes and the United States government. Governor Simcoe saw him at the Council House in Mohawk Village on the Grand River in 1793 and later Brant conferred with the United States commissioners at Navy Hall and at Detroit.

5. Either Antonio de Guevara (1480-1545) whose "Dial of Princes" was several times translated into English, or the poet Louis Velez de Guevara (1570–1644).

6. William Osgoode (1754–1824) was the first chief justice of Upper Canada in 1792; on the death of William Smith he succeeded as chief justice of Lower Canada in 1794.

7. No diary entries appear from December 31, 1792, to February 3, 1793. On January 16, Katherine, Mrs. Simcoe's seventh child and sixth daughter, was born at Niagara. The birth is recorded in Dunkeswell Parish Church, near Wolford, and in Mrs. Simcoe's letters to Mrs. Hunt. Katherine died in York on April 17, 1794, and was buried there. Her name never appears in the diary.

8. Captain William Mayne of the Queen's Rangers often attended Mrs. Simcoe when Lieutenant Talbot was away.

9. Governor Simcoe's proclamation of July 16, 1792, transformed the La Tranche River into the Thames but failed to transform the Grand into the Ouse.

10. Robert Pilkington (1765–1834), lieutenant in the Royal Engineers, was on Governor Simcoe's staff from 1793 to 1796. He built the fort on the Maumee under the governor's instructions. Like Mrs. Simcoe he drew many maps and made sketches, some of which she copied.

11. Sir Joshua Reynolds's popular discourses delivered to students of the Royal Academy from 1769 to 1790.

12. The Natives were disturbed by American encroachments on their lands and three commissioners were sent by the United States to meet a party of Natives under Joseph Brant. Meetings were held at Sandusky and at Navy Hall on July 7 and 8 but negotiations failed because the Natives insisted on holding the land beyond the Ohio River.

13. Governor Simcoe treated the commissioners with great courtesy but after they left he wrote to General Alured Clarke, "Glad to get rid of the commissioners after six weeks of their company. Lincoln was civil, Randolph a Virginia rake, Pickering a violent, low, philosophic, cunning New Englander. Pickering maintained at table that a state has the right to set up for itself just as the son in a family." *Correspondence of Simcoe*, Vol. I, 400.

Chapter 5: Life at York

1. Mrs. Simcoe means that there was no one on board capable of piloting the ship into the bay.

2. This site was east of the present Old Fort York near the shore of the bay. The creek has been drained; the grove of oaks where the town was to be built was in an area bounded by Queen Street on the north, George Street on the west, the modern Berkeley Street on the east, and the bay shore.

3. The present island was joined to the mainland until the waves of Lake Ontario broke through the low neck of land. The Eastern Gap, gradually widened, was first used by commercial vessels in 1858.

4. Now Scarborough Bluffs.

5. Fort Rouille, located at the foot of the present Dufferin Street, destroyed in 1759.

6. The government mill stood on the site of the present "Old Mill" restaurant.

7. What is now Hanlan's Point; it was named Gibraltar Point on government maps after 1796 and is so marked on some maps at the present day.

8. In a letter to Sir James Bland Burges dated September 23, 1793, Governor Simcoe thanked him for sending "a copy of Alfred." Three letters on political subjects signed "Alfred" were addressed to the people of Great Britain. Sir James was suspected to be the author.

9. *Mémoires de la Vie du Comte de Gramont*, published 1713.

10. Castle Frank was built overlooking the Don Valley near what is now the north boundary of St. James Cemetery. Colonel Talbot wrote to Colonel Simcoe in 1803, "I paid a visit of duty to Castle Frank, which I am sorry to add is uninhabited and going to ruin." In 1829 it was accidentally burned down.

11. Probably smoke from forest fires.

12. This house at Queen Street and the Don River was one of the earliest in Toronto. John Scadding, who was manager of the Simcoe estate at Wolford, came to Upper Canada soon after the governor's arrival. His son, Henry, a clergyman, wrote many historical works about Toronto. A later Scadding cabin was moved to the exhibition grounds in Toronto where it may still be seen.

12. A widow in the Ojibwa or Chippewa tribe was obliged to carry about after her husband's death a "spirit bundle" containing a lock of her husband's hair or nails from his fingers or toes, pieces of wood he had chopped, bits of cloth or leather that had been his. It was intended to comfort her with the reminder that her husband was not entirely gone. She had to carry it for from one to three years. Diamond Jenness, "The Ojibway Indians of Parry Island," National Museum of Canada Bulletin 78, 106–07; Frances Densmore, "Chippewa Customs," Bureau of American Ethnology, Bulletin 83, 77–8.

14. Queen Marie Antoinette was guillotined on October 16, 1793.

15. *"Que diable allait-il faire dans cette galère?"* from Molière's *Les Fourberies de Scapin.*

16. Miami so called, actually the Maumee River in Ohio, runs into the western end of Lake Erie. Governor Simcoe built the fort on the left bank near the river-mouth near the present town of Maumee.

Chapter 6: Life at Niagara

1. The *Governor Simcoe* was built at Kingston in 1794, eighty-seven tons burden. Used for trade on Lake Ontario, this schooner was armed during the War of 1812.

2. There is no agreement as to where the Legislature met, whether in Freemason's Hall, in a marquee, at Navy Hall, or elsewhere. There is some likelihood that the first session may have met in Freemason's Hall, and the succeeding ones in an addition built on to the barracks of Butler's Rangers — a shed of rough lumber, provided with tables and benches.

3. The third session of the Legislature prorogued on July 9, not July 7.

4. Forty Mile Creek (at what is now Grimsby) was visited by the duc de la Rochefoucauld-Liancourt in 1795; he wrote that the creek "turns a grist mill and two saw mills which belong to a Mr. Green, a Loyalist of Jersey, who six or seven years ago settled in this part of Upper Canada. — His estate consists of three hundred acres, about 40 of which are cleared of wood." Vol. I, 258–59.

5. The Tuscarora village was near Lewiston, New York.

6. Right Reverend Jacob Mountain, first Anglican bishop of Quebec.

7. Sir Alexander Mackenzie of the North West Company was returning from his famous journey to the Pacific "from Canada by land."

Chapter 7: Visit to Quebec

1. Mr. Thomas Carleton, son of Lord Dorchester, 1774–94.

2. Johnstown was east of Prescott, not New Johnstown, the early name of Cornwall.

3. This may mean that the loss of the sleigh had occurred the previous autumn and news of the accident had just come by a boat from Montreal.

4. Beyond Castle Frank woods was the land of Captain George Playter and directly across the Don that of his son, John. Both were settlers from Pennsylvania.

Chapter 8: Niagara

1. Louis Hennepin, *Nouvelle Découverte d'un Très Grand Pays* (Utrecht, 1697).

2. The Indian ladder, as Mrs. Simcoe explains, was a notched tree. The ladders Mr. Pilkington placed for Mrs. Simcoe were giving good service two years later. In 1797 Isaac Weld in his *Travels Through …North America* (2 Vols. London, 1800), Vol. II, 123, speaks of "Mrs. Simcoe's ladders having been originally placed there for the accommodation of the lady of the late governor." These were more used, he adds, than the Indian ladder.

3. A snow was a small sailing vessel resembling a brig.

4. Governor Simcoe proposed to build a fort at Long Point or Charlotteville but Lord Dorchester objected.

5. Perhaps the Servos mill at Four Mile Creek.

Chapter 9: York and Niagara

1. John Brown Lawrence had been a fellow prisoner with General Simcoe during the American Revolution. General Simcoe invited him to visit Upper Canada where he took up land.

2. The Pine Fort at Holland River, then the end of Yonge Street, was called Gwillimbury for Mrs. Simcoe's maiden name.

3. Timothy Skinner's mill stood on the east bank of the Don, south of Pottery Road.

4. Sarah, the widow of Jonathan Ashbridge, came from Pennsylvania in 1793 and settled in York with her family near what is still called Ashbridge's Bay.

5. Dr. James Macaulay chose his lot in the summer of 1793; it was bounded by Bloor, Yonge, Queen, and (approximately) Bay streets.

6. Jay's Treaty provided among other things that British troops should be withdrawn from United States Territory by June 1, 1796, and that the fort on the east side of the Niagara River should be given up by the British.

7. The King's Head Inn stood near the southern end of Burlington Bay; it was built by order of the governor to accommodate travellers.

8. Richard Beasley was a Native trader who was the first settler at the head of the lake, on land later known as Dundurn Park.

Chapter 10: Departure

1. Probably rhubarb.

2. Lord Dorchester had been recalled and he and Lady Dorchester had left Quebec on the ill-fated *Active* on July 9, 1796. General Robert Prescott had succeeded as acting governor. He was formally

appointed in April 1797 and served for two years. His wife and daughter were attentive to Mrs. Simcoe.

3. "Caissa" by Sir William Jones was a poetic introduction to the game of chess, in *Poems*, published in 1772.

4. Joshua Barney, American naval officer, then in the service of the French.

5. The part of the sea off the east coast of Kent.

SELECTED READING

Bassett, John M. *Elizabeth Simcoe: First Lady of Upper Canada.* Toronto: Fitzhenry & Whiteside, 1974.

Cruikshank, Brigadier E.A., ed. *The Correspondence of Lieutenant-Governor John Graves Simcoe.* 5 vols. Toronto: Ontario Historical Society, 1923–31.

Fryer, Mary Beacock. *Elizabeth Posthuma Simcoe 1762–1850: A Biography.* Toronto: Dundurn Press, 1989.

_____. *King's Men: The Soldier Founders of Ontario.* Toronto: Dundurn Press, 1980.

Fryer, Mary Beacock, and Christopher Dracott. *John Graves Simcoe 1752–1806.* Toronto: Dundurn Press, 1998.

McLaughlin, Florence. *First Lady of Upper Canada.* Toronto: Burns & MacEachern, 1968.

Riddell, William Renwick. *The Life of John Graves Simcoe: First Lieutenant-Governor of the Province of Upper Canada, 1792–1796.* Toronto: McClelland & Stewart, 1926.

Robertson, John Ross, ed. *The Diary of Mrs. John Graves Simcoe, Wife of the First Lieutenant-Governor of the Province of Upper Canada, 1792–1796.* Toronto: William Briggs, 1911. Reprinted in 1934 by Ontario Publishing Company and in 1973 by Coles Publishing Company.

Van Steen, Marcus. *Governor Simcoe and His Lady.* Toronto: Hodder & Stoughton, 1968.

INDEX

INDEX